A Summer in Kintyre: Memories and Reflections

Previous books by Angus Martin

History

The Ring-Net Fishermen
Kintyre: The Hidden Past
Kintyre Country Life
Fishing and Whaling
Sixteen Walks in South Kintyre
The North Herring Fishing
Herring Fishermen of Kintyre and Ayrshire
Fish and Fisherfolk
Memories of the Inans, Largybaan and Craigaig, 1980-85
An Historical and Genealogical Tour of Kilkerran Graveyard
Kintyre Birds
The Place-Names of the Parish of Campbeltown *(with Duncan Colville)*
The Place-Names of the Parish of Southend *(with Duncan Colville)*
Kilkerran Graveyard Revisited
Kintyre Families
Kintyre Instructions: The 5th Duke of Argyll's Instructions to his Kintyre Chamberlain, 1785-1805 *(with Eric R. Cregeen)*
By Hill and Shore in South Kintyre
Kintyre Places and Place-Names

Poetry

The Larch Plantation
The Song of the Quern
The Silent Hollow
Rosemary Clooney Crossing the Minch
Laggan Days: In Memory of George Campbell Hay
Haunted Landscapes
Paper Archipelagos
Always Boats and Men *(with Mark I'Anson)*
One Time in a Tale of Herring *(with Will Maclean)*

A Summer in Kintyre:
Memories and Reflections

Angus Martin

The Grimsay Press

Published by:

The Grimsay Press
An imprint of Zeticula Ltd
The Roan
Kilkerran
KA19 8LS
Scotland
http://www.thegrimsaypress.co.uk

First published in 2014

Text © Angus Martin 2014

Front cover illustration. The author pouring a cup of tea beside the Old Road, 28/7/2013.
Photograph © Amelia Martin.

Back cover illustration. The author with cliffs of Rubha Dùn Bhàin behind him, 26/3/2014.
Photograph © James MacDonald.

ISBN 978-1-84530-153-8

All rights reserved. No reproduction, copy or transmission of this publication may be made without prior written permission.

For all who will never see these places again, except in memories and dreams.

Acknowledgements

I am indebted to the following for assistance with this book: my wife Judy, Teddy Lafferty, Agnes Stewart, John MacDonald, Jimmy MacDonald, Murdo MacDonald, Amelia Martin, George McSporran, Barbara Docherty, Barbara Matheson, Hartwig Schutz, Wiebke Schutz, Sandy McSporran, Sandy McMillan, Davie Robertson, Kathleen Wallace, William Crossan, Jim Edgar, Archie K. Smith, Duncan Macdougall, and the patient and attentive staff of Campbeltown Public Library, without whose resources – particularly the back issues of local newspapers – this work would have been much the poorer.

Contents

Acknowledgements   vii
Subjects   xi
Illustrations   xv
Introduction   xix

A Summer in Kintyre: Memories and Reflections   1

Appendix 1
Holding on to Time: Poetry and Midden Refuse in
   the Life of Angus Martin (1991)   246
Appendix 2
   A Trip to the Largieban Caves   253
Appendix 3
   A Journey to Cnoc Moy   255
Appendix 4
   A Winter Adventure in Glencoe   258
Appendix 5
   A Song for Jamie's Wedding   267
Appendix 6
   The Cara Broonie and relatives   268

Sources   277
Index   279

Subjects

A rock on Sròn Gharbh	3
With Barbara Matheson	12
The green oar	14
'Not the goat'	15
Long walks	16
A camp at the Inneans	18
Willie MacArthur	22
First visits to the Inneans	25
1984	30
Evasive tactics at Largiebaan	34
Frights at Largiebaan	38
Bruach Dearg	42
Largiebaan, 1967	44
Largiebaan, 1980	46
Choughs	50
1983 and 2013	54
Binnein Fithich	59
Butterflies	61
High point at Largiebaan	64
Silence	68
Malcolm	68
Weather factors	70
Largiebaan, 17 June 2013	72
A sheep below the Aignish	77
The Aignish	78
Earadale	80
A visit to the Largieside	81
Achadh na Sìthe	83
John McQuilkan	84

Psychedelia	87
Duncan and earlier McQuilkans	91
McIntyre family	95
Cladh Mhìcheil	96
Miss Lucy Campbell	98
Killypole	99
Graffiti	104
Alec	107
Snow on the moors	111
The Weigh-Hoose Folk Club and Dick Gaughan	113
Hamish Henderson	115
Auchenhoan	120
Boulders and scares	124
Balnatunie	137
Langlands and Lang	141
Balnatunie ruins	143
A roadside spring	144
Campbell Macarthur	145
The Macarthur family	150
Sweetie Bella's Quarry	153
Ben Gullion	155
Litter and vandalism	156
Afforestation of Ben Gullion	165
Largiebaan, 18 July 2013	166
Mist	169
The Hidden Crag	173
The bone temple	175
Conical Hill and harebells	177
Dragonfly Lochan	181
Benjie's Drinking Pool	182
The Hawk's Peak	182
'Foot and mouth' restrictions	186
Fin Rock	188
The Willows	196
A trip to Cara	199
The *Aska*	207

A visit to Cara in 1953	209
A larch and a rowan	212
'Sheggans' and Seamus Heaney	215
'Shelisters'	218
Ròideagach	222
A walk above Killean	225
Rubha Dùn Bhàin	230
Barr Glen	233
William Gilchrist	234
Garvalt	235
Sròn Gharbh II	238
Laggan Loch at last	241

Illustrations

1. Benjie on rock at Sròn Gharbh, 2006. — 5
2. The bench-shaped rock at Sròn Gharbh, 2013. — 8
3. Barbara Matheson in the Inneans Glen, 2013. — 12
4. Willie MacArthur and nephew beside tent in Inneans Bay, c. 1975. — 19
5. Willie MacArthur and nephew beside oar on moorland, c. 1975. — 21
6. The Hamilton tent in the Inneans Bay, 1967. — 26
7. Angus Martin and tent in the Inneans Bay, 1967. — 28
8. Jimmy MacDonald and Angus Martin near the Gulls' Den, 1984. — 32
9. Jimmy MacDonald at the triangulation pillar on Cnoc Moy, 1984. — 34
10. Neil McKellar and Bob Halbert at Largiebaan Caves, 1982. — 43
11. A party on Largiebaan shore with Layde Church notice-board, 1980. — 47
12. Teddy Lafferty on Aonach Eagach, Glen Coe, c. 1975. — 49
13. Donald Docherty on precipitous track to Largiebaan shore, 1982. — 51
14. Chough hunters on Largiebaan shore, 1984. — 52
15. Michael Claffey and John MacDonald in old steading, Glenahanty, 1983. — 57
16. Robert McInnes, Angus Martin and John MacDonald at Lochorodale peat bank, 1986. — 58
17. Binnein Fithich, 2013. — 67
18. Amelia Martin, Murdo MacDonald and Sandy McMillan at Largiebaan, 2012. — 75

19. The author disguised as a hippie, 1973.	88
20. Murdo MacDonald in Cladh Mhìcheil, 2013.	97
21. Killypole steading, 1986.	100
22. John MacDonald with bog cotton below the Slate, 1983.	103
23. Billy McTaggart in the Inneans Bay, 1985.	105
24. Alec Honeyman with Judy and Sarah Martin on the Old Road, 1991.	108
25. Amelia Martin at Killypole steading, 2013.	110
26. The Weigh-house, Campbeltown, c. 1970.	112
27. Georgina Anderson and Davie Robertson playing in Royal Hotel, 1981.	115
28-30. Ceilidh with Hamish Henderson in the Mitchell house, Campbeltown, 1956.	118-119
31. Robert McMullen, Donald Docherty and Malcolm Docherty below the Aignish, 1983.	121
32. Boulder marking the boundary of Lossit and Ballygroggan, 2013.	125
33. John MacDonald at boulder near Glenmurril, 1981.	127
34. Angus Martin at Craigaig boulder, 2011.	129
35. Road-marker boulder near Innean Beag, 2012.	134
36. Baden-Wurttemberg boundary stone in Black Forest, 2014.	136
37. Jimmy MacDonald in Balnatunie fire-place, 1984.	138
38. Campbell Macarthur, self-portrait, c. 1966.	148
39. Fraser and Robert Macarthur in India, 1943.	151
40. Martin sisters egg-rolling at Knockbay, Easter 1993.	163
41. The camp-site in the Inneans Bay burnt by vandals, 1982	164
42. Conical Hill under snow, 1970.	177
43. Amelia Martin on Conical Hill, 2011.	179
44. The harebell rock on Conical Hill, 2011.	180
45. The Hawk's Peak, 1991.	185
46. Bella and Angus Martin on The Hawk's Peak, 1996.	186
47. Foot and Mouth warning notice, Narrowfield gate, 2001.	187

48. Benjie on Fin Rock, 2008.	189
49. Pony-riding at Kilkerran, 1992.	190
50. Mike Smylie in the Inneans Bay, 1992.	194
51. Lodgepole pines on Ben Gullion, 2012.	197
52. Duncan Macdougall at the helm of *Faoileag* crossing to Cara, 2013.	200
53. Duncan Macdougall and Sandy McMillan on the Mull of Cara, 2013.	202
54. Angus Martin on the Broonie's Chair, Cara, 2013.	203
55. The Mull of Cara, 2013.	205
56. 'Sheggans'/ 'Shelisters' at Knockbay, 2011.	220
57. Twinning-pen at back of Ben Gullion, 2012.	227
58. Twinning-pen, Largiebaan Glen, 1984.	228
59. Carradale Girl Guides in Barr Glen, c. 1983.	237
60. John MacDonald at Laggan Loch, 2013.	242
61. Looking back on Laggan Loch, 2013.	243
62. Benjie and Angus Martin above Sròn Gharbh (Tarbert), 2007.	245

Introduction

I explain the origins of this book on the very first page, but there was another motivating factor which I'll declare now. Since 1991 I have been writing a regular feature, 'By Hill and Shore', for the *Kintyre Magazine*. These contributions contain a mixture of natural history, archaeology, history, folklore, place-names, genealogy, and dialect. In short, all my interests are in there, connected by a continuous thread – my journeys in the outdoors. I can honestly say that no literary activity, poetry excepted, has given me more satisfaction than the writing and assembling of these chunks of observation. Gratifyingly, in 2011 a selection from twenty years of these writings was published, with photographs, as *By Hill and Shore in South Kintyre*.

In 2013, however, I was already a year retired and so often in the hills, enjoying the exceptional summer weather, that I quickly realised that the usual six or seven pages of 'By Hill and Shore' would never accommodate all the experiences and thoughts I was accumulating. This book, therefore, is in great part a response to that concern. As anyone familiar with 'By Hill and Shore' will realise, *A Summer in Kintyre* is essentially a greatly expanded version of that *Kintyre Magazine* staple.

Yet, it's more than that. With the wider scope allowed to me, I have looked more into my past – at places, people, and events – and tried to understand how my interests have developed in the ways they have. So, there could be a little philosophy in here, though I hesitate to press that claim. There is one certainty in my life – I am now completely rooted in Kintyre. I do enjoy a very occasional trip away, to visit my daughters or to watch a football match, but, like ripe fruit, I do not travel well.

Towards the end of the writing of this book, I happened to come across a copy of an article I'd written in 1991 for *The Scottish Book Collector* at the request of its editor, Jenni Renton. The title, 'Holding on to Time', caught my attention at once, since I'd used a similar expression in the opening page of this book; and when I read through the article it seemed to fit the scheme of *A Summer in Kintyre*. Or it perhaps does as an appendix, which is what I've made it. I hadn't exactly forgotten that I'd written the article, but I hadn't read it in two decades and its rediscovery seemed fitting. If nothing else, it reveals a mind already working on some of the themes I have been exploring in this book.

Agnes Stewart, my wife Judy, and Jimmy MacDonald cast a critical eye over the penultimate draft, for which special thanks are due, but I have no doubt that errors still lurk in this book: 'Age does not come alone.' To the reader: I would welcome corrections – also, indeed, information and anecdotes – for inclusion in any subsequent edition.

If enough people buy this book and enjoy it, I'll write another in much the same vein; there are many more places in Kintyre to be explored or revisited. And if any readers can suggest subjects for that further literary excursion, I'd be grateful to receive these suggestions.

13 Saddell Street, Campbeltown, Argyll PA28 6DN
e-mail: judymartin733@btinternet.com
Angus Martin, 13 April 2014.

A Summer in Kintyre: Memories and Reflections

A rock on Sròn Gharbh

The conception of this book can be dated to 10 July 2013, 6.30 p.m., at Sròn Gharbh. The day had been very warm, and I'd come from the Inneans shore and was heading slowly north to Machrihanish to catch the last bus home. I had ample time to complete the walk and decided to sit for an hour on the ridge at Sròn Gharbh. I'd sat there the last time I walked that coast and had discovered an unexpected sense of connection with the place. Jimmy MacDonald, a walking companion, was fond of resting on a grassy slope under the ridge on its south side, and I had sat there with him several times in recent years; but I now preferred the ridge itself – a testimony to that glorious summer of 2013. Under the ridge was often a place of shelter – from wind and perhaps also rain – but on that evening in July my desire was for moving air to cool me and to help deter clegs and midges.

In my rucksack I was carrying a notebook I call my 'hiking journal'. It was the latest in a succession of notebooks extending back to 1980, when exploring the hills and shores of my native Kintyre became, at the age of twenty-eight, a kind of creed. I have, since boyhood, been both an avid collector of memorabilia and a writer, and each of these complementary compulsions, I now recognise, helps me to hold on to the past ... or, put another way, to hold back the future. Futile endeavours, to be sure, but they work for me in precious moments of illusion, when the past

3

returns complete in memory. Sometimes these heightened memories can be induced by a photograph or a bus ticket or by a few handwritten lines embodying a moment which would otherwise have been lost.

That journal contained a photograph which had exercised my curiosity for much of the summer: the family dog, Benjie, standing on a rock, wind sweeping through his fur. The background was Tòn Bhàn – or Dùn Bàn, as some authorities prefer – the headland north of Sròn Gharbh, and I was certain that the photograph had been taken on Sròn Gharbh – but where was the rock? I had looked in vain for it that summer. The photograph had been taken on 17 April 2006 – Easter Monday – by a German friend, Hartwig Schutz. I hadn't realised he'd taken it until a copy arrived at the end of that year in his annual home-made calendar. I appreciated the photograph, and appreciated it all the more after Benjie's death at the end of 2008.

My wife Judy and I visited Hartwig and his wife Elisabeth in Engelsbrand in April 2013 – seven years later – and Hartwig printed another copy of the photograph and gave it to me one evening mid-way through our visit. We stayed for only a week, and spent most of that period walking in the Black Forest near Hartwig's home. Lovely and different, but not my home. Hartwig is aware that travel unsettles me, and he perhaps sensed that an image – tangible, transportable – of Kintyre would assuage my nostalgia for home. It did, and I carried it all the way back, as a kind of talisman, through Paris, London and Glasgow, cities whose traffic noise and tides of humanity distressed me in equal measure.

I had resolved in Germany to find that rock and to celebrate there my safe return. There was nothing particularly 'mystical' in the desire – I simply wished to see it again and to transfer the image of Benjie from paper to stone, which, now that I consider it, had served as a kind of plinth for the living dog. I wished, by the power of imagination, to place him there again and to 'see' him as the camera saw him in that moment in that day seven years before. Memory alone could have been of no service to me, since I didn't remember his being on the rock. Hartwig alone noticed him there and recognised a photographic opportunity.

I was back on Sròn Gharbh for the first time in 2013 on 14 May, with Jimmy MacDonald and his dog Kosi. We took a bus to Machrihanish and crossed the Galdrans, stopping first at Craigaig, for lunch, and again at Sròn Gharbh, where we searched for the rock – I had shown Jimmy the photograph – and failed to find it; but we did find a badger's skull on top of the ridge. I've yet to see a badger, living or dead, so the skull was a start! How it got there is the unanswerable question. I was back on 24 May, alone; on 29 May, with Judy; on 19 June, alone; and on 25 June, alone, without success in my searches. On 10 July I found it.

1. Benjie on rock at Sròn Gharbh, 17 April 2006. Photograph by Hartwig Schutz.

My success was accidental. When I emerged on to the ridge on the sheep-track which crosses the south face of Sròn Gharbh, I unthinkingly continued straight ahead for three or four steps ... and there was the rock ahead of me. Normally I'd turn sharp right and climb higher on the ridge, and higher is where I'd concentrated my searches for the rock. Just to be certain, I took out the photograph and compared it with the scene in front of me. The background was correct when I stood where Hartwig must have stood to take the photograph, but the rock itself didn't look quite right. The differences were slight, and attributable, I decided, to botanical change – seven years had passed and, additionally, spring then was summer now and plant growth more vigorous.

As I noted in my journal: 'An emotional moment.' Since Benjie was 'put down' on 22 December 2008, I believe that not a day has passed without my remembering him. The act of remembrance is now largely mechanical, a mere nod to his reappearance in memory; but sometimes, even yet, I am momentarily overcome by a surge of nostalgia, occasioned always by a spot on the landscape which was a once-familiar haunt of ours.

I placed my rucksack on top of the rock, where Benjie had stood, and propped the photograph against it, facing me, so that I could frame a photograph of my own, using the original image. Having taken a couple of shots, I shouldered the rucksack and climbed the ridge to my intended resting-place. I had noticed, on my previous visit, a bench-like rock opposite another rock, on the ridge itself, into which an oar had been wedged. Whoever was responsible for planting that skyline marker must have carried it a fair distance from the shore.

Back in 1981, both Teddy Lafferty and Willie MacArthur told me about a marker, but neither of them knew who had placed it there, and in any case it wasn't an oar. Willie remembered seeing a kind of flag on it for a time. He is long dead, and Teddy hasn't seen the Inneans in ten years owing to damaged knees. He laments his condition, but he is approaching his eightieth birthday, and I chide him when I meet him: 'But you can't go on for ever, man.' He knows that, but finds no consolation in the truth. I can't blame him – I'll feel the same myself if I live long enough to be denied mobility – but he has his memories, and, if one lives long enough, memories are all that remain, the sweeteners before death.

He has his photographs, too, patiently taken. He thought nothing of sitting high on Beinn na Faire for hours, looking down on the Inneans Bay and watching for the play of sunlight which he knew would enhance the image. He is a man who is content to sit, and I share his philosophy. I have encountered walkers in remote parts of Kintyre, hurrying from place to place, and wondered why they were there. Were they engaged in a test of stamina, and what memories would they take home with them?

Teddy carried a good camera with him when few others had a camera of any kind, and his photographs of the Inneans are among the best I have seen. Now that photography is accessible to all, a mobile phone being all that's needed, there must be thousands of photographs of the place. The earliest I have seen was in the *Campbeltown Courier* in October 1936, a decade before the bay became a popular destination. It was taken mid-way down the glen and frames the bay and a sunlit ocean. There are two walkers in the foreground, one carrying a little knapsack, and they stand, looking westward, backs to the camera, on a grassy spur which is clearly recognisable. Titled 'The Aoineans', it is an evocative composition, even microfilmed from newsprint, but its quality isn't adequate for reproduction here.

From 7 December 1935 to 29 September 1939, an unknown photographer was contributing images of remote parts of Kintyre to a regular feature in the *Courier* titled 'A Kintyre Beauty Spot'. Both the first and the last image in the series is of the Inneans, and the caption to the first may be the earliest published description of the bay: 'Between the sea and cliffs is a small sward of turf through which a stream meanders. An unknown victim of the Great War lies buried here with a simple memorial in his honour, a wooden cross surrounded by a lifebelt and on the cross "God Knows".'

All these photographs of the Inneans illustrate a landscape which remains recognisable in every detail, but many other images in the series demonstrate the tragic changes wrought by coniferous afforestation and depopulation of the remotest glens.

2. On Sròn Gharbh, looking south to the 'bench rock' in foreground and the barely discernible marker-oar on the ridge, 10 July 2013. Photograph by the author.

Sròn Gharbh was ever a transit point, en route to or from the Inneans by the coast. Most visitors to that loveliest of Atlantic inlets cross the moors from Ballygroggan to reach it, and return by the same way. Since the Kintyre Way – a walkers' route through the peninsula – was established, access has been simplified for the uninitiated; the coast, however, offers an alternative route, rugged and more difficult, but also more varied in its beauty.

No one, to my knowledge, has ever gone to Sròn Gharbh for its own sake, but increasingly I stop there for lengthier periods and enjoy the place on its own austere terms. The name translates from Gaelic literally as 'Rough Nose', a fitting description. Nose here equals 'point', and Norse *nes* is also 'nose' projected on to a landscape feature. There is a *nes* at Largiebaan, to the south, in 'Aignish', which I'll look at later. The specific *garbh*, 'rough', explains itself in the landscape – the promontory viewed from the south is studded with rocks.

I sat on the 'bench-like rock', ate the last of my filled rolls and drank two cups of tea. Then I filled my pipe and lit it. The air, even that high on the ridge, was so still that one match was enough to ignite the tobacco, a detail which I suspect will impress few readers. I mention it, anyway, because the accomplishment is rare in the outdoors. Wind is the norm, and even when one has taken precautions, by turning one's back to the wind and shielding the pipe bowl with one's hands, match after match tends to blow out until perhaps the seventh or eighth strike stays lit long enough to do its work. Or one might strike two matches at the same time, which often works when they keep each other alight. I thought of Hugh MacDiarmid's poem, 'Dìreadh III', with its description of the poet standing on the summit of Sgurr Alasdair and gazing on the peaks of the Cuillin of Skye.

> I light my pipe and the match burns steadily
> Without the shielding of my hands,
> The flame hardly visible in the intensity of light
> Which drenches the mountain top.

Since MacDiarmid considered the phenomenon worthy of comment, I consider my own little prose testimony validated.

Smoking, of course, has become a social disgrace, a habit to be concealed unless accompanied by self-condemnation; but I enjoy my pipe and, while troubled occasionally by twinges of guilt, can no more conceive of relinquishing the indulgence than I can of giving up hiking or writing, both of which are unfortunately linked to the tobacco habit.

Another and better known poem of Hugh MacDiarmid's had earlier come to mind on that ridge. On 19 June, the profusion and variety of the botany at Sròn Gharbh prompted me to explore a passable ledge under the ridge itself. I was hoping for a rarity and imagined I had one, when, peering over, I noticed a cluster of white cup-shaped flowers. From overhanging rocks and at the very limit of my nerve, I took a series of photographs. When Judy transferred the images to her computer the following day and we were able to focus in on the colony, the species transpired to be the burnet rose (*Rosa pimpinellifolia*), MacDiarmid's 'little white rose of Scotland'.

> The rose of all the world is not for me.
> I want for my part
> Only the little white rose of Scotland
> That smells sharp and sweet – and breaks the heart.

Strangely enough, I'd looked at a sprawling mass of these roses near High Lossit that very day on my way to the top of the brae. Agnes Stewart had told me about them, and when I studied the Sròn Gharbh flowers, albeit from a distance above, the burnet rose flashed into my mind; but subconsciously, perhaps, I was seeking a rock-dwelling rarity and a measure of glory. Looking back, however, the real glory was in that summer evening, as I clambered around the rocks, absorbed in the nature of the place and breathing its elemental silence.

Next to the roses there was another species of flower which I examined through binoculars and photographed that day, and on subsequent days, but it ultimately eluded identification. Photography is never a satisfactory substitute for the physical examination of a flower, but, particularly when expertise is lacking, as in my case, photographs secured at close range can be useful aids to identification. So far, however, I haven't figured out a safe route to that spot, which is directly above Jimmy's sitting-place under the ridge. From above, the ground appears fairly level, but, from below, sloping. I've never seen sheep, or even goats, on it, so I'm probably never going to reach it unless on a rope. It still seems to me an odd place for roses and I wonder how the seeds arrived there. Probably in a bird's dropping, and – who knows? – the bird may have brought the seeds in its gut all the way from Lossit.

While sitting smoking on the rock – I am back to 10 July – I was startled by the sudden appearance of a gull which materialised over the ridge, saw me, and, itself just as startled, stalled momentarily in flight, then instantly turned around. I was thinking all the time about Benjie's rock and fretting over certain details which appeared in the photograph but were absent in the present reality, in particular a tiny lichen formation. So, I returned to the rock and was able to find the ring of lichen, which had been obscured by heather growth. While there, I lifted a flake of schist from the rock and took it away with me to add to the little cairn I'd built on Ben Gullion in Benjie's memory.

I had first noticed, and sat on, the bench-shaped rock on 25 June. That, too, was a still day, but cloudy, with the sun's appearance erratic in blinks. I watched, while smoking, a two-masted sailing ship, which I later identified in Campbeltown harbour as the *Royalist*, a sail training brig operated from Plymouth by the Marine Society and Sea Cadet Charity.

She was heading slowly towards the Sound of Islay across a calm sea. From my high vantage point, it was also a wide sea, and the ship had a toy-like appearance far below me. There were, of course, people aboard her, and I had met no one all that day, but I would never know who they were, far less communicate with them, and I doubt if any one of them gave thought to the possibility that human eyes on the distant blue coast, disappearing slowly astern, might be following their leisurely passage.

The notion occurred to me, too, that I could be sitting on my rock in the year 1813 watching the ship, for all that the twenty-first century intruded on the scene. If I looked past the rucksack, my own century might not exist. And there was that profound silence, which fills solitary places on such days. It has several registers, I imagine, of which the moorland one is the most intense, but I shall return to silence in another, later place on this journey through landscapes of memory and emotion.

With Barbara Matheson

3. Barbara Matheson enjoying lunch in the Inneans Glen before the rain came, 2 August 2013. Photograph by the author.

I was at Sròn Gharbh on 2 August with a niece, Barbara Matheson, from Skye. We sat under the ridge that day because the wind was strong southerly. There was no lingering or, for me, smoking. We had walked out from Ballygroggan to the Inneans Glen and stopped for lunch close to the end of Gleneadardacrock. We chose our spot in sunshine, but as we ate our 'barms' – those sweet provincial rolls beloved of 'exiles' – and drank our flask tea, we began to notice ominous sheets of rain slanting miles out to sea. I thought the showers might miss us, but we soon felt spits. Then came a distant peal of thunder and a lightning flash, which I noticed but Barbara, looking elsewhere, didn't. Then a downpour began and we gathered our stuff – the meal, by then, was over anyway – and hastened towards the burn to our left. By good fortune, we found at once a rock overhang and installed ourselves under it. Some rain was driving into our space, but we were able to keep the rucksacks dry and enjoy a modicum of comfort.

When the shower passed, we emerged from under the rock, crossed the glen to its north side and climbed to the old road which runs past the scant ruins of Innean Beag and the later sheep-fank, built, I suspect, from the township rubble. We were heading west for the skyline boulder which marks the northward turn in the road, and before we reached it I noticed in a wet spot a little colony of grass-of-parnassus, one of the later flowers of summer and a white-petalled beauty which ranks high in my list of favourites. I encouraged Barbara, who was unfamiliar with the species, to photograph one of the flowers, which she did, while I held its stem to steady it in the wind.

Further on, as the Inneans Bay opened out to our vision, she needed no encouragement to reach again for her camera. That view – of a cliff-bound green bay fringed by sand and breakers – was special to her because she was seeing it for the first time in over a quarter of a century. Back in the early 1980s, as a student nurse, and before she married Alistair Matheson and had their family, now grown to adulthood, she was a frequent companion of mine on hikes around south Kintyre. The Inneans was one of my favourite destinations, and became one of hers too, but on that day we would only look down into the bay. It was enough, however, for her, as it was for me. Habits change, and for me the compulsion to visit shores has receded, unless I am out to collect driftwood for the domestic fire.

Time was when no walk was complete without the ritual of wood-gathering and a kettle of tea brewed on a stick fire. A flask suffices now for me, yet Barbara, as she told me, preserves the tradition in her adoptive Skye, and she asked me if I still carried a kettle sometimes. The answer was 'No', but that's not to say that a soot-blackened kettle won't again find a place in my rucksack.

We lingered only minutes at the road-marker boulder but I shall return to it, for it too is a rock with a history, personal and conjectural. The wind was fierce there. No, plural – winds. There was one blowing westward through the glen and another blowing northward over the sea, its gusts apparent as scurrying ruffles on the surface; and when we faced northward to follow the old road up the coast, yet another wind met us.

The green oar

I showed Barbara the photograph of Benjie on the rock at Sròn Gharbh, then the rock itself, and finally the bench-shaped rock, with room for two persons to sit with feet planted comfortably on the ground. I had mentioned the marker oar and we looked at that. Days earlier I had remembered a poem I'd written, titled 'The green oar'. She asked what book it had been published in, and I told her it had never been published but that I'd look it out. Was this the same oar I'd written about? When we examined it, we saw green flakes of paint still adhering to the slowly perishing wood.

Three days afterwards, I looked for that poem which I couldn't remember, and found it in a ring-binder. There is nothing to it – mere whimsy – which explains why it was never published ... until now. Its time has come, on the back of a memoir. It was dated 4 October 1990.

> The green oar with the broken blade
> on the Atlantic shore is laid
> and I cannot help but wonder who
> was last to dip the green in blue.

I checked my hiking journal for particulars of that day and found that I had taken the 10 a.m. bus to Machrihanish and walked the coast to the Inneans. I'd been on Craigaig shore and had written the poem there while sheltering from wind. The oar, therefore, was on the beach and not stuck on the top of Sròn Gharbh, which I wouldn't have passed until later. Who carried the oar there and jammed it in the rock as a replacement for an earlier marker? I don't know, but I am certain it's the same oar that stands there to this day. Green oars are rare – I've only ever seen one!

I noted, while sheltering at Craigaig: 'My head is full of the desire to write, but I'm finding difficulty.' I'd already produced 'Spindrift' – a failure. Then came 'The green oar' – another failure. 'Not the goat' followed, but indecency of execution warped its potential.

'Not the goat'

> A musky whiff and I was with him
> black goat in the grip of dying,
> flat on his side and feebly kicking,
> snorting against his weight of horn,
> the visible eye half-shut and dimmed
> that he might lose the world
> by a slow and kindly fading.

By my standards, it wasn't a bad start. The scene-setting elements are exact, and that's because, as I admit in the second verse

> I'm huddled down behind a rock
> a minute from the bracken-rimmed
> and muddy hole he's lying in ...

By the end of the poem, the game is up:

> in truth, it was the poem I saw
> and not the goat.

I'd come upon the billy south of Craigaig and assumed that he was dying. He was, and I saw his bones amid slime and scattered wool in March of the following year. Injured or ill animals encountered on the hills are always vexing. If domestic, one can report them to the farmer, who might act responsibly or might not, depending on who he is. Increasingly, animals die unaided. There are no doubt more reasons than I can identify, but one of them is surely lack of manpower. I can think of big sheep farms which thirty or forty years ago employed three experienced shepherds and on which one man now does everything, hiring assistance only when he needs it. At bottom, altered markets and economic pressures are to blame.

Long walks

I was walking longer distances in the hills that summer than I'd walked in nearly thirty years. At the age of sixty-one ... but, wait, let me ponder that number and try to figure out what it means to me. *Nothing much* is the answer. Physically, I feel much as I did at the age of thirty-one. The legs are still muscular and stamina still takes me to the destinations I choose. Some parts of the 'soft machine' which is Angus Martin now function less efficiently, but that's to be expected. I take no medication of any kind, which at my age is probably unusual. I am not, however, complacent. Death is ahead of me and I need no reminders besides those I invite. I do not (yet) fear it, but I am conscious of its approach. Ten years away? A year? Six months? A day? I am more concerned with mental decline and final years languishing in a care home or psychiatric ward, lost to myself and those who knew me – a wrecked mind on an unrecognisable shore.

At the age of sixty-one I have been walking respectable distances and I admit to a feeling of quiet satisfaction on completion of one of the longer hikes, though I realise that there are contemporaries of mine, and others far older, who will cover much more ground in a day than I do.

On 12 July I caught, as I usually did, the 1 p.m. bus to Machrihanish and headed for Largiebaan cliffs by the Kintyre Way. Rather than return by the same route, I resolved this time to head for Glenahanty and take the hill road by Lochorodale to catch the last bus from Southend at Auchencorvie around 10 p.m., and I managed it comfortably, even with my two customary stops for refreshment. That became a round trip I was eager to repeat, and did. Since I turned sixty, I have possessed a bus pass which entitles me to free travel anywhere in Scotland. I'm not particularly interested in greater Scotland, but that wafer of plastic with my photo on it gets me around Kintyre at no personal expense. It's a privilege I'm grateful for, but not one, I suspect, that my daughters will ever enjoy.

I've been trying to recall my longest ever hike in a day and I believe I have it, though I've yet to find a record of it in any notebook and I can't suggest even a year, never mind a date. I'd walked from town to Machrihanish and from there to the Inneans, where I remember meeting Allister Stewart (but not Agnes, though no doubt she would have been there). I was clearly still a novice and asked Allister how I might get back to Campbeltown by a different route. He suggested I follow the iron fence posts which marked the march of Ballygroggan with Largiebaan on the south side of the glen. I seized on his advice and followed these posts – they still stand, though the march apparently has since been adjusted – which led me through Gleneadardacrock to Glenahanty. But instead of turning left at the end of the track, I turned right into Glenbreackerie and added miles to the journey. I suppose I must later have turned north at Drumavoulin.

Whatever, I found myself walking in a late summer's evening which has assumed, in memory, a magical – or mythic – dimension. The hills had turned a hazy blue all around and the whole landscape was steeped in the profoundest silence I have ever known, so that I felt myself transported into another world. Not even a bird sang, or so I remember – nature herself seemed awed into a total silence. I was still far from home and night was near, but I felt myself wrapped in an exquisite sense of spiritual well-being, as though I had arrived at a state of perfect acceptance in which nothing mattered but being in that unimaginable passage of time. On Killellan brae, however, a kind lady, Elsie McPherson, stopped in her car and offered me a lift into town, and I accepted with a sense of gratitude which remains undiminished to this day.

A camp at the Inneans

On 6 August 2013, I called in at George McSporran's house in Campbeltown and enjoyed coffee and conversation with him and his son Sandy. On my way home, I noticed Teddy Lafferty sitting on the bench under the Town Hall clock. I sat beside him and we were joined soon after by Iain MacGillivray, who proposed, in the passage of conversation, that his native Glenelg was the only Scottish place-name which spells itself backwards (though not in its Gaelic form, as Iain would know). I'd had no lunch, so I suggested we repair to the little café on the opposite side of Main Street. Iain was going home, so there was just Teddy and me for tea and scones.

4. Willie MacArthur and nephew beside tent in Inneans Bay, c. 1975. Photograph by Teddy Lafferty.

I mentioned the oar at Sròn Gharbh and Teddy immediately remembered taking a photograph of Willie MacArthur beside an oar about forty years back. I was curious as to how two 'loners' happened to be together that day, and Teddy explained the circumstances in thoroughly memorised detail.

He was camping in the Inneans Bay one summer with his little blue tent, and about 11 p.m. heard movements outside. While listening intently to try to interpret the disturbance, he heard a voice hail him: 'Hello, the camp!' This was Willie MacArthur and a young nephew, and Teddy was astonished at the lateness of their arrival; but Willie explained that he had received a new tent from a sister in Wales and that he took a notion that evening to try it out, so he asked his brother Hugh to run him to Glenahanty. And so he appeared in the bay at nightfall. Teddy had a torch and helped him pitch the tent. It was a big one, by ordinary standards, and after they put it up Teddy noticed that it was squint and cautioned Willie to be sure to straighten it out in the morning in case visitors came and noticed the state of it.

Visitors did come – Allister and Agnes Stewart – but they remarked only that they'd never before seen two tents in the Inneans at the same time. Agnes would have photographed the blue tents side by side from high ground on her way in, but had left her camera in the car. (A few days later, I asked Agnes if she had any memory of that day. She hadn't, and explained that she had discarded her diaries while moving house in 1980, but she reckoned the year would have been about 1975.)

Teddy packed his gear before Willie did, and set off on to Beinn na Faire to compose a photograph of the bay. Then he lay back with his head resting on the rucksack and fell asleep in the sun. He woke into startling glare, hearing Willie's voice: 'There he is, lyin there.' Willie and his nephew had been delayed when the boy dropped a roll of gear on the hill-slope; it bounced back to the bottom and Willie had to retrieve it. Carrying the tent in a kit-bag slung over a shoulder, he looked exhausted. All three made their way north and Teddy took a photograph of Willie and his nephew beside an oar they encountered. I asked him to look it out for me.

When I visited Teddy in September to see the photograph, it was immediately obvious that this was an oar in another place. It was stuck in the middle of moorland, roughly inland from Sròn Gharbh, and its purpose there was ambiguous, to say the least. Had someone found it on the coast and begun carrying it home and then wearied of the task and left it standing, to be located and shouldered another day? What became of it? Teddy enquired at the time, but no one had an answer.

5. *Willie MacArthur and nephew beside oar on moor inland from Sròn Gharbh, looking north, c. 1975. Photograph by Teddy Lafferty.*

Willie MacArthur

I met Willie MacArthur for the first time on 31 August 1980 at the Inneans and realised at once, from talking to him, that he had knowledge which I wanted. I entered the following in my journal:

> Went across to the Gulls Den with John [MacDonald]. On my way back met Willie MacArthur with Donald MacVicar's two sons. He was on his way to a lythe fishing rock with line. His was an unusual lure – sheep's wool, which, initially, he had used for tying on bait; but, by observation, he discovered that when the bait had been 'sooked oot', the lythe would continue to attack the wool.
>
> He showed me the wee burn that flows down by Innean Mor – and which, I assume, served that community – and advocated its water, a couple of bottles of which he customarily carries home with him. He told me that he formerly camped here with the lads from Drumlemble.
>
> An incident which he recalled: one time a rat was washing itself when a falcon swooped upon it and lifted it perhaps 60 feet into the air, and dropped it on the shingle. And the rat raced off ...
>
> Wood Bay is to the north around the point.

Willie took John MacDonald, Donald Docherty and me from Largiebaan over Cnoc Moy and into the Inneans on 19 April of the following year, when I noted that his legs were 'still stiff after his serious accident'; he had been struck by a car. The following also went into my journal: 'Willie pointed out a bluish haze on the tops of the peaks to the south of Largybaan and affirmed that the phenomenon indicated, by his experience, two or three days' good weather. Goose pimples on the bare flesh in warm weather portended rain, he found.'

I had already, in February 1981, tape-recorded him at the Flush, where he lived with his brother Hugh and family. I would use a little of what he told me in *Kintyre: The Hidden Past*, but most of his stories didn't fit.

He was taken to the Inneans for the first time around 1948 by Eddie Kerr and Don Thomson from Drumlemble. Some of the campers at that time went with nothing, not even a blanket. In fine summer weather Willie himself would lie in the open beside a fire and manage some sleep. His tiredness, after the hike out there, helped, and, anyway, by four in the morning the sky had lightened and night was over.

Willie kept 'bags o' gear' beside the burn, but one year 'at the gull eggs time' (p 70) a gang of lads threw all his pots and pans on the beach and broke them up, a bout of mischief which one of the Ballygroggan shepherds, Donald Sinclair, observed from a hilltop. Another year, a party of soldiers 'stole' all Willie's rabbit snares and removed a tent which belonged to Duncan McLachlan. Duncan was furious, but Willie and Malcolm Hamilton later recovered the tent, lying wet at the north end of the bay. Willie went to RAF Machrihanish and lodged a complaint, but to no effect. 'The buggers,' Willie said, 'were supposed tae be roon on a survival course – they survived on the stuff I left!'

Willie also complained of 'loafers' who would appear in the bay expecting free food and shelter, but unwilling even to gather firewood. Malcolm once brought back a fellow in a suit he'd met in town and took pity on because he seemed 'lonely'. Willie was annoyed and told Malcolm: 'Well, by Christ, you can cook for him!' When he had calmed down, he said to Malcolm to tell the visitor there were only three slices of bread left and that 'Willie's up first – he eats hell of a breid in the moarnin'. Sure enough, at dawn, when Willie emerged from the tent to start the fire, the guest was at his back, 'so that he winna miss his slice o' breid'.

Willie, who was a lime-burner at Fort Argyll, spent summer holidays at the Inneans with Malcolm. The two would meet at Machrihanish and then set off. If the weather was good, the first week would fly in, but if rainy it was a weary sojourn.

He and Malcolm would retreat under a cliff in heavy rain, but by then Malcolm might already be soaked to the backside. 'I don'know how thon man dinna feenish up with pneumonia,' Willie remarked. But Malcolm was hardy and 'never stopped' when walking the hills. He told Willie once that he was at the Inneans as a teenager and there was only a gill of whisky between five of them. 'These were the hard days,' Malcolm joked.

A little of the magic of the Inneans seeped into Willie's recollections when he mentioned taking newcomers there. Before descending into the bay, he'd say to them, 'Aw, sit here for a while – A'm waantin tae look doon at that sea' – it was all blues and greens in the bright sun.

Towards the end of the recording, Willie asked me if I'd ever read any of Jack Kerouac's books. He had bought *Big Sur* in the Courier Office and it was just like reading about the Inneans, he enthused. The 'bit wid come on him – the coast!', and he'd 'bugger off in the dark' with his pack and a torch, and 'You'll be over and he'll be over'. I've never read the novel but that's how Willie described it.

Willie, with a full cast of other Inneans stalwarts, makes three appearances in the forty-verse comic poem which opens with 'A bunch of boys to the Aonans came'. It was signed 'Gruachan Ben', which I assume to be a corruption of 'Ben Cruachan', so perhaps the author was a Campbell. I enquired after his identity, but without success. Perhaps some reader knows and can also provide an original copy of the ballad, which is incomplete in all the versions I have so far seen. It's a competent piece of versification as to rhyme and scansion, notwithstanding some missing and garbled lines, and it's also very entertaining in its character-by-character portrayal of a merry night around a camp-fire in the bay. These are two of Willie's appearances.

> Then Kerter went for loads of sticks
> And they were hard to get.

> He said to Brown, 'We're in a fix –
> The sticks are soakin wet.'
>
> 'The Parson's Son' was read aloud,
> We murdered 'Old Fantown'.
> McArthur seemed upon a cloud
> wi' 'The Star o' the County Down'.

Agnes Stewart, a singer herself and a member of the noted Mitchell Singers, recalled Willie as 'a real good singer when he had a dram or two'. The Stewarts met Willie at the Inneans on several occasions, and here Agnes contributes two culinary anecdotes from those distant summers.

> He was making stew – probably rabbit stew – one day when we came on him in the bay. As he stirred the pot, a piece of meat fell on the ground. He lifted it from among the sheep shit, rubbed it on a rather doubtful pullover, and said, 'Dae ye want a plate o' stew?' We politely declined.
> On another occasion, when he was cooking with a different pot, he told us that he had found a full set in the 'toon dump'. 'I'll jeest show ye where I hide them – use them any time ye want.' They were solid but rusty pots, and again we declined the offer.

William MacArthur died in Lorne Campbell Court sheltered housing, Campbeltown, on 20 March 1989 at the age of seventy-two.

First visits to the Inneans

As related in *Kintyre: The Hidden Past* (p 146), Willie's pal Malcolm Hamilton and brother Stewart Hamilton pitched a bell-tent at the Inneans in the mid-1960s. It was undoubtedly the biggest tent ever known in the bay, and Teddy Lafferty told me that they got it there, assisted by Johnny Coffield, in short stages. Each man took a turn at lugging the heavy canvas until they had all reached the limit of their endurance, when the load would be abandoned. Next time they were heading to the Inneans, the tent would be located and the effort renewed until it arrived in the bay months later, having been rolled downhill at the very last. Teddy remembers seeing it, years afterwards, collapsed and rotting in the bay.

6. The Hamilton tent in the Inneans Bay, looking north, 24 September 1967. Photograph by the author.

My boyhood friend Iain Campbell and I went to the Inneans on 23 September 1967 with our own little tent, in which we spent an uncomfortable night, not realising that the big tent we could see already pitched in the bay was unoccupied. We could have spent the night there instead – in the spirit of the coasting fraternity, no one would have minded as long as we left things as we had found them – but teenage inhibitions held us back.

In *Kintyre:The Hidden Past* I record this as 'my first experience' of the Inneans, but I was mistaken. I'd been there exactly a month earlier with a group of friends, a fiasco which took us on to the summit of Cnoc Moy before we saw the bay below us and were able to orientate ourselves. We 'saw the unknown sailor's grave' and met 'R. Hamilton & J. McCallum etc. camped there' – presumably in the big tent! On reflection, that encounter probably inspired my own camping trip later that summer.

Both records are in a slim red-covered 'Silvine' exercise book which had been stored in a filing cabinet in the old shop below our flat in Saddell Street. When I looked in that cabinet in 2012, I found to my horror that mice had nested in the drawer and that the bottom left-hand corner of the notebook had been nibbled away for bedding material. The earlier record in its entirety and the greater part of the later record survived the mice's depredations – other diaries were completely shredded – as did two little photographs, taken with my 'Brownie' camera and reproduced here.

> 23 & 24 September 1967. Left on the Saturday afternoon, taking bus to Drumlemble, where we purchased ice lollies. Were exceedingly heavily laden but after about 4 or 5 hours walking over moor and bog we arrived, in smirr, at our destination, to discover that there was already a tent up (but unoccupied, as we were later to find out). Unable to light fire, so ate supper of cream and mixed canned fruit. Forgot groundsheet (or rather no groundsheet existed) so slept on wet grass in wet clothes. Wakened up periodically during night, switching on transistor now & then.

Still wet in morning, so decided after lighting a fire and cooking 1 tin beans, 1 tin spaghetti, and 4 beefburgers to leave for home. Most miserable homeward journey, progressed painfully slowly over moor and mire, soaked, despondent and tired. Reached Killypole Loch eventually, then went on the road and were picked up by farmer and taken to Stewarton, where we were lifted again from bus shelter [remainder of narrative destroyed by mice.]

7. *The author with tent, fire and cooking pots beside Allt Dubh, the Inneans Bay, 24 September 1967. Photograph by Iain Campbell.*

The 'transistor' which Iain and I were 'switching on now & then', when we woke in our damp prison, was of course a portable radio, which must have provided us with some spiritual comfort in the night. We were in the 'summer of love', though we didn't know that at the time, and the songs I noted in my jotter reflect the mood of the times: Bobbie Gentry's 'Ode to Billy Joe'; Scott McKenzie's 'San Francisco (Be Sure to Wear Some Flowers in Your Hair)'; Flowerpot Men's 'Let's go to San Francisco'; Traffic's 'Hole in my Shoe'; Small Faces' 'Itchycoo Park', and one out-of-the-ordinary specimen, which failed to register on the chart, 'The Madman Running Through the Fields' by Dantalian's Chariot, which Zoot Money formed after his Big Roll Band broke up.

I would have done well to have remembered, in later years, that radio Iain and I carried to the Inneans and back, because I subsequently developed an antipathy to technological intrusion in wild places. I can cite an example, noted on 16 May 1992. I was cycling to the family caravan at Polliwilline and stopped at the Second Waters to enjoy a peaceful lunch.

> Minutes after I got here, two carloads of noisy youths arrived & took over the lay-by. They are on the grass around the cars, music blaring. I'm across the burn, on the south side, concealed more or less by trees, though they know I'm here. In a way, it's better to be entirely visible – one feels less surreptitious. Their idiotic singing irritates me. There's the music of the burn & of the birds – quite sufficient. I must be getting old and intolerant, but I'd like these people banned from the countryside.

There was another late '60s camping trip which should have ended at the Inneans, but didn't. It isn't recorded in my red jotter and all I remember of it is that Michael McGeachy, a boyhood neighbour, was with Iain Campbell and me on that adventure, and that when I crawled out the tent in the morning I was startled by a vision of total blue – the tent was pitched on a grassy slope, with nothing but sea and sky beyond the doorway. I assume we must have run out of time on our way to the bay and had to settle for that crazy site, but I have no recollection of where we were. Michael remembers a little more.

He agrees that the tent was on a slope, but also remembers that it was close to a cliff. We all had a stroll before setting up the tent, he says, and after eating an 'Aztec' bar, he carelessly dropped the wrapper, which, when he was out again during the night, he ground into the turf with the heel of his shoe. In the morning, he rediscovered the wrapper 'about three feet from the cliff-edge'. It was a windy night and 'we couldn't have pitched the tent in a worse place if we had tried', he remarked. He remembers that we did visit the bay, next day, and the Sailor's Grave is clear in his memory, along with 'about three million rabbits running about'.

Rabbits have been extinct there for several years, for reasons which elude my understanding. Predation seems the obvious cause – eagles, buzzards and mink for a start – but was the colony perhaps first depleted by an outbreak of myxomatosis which went unnoticed? And how did the rabbits arrive in the Inneans Bay in the first place? Migration of even a minimal breeding stock across miles of moorland or along a rocky coast seems unlikely to me. Perhaps they were introduced to provide a food source for the post-war camping fraternity, which certainly shot and trapped them. Had I asked the likes of Willie MacArthur, an answer might have been forthcoming, but it's probably too late now for answers.

1984

During the writing of this book, I read, among many other books, Derek Cooper's *The Road to Mingulay*, in which I found the following recollection which prompted one of my own: 'I sat on Skye for most of the summer of 1984; it was the hottest and driest period in living memory. The sun had come out of the clouds on Easter Saturday and with a few striking exceptions it had gone on shining ever since.' That's exactly as I remembered that summer, which started for me at the Inneans on Saturday, 21 April.

I was with Donald Docherty, Ruari MacLean and Jimmy MacDonald, and we arrived in the bay an hour before sunset. We had two tents, which we began pitching right away. I had come without tent poles, which were to hand when I began packing, but had inexplicably disappeared by the time I'd finished. I improvised using two sticks from the shore, whittling them to points to fit the eyelets on either end of the little tent. Having set up camp, we dined on cheese and tomato rolls and then opened a quarter-bottle of 'Black Bottle' whisky – 'scarcely adequate', as I noted ruefully in my journal – and a couple of bottles of 'Belhaven' pale ale. When we retreated from the fireside to our tents, the sky was 'full of stars – a veritable plethora – and the air chill'.

I was sharing a tent with young Jimmy and 'slept remarkably well, waking at intervals of an hour or an hour-and-a-half when the particular discomfort of my position became unbearable'. After a simple breakfast of cheese and bread, we set out for the Gulls' Den in the south and looked into it from various points along the ridge. 'En route there,' I added, 'we saw an eagle hustled out of its course by several ravens; one in particular dived repeatedly at its back and turned it swiftly towards Largybaan whence it had come.'

I didn't comment on the weather, but memory and the photographs I took that week-end attest to clear skies and unseasonable warmth. Nor did I mention that I would be setting out the next week on a journey to the Glens of Antrim, which took me two days by public transport – by bus to Glasgow and thence, after an overnight stay, by train to Stranraer to catch a ferry to Larne. I remember sitting at the camp-fire in the Inneans and looking across the North Channel to my very destination. At that time, there was no ferry-link from Campbeltown. The previous one was thirteen years in the past and the next one thirteen years in the future.

8. *Jimmy MacDonald (L) and the author on the cliff-top near the Gulls' Den, 22 April 1984. Photograph by Ruari MacLean.*

I was in County Antrim to deliver a lecture to the Glens of Antrim Historical Society, and it didn't go well. The lecture was titled 'The Irish in Kintyre', and I decided to use the chapter of that name in my book *Kintyre: The Hidden Past* as the basis. I belatedly realised that the text was too stodgy to read aloud, but that's what I had to do, to a large expectant audience which frankly intimidated me. Being rather new to the lecturing business, I hadn't thought to assemble a set of illustrations, and so denied myself that simple means of enlivening the material. I spent a week in the Glens, the pre-lecture part of which was devoted to worrying about what I'd let myself in for, and the post-lecture part to reproaching myself for having betrayed the faith of my generous hosts.

It was during that week in County Antrim that I was introduced to poteen of a quality I hadn't suspected could exist. I'd first sampled the stuff in a house in Edinburgh in the 1970s, and if I hadn't been told what it was, I'd have guessed that it was a lavatory-cleaning fluid and that my host wished me dead. On the second occasion, my host was an Irish speaker, lived on the Antrim coast and was a respected member of the community. His source of poteen was an elderly widow living in a remote part of the countryside. Her standards were high, and her product, distilled from potatoes, was as smooth on the palate as the earlier one had been harsh. Judy and I, on our honeymoon in 1985, spent a few nights as guests of that same gentleman and his wife, when Judy too was introduced to the superior spirit. Occasionally, in later years, one of our host's daughters, when visiting Campbeltown, would bring us a little deceptively labelled plastic bottle containing a certain clear liquid.

On 7 May, I was on the summit of Cnoc Moy, en route to the Inneans with Jimmy MacDonald, and noted in my journal:

> This time last week I was preparing to leave Glasgow by bus for home, having ended my week in County Antrim. Here I am – 12.50 p.m. – on top of Cnoc Moy, with my back resting on the trig point, on which I have pencilled the names of myself and Jimmy, and looking across to the bluest Ireland, so blue it is almost diaphanous. I wonder if anyone will read this after my death and understand the satisfaction of such a feeling.

Never mind 'after my death' – here it is! My euphoria, however, was not shared by my eight-year-old companion: 'Jimmy is lying in the foetal position, suffering from his not infrequent nausea. He probably ate and drank too quickly after the exertion of the climb.' When Jimmy got to his feet again, I photographed him, looking queasy, at the triangulation pillar. Thirty years on, Jimmy is the one with camera in hand and serious intentions in mind. He provided the front cover for this book, but neither landscape nor portraiture is his main interest. In the past five years he has been assembling an impressive collection of wildlife photographs, many of them won from nature's extremes.

9. *A queasy Jimmy MacDonald at the triangulation pillar on the summit of Cnoc Moy, 7 May 1984. Photograph, taken facing north, by the author.*

Evasive tactics at Largiebaan

Earlier in the day – 6 August – that I met Teddy Lafferty, on my way across town I'd met another hill-walker. I withhold his name for fear of embarrassing him, but I trust that if he reads this his response will be one of amusement – no hard feelings, brother! His first words, 'I must apologise to you', puzzled me at once. I hadn't seen him for years (or so I thought), so what was he apologising for? The explanation followed immediately – he'd avoided me at Largiebaan. I remembered the encounter very clearly. It had happened less than a month back, on 12 July.

I took the 1 p.m. bus to Machrihanish, and when I sat, two hours later, on an airy rock close to the old Ballygroggan peat-bank, I noted in my journal 'a sweltering day' and a bus unusually busy, with passengers, young and old, travelling to the beach for sunshine, sand and sea.

As I toiled up Lossit brae I had seen two men approaching downhill with backpacks. One of them was James Lafferty, Teddy's nephew, who remarked that he had recognised me from a distance by my gait (identical, I am assured by my sister Barbara, to that of a maternal uncle, John McKenzie). He and his friend had camped the night in the Inneans Bay and were now heading for the Old Clubhouse for a refreshing beer. One bottle of beer, remaining from the supply they had carried with them to the Inneans, had been deposited in the burn which runs past the camp-site. In that information was the implicit invitation to help myself to it. I told them I didn't intend going into the bay, but was heading for Largiebaan.

Beer in the burn is, I suppose, a tradition of sorts out there. I have found bottled and canned beer there in the past and drank it. Some visitors may leave it in the hope of its still being there on a subsequent trip, but the cans and bottles are seldom concealed and the real motive, I suspect, is just to lighten the load for the return journey.

James reported having met Alex Docherty that day, and I wasn't surprised, since Alex, in his own quiet way, is one of the most active cyclists and hill-walkers in Kintyre and I'd expect to see him myself at least once a year in some more or less remote spot. Meet him I did that day. I had reached the point in the Inneans Glen where the track dips to the confluence of two burns, when I saw a figure approaching from Innean Mòr sheep-fank. Close to my observation point, three weeks later, I would sit out a thunder plump with Alex's cousin, Barbara Matheson. Alex's father John Docherty and

Barbara's father Malcolm were brothers. The coincidence pleases me for no other reason than that I am able to make the connection; and, in years to come, if I have years left to me, I shall 'see' these blood relatives together in a shared landscape, be that landscape actual or in memory.

Alex and I met half-way down the glen and stopped for conversation. I remarked on the heat of the day, a subtle complaint, but he countered wisely that such weather was so rare it demanded to be enjoyed. His big news from the bay I would not be descending into was that two canoeists had earlier landed there. They were both women and had paddled round the Mull heading for Machrihanish, a bold undertaking, I am assured by a canoeist friend.

An hour and a quarter later, from the cliff-top at Largiebaan, I watched a lone canoeist slipping northward. I was on the highest point of the cliff – a feature to which I shall return – and stood there, intending to be seen against the skyline should the canoeist happen to look landward. To increase the chance of being noticed, I decided to shout, but shouting is something I very seldom feel I have to resort to, and the result was self-consciously tame and elicited no response. Had I tried again, I could have improved on the performance, but Largiebaan is a vast and echoing place and I already felt insignificant and foolish. I left the cliff-top earlier than I'd have wished, at 6.15, but I was aiming to reach the main road at Auchencorvie before 10 to catch the last bus into town. I'd never before attempted that circular route and was uncertain about time and distance. I needn't, however, have worried – the walk was completed with half an hour to spare.

Between cliff and forest, I saw a man walking briskly towards me on the same track. The walk had already turned out to be sociable, and here was a third encounter about to happen. Except it didn't happen, because he abruptly veered south-west without acknowledging me and kept going without a backward glance. I watched him disappear towards the cliffs, noticing his proper outdoor gear and his rucksack with something suspicious-looking protruding from the top of it (it was a walking-pole, I later found out). I felt cheated, and, when he drove past me later, I was facing the roadside, notebook in hand, recording the co-ordinates of a ringlet butterfly, but more especially turning my back to him.

I hadn't recognised him, and his identity would probably have eluded me for all time had he not offered his apology in the street weeks later. He had recognised me, but not on the track to the cliff, otherwise he would have spoken. The explanation for his reaction – which I respect, but do not share – is that, having had unfortunate experiences with landowners and their employees, he prefers to avoid walkers unless he knows them ... and at 6.30 p.m. on 12 July 2013 he did not know me.

I have often thought about the wide range of responses experienced when meeting people in remote places. My philosophy is this – if they are doing what I am doing, then they'll probably be interesting, and, equally, will probably find me interesting, particularly if they are strangers to Kintyre. And, indeed, I have met many interesting – even exotic – fellow-walkers, though lifelong friendships are rarely formed on the strength of a ten-minute conversation. At the opposite extreme, I have known other walkers avoid me.

One example has lodged firmly in my memory and it's the one I dislodge for discussion should this subject come up. When Jimmy MacDonald accompanied me on a hike from the Mull to Machrihanish on 4 April 1984, we weren't long started when we noticed a couple of other walkers ahead of us. I adjusted our route so that it would intersect with theirs, but they clearly weren't having it and turned away in a direction that took them clear of us. I was annoyed, since I've always considered it a courtesy to engage with other hikers in lonely places where humans are rarely encountered. I admit that curiosity is part of my motivation. Who are they, where are they from and why are they here? 'They', however, sometimes don't share that curiosity and prefer to be solitary in solitude. Having said that, a couple of good friends of mine are certain to be emotionally crushed if they arrive at a destination – the Inneans, say – and find others already in occupation. I am delighted with the prospect of a chat; they are inconsolable!

The same principles apply at sea, another kind of wilderness. When herring fishing was slack, boats would come together so that crews could mingle and pass the time. I recall one night in the 1970s, in the Kilbrannan Sound, when the moon was too bright for ring-netting, and we tied alongside our neighbour-boat. It was a lovely interlude, which I chose to spend on deck, taking in the beauty of the scene: the moonlit waters with the black backdrop of the Arran mountains in the east, and the pure silence, with the engines switched off and the boats drifting together. I remember reflecting that this would have been how it was in the days of the skiffs, before the invention of noisy engines.

When sailing ships met in mid-ocean, they'd signal to each other with flags, and, if sea conditions permitted, would heave-to, lower out a life-boat, and the two captains would meet and exchange news. Fresh faces were rarely encountered on long voyages and such opportunities were seized. Herman Melville, in *Moby Dick*, devoted an entire chapter to the custom.

Frights at Largiebaan

By mid-July, I had been out to the cliffs at Largiebaan five times, surpassing the total of any previous year, and without the involvement of any car. Not that I was trying to establish a 'personal best'. There are easy explanations – the rare sunny summer of that year, and, no doubt fuelled by these conditions, a rekindling of my passion for the place. Not that I descended to the celebrated caves. It's a rocky, inhospitable shore and can be difficult to reach. I know it well enough, and had no great desire to return there. Perhaps age is a factor. Perhaps the increasing solitariness of my walking is also a factor. Should someone ask me to take him, or her, to these shores, I would agree – the role of 'guide' pleases me – but few such requests reach me, and my hiking companions of the past have rather dropped out, lost to other pursuits or themselves preferring solitary ways.

I had a fright at Largiebaan in 2012. On 3 June I went with Jimmy MacDonald to the coast south of Rubha Dùn Bhàin and sat with him for an hour or two of bird-watching. From there we headed north and crossed the burn on to the shore and looked around the caves. When it came time to leave, Jimmy recommended a route which he had taken before. I was all set to climb straight out from where we were – my usual route – but agreed to try his way, which involved going north a bit from the caves and up from there. The initial stage – surmounting a rock-face, modest though it was – I found difficult, but not alarming. It was when I followed Jimmy to his chosen point of ascent that my problems began.

As he was scaling the rock-face, I happened to look away from him and suddenly realised that I was standing on a ledge above a drop into the sea. A slip would almost certainly have meant death, and I reached an instantaneous decision – I wasn't going any further ... I was going back ... and at once! Jimmy was surprised, but understanding, and decided he'd accompany me back, but when he looked down the way he had come, he, in turn, changed his mind. So we quickly agreed that he'd continue, while I retreated, and that we'd meet on the top. He'd tell me later that his one anxiety was how I'd cope with that rock-face at the caves. He needn't have worried – I scrambled down it in seconds, desperate to put the place firmly behind me.

I took a winding route up the scree slope, stopping to examine flowers on the way, and when I reached the top Jimmy was waiting for me. He admitted that he'd never been so glad to see anyone in his life before. I enjoyed the climb out, its familiarity enhanced by a sense of intense relief, and close to the top sighted a little fox eyeing me curiously from a rock pile I'd dodged around. Largiebaan, I concluded that day, is not for the faint-hearted ... or, perhaps, the ageing.

I'd had similar experiences before. I remembered climbing down a rock-face to retrieve a walking-stick I'd dropped, and being unable to find foot-holds below or hand-holds above; I remembered fear, a scorching sun, and flies buzzing around my face. I didn't, however, remember how I escaped the trap I'd descended into. When I looked in my journals, I discovered, in a curiously flat account, that I'd got back up the way I had come: 'I got stuck mid-way down a rock face and was forced, after increasingly perturbing indecision, to climb back on to the grass ledge.' For 'increasingly perturbing indecision' read *mounting panic*! The date was 29 August 1981 and the incident took place on the south side of Uamha Ròpa. I was heading for Largiebaan with a nephew, Malcolm Docherty, who was camping with me in the Inneans Bay, but in memory I was alone that day. In the end, I found an easier way down and managed to retrieve my stick.

Benjie had a fall on that coast, at Largiebaan. We had gone there with Hartwig Schutz on 23 October 1999 and were descending to the shore when his paws slipped on a rock. He didn't fall far, about twenty feet I reckoned, but he was bouncing off rocks on his way down. He seemed unharmed, but had injured an ear which would discharge periodically and foully for the rest of his life.

Back in October 1993, after a visit to the Largiebaan caves with George and Sandy McSporran, I called on ninety-year-old Alex Colville in Campbeltown to tell him that I had seen his name in the main cave, marking a visit in 1931 with A.P. MacGrory, M. C. Watson, A. Watson and J. S. Richmond. He told me a story about a minister – relieving the Rev B. B. Blackwood in Lochend U.F. Church – who had taken his two grandsons to Largiebaan in the late 1920s. One of the boys broke a leg there and the other was sent to Largiebaan steading to fetch help. The brothers Jamie and Alistair Beattie answered the summons, and carried the injured boy on a 'fleck' – a portable gate – all the way from the shore, a remarkable feat of strength.

A report of that accident eluded me until the final stages of this book, when, in the *Campbeltown Courier* of 12 September 1931, I noticed a news item headed 'Boy's Narrow Escape'. The accident had happened not in 'the late 1920s', but in the same year Alex had gone to the caves, and other details had become similarly muddled in his memory. There was only one boy, whose name was Peter Gordon-Dean. He was twelve years old and a grandson of the Rev John MacNeill, D.D., who was spending the summer at Westport. The party which visited the caves included the boy's mother and a MacNeill uncle. Peter, while 'exploring the cliff face', fell about twenty feet and then rolled a further three hundred feet. 'The incident created great alarm' – I'll bet it did! – and 'assistance was obtained from the shepherd's house at Largiebaan'. 'Mr Beattie jnr.', the report continued, 'rendered valuable aid in conveying the boy from the difficult spot at which the accident occurred to Gartnacopaig House, whence, after first aid had been rendered, he was taken to Campbeltown Cottage Hospital.' His injuries consisted of a fractured left wrist and 'bruises and abrasions on various parts of the body'.

There was a sequel to the accident, which Alex remembered clearly because he was involved in it. The minister, to express his gratitude, asked A. P. MacGrory – owner of an electrical shop in Main Street – to install a wireless set at Largiebaan for the Beattie family, and Alex helped 'Tony' MacGrory carry the set up the brae from Glenahanty. The father, John Beattie, who wore a long patriarchal beard, remarked of the wireless: 'I can sit at the fire noo and listen tae the word o' God.' By then, it was taking him the greater part of a Sunday to walk to the church in Southend and back. He died, aged seventy, on 14 March 1935, at Largiebaan, in the very house in which he'd been born. He was a thoroughbred Borderer by lineage, his mother having been a Todd, though the Todds, by virtue of an earlier arrival in Argyll than the Beatties, 'became Gaelic speakers and Highlanders to all intents and purposes'.[1]

Bruach Dearg

The steep road up from Glenahanty has a Gaelic name which isn't on any map – I heard it from shepherds who had lived at Largiebaan. It is known as Bruach Dearg, 'Red Brae', from the reddish soil that forms the road; but there is more than soil on the road – it's stony, and has been ever since I can remember. I was on the Southend postal delivery intermittently for a few years in the late 1980s and at first found that brae very intimidating. It was a case of into first gear at the bottom and keep the foot on the accelerator all the way to the top. If the motor should stall, there was no choice but to reverse all the way to the bottom and try again.

That said, my journal for 1980 tells me that on 31 August John MacDonald and I got a lift in Allister and Agnes Stewart's car to Gartnacopaig, and that they drove all the way to Largiebaan, to walk from there to Machrihanish, so the road was clearly in tolerable condition then. Sitting in the doorway of Gleneadardacrock, I noted an 'exceptionally fortuitous launch' to that day's outing. John and I had been standing at the Witchburn 'thumbing a lift' for almost half-an-hour when the Stewarts stopped for us and took us as far as we wished to go. That was the day of my first encounter with Willie MacArthur at the Inneans (p 22). He was one of five other visitors to the bay that afternoon, and we also saw two figures on the skyline, whom we assumed to be Agnes and Allister. 'We waved and they returned the gesture.'

I remember returning one evening from Largiebaan, around the same time, and seeing a car abandoned at the bottom of the Bruach Dearg. I discovered later that an elderly lady from Southend had been trying to get to Largiebaan to join a Kintyre Antiquarian Society outing, had driven into a ditch and burned out the clutch in repeated efforts to get the car back on the road. She had been told to park above Dalsmirren and await a lift to Largiebaan, but ignored the advice and paid the penalty.

10. Neil McKellar (L) and Bob Halbert at the mouth of the big cave at Largiebaan, 8 August 1982. Photograph by the author.

I was in a car which unexpectedly ran out of fuel on the brae. It belonged to Neil McKellar's mother, Jenny, in Campbeltown. I had met Neil, who was then a fisheries economist in Edinburgh, in the Ardshiel Hotel, and we arranged a trip to Largiebaan the following day. Also with us that day, 8 August 1982, was his friend Bob Halbert and a young neighbour of mine, John MacDonald. The day was misty and damp, but we 'went through the motions' – built a fire, brewed a pot of tea, and then explored the caves using a small torch Neil had brought with him. Our exit from the shore to the cliff-top was by the scree slope on the south side of the caves. That I was carrying a bag of goat dung for the leeks and onions in my garden didn't make the climb any easier for me. The farmer at Gartnacopaig, John Harvey, kindly siphoned two bottles of petrol from the tank of his own car, which was enough to get us back to town.

I'd met Neil, who was several years older than me, through his sister Margaret. Their father, also Neil, who belonged to Greenock, retired in 1969 from the Royal Bank of Scotland after forty-four years in banking.[2] He and my own father died within three months of each other in the first quarter of 1975, aged sixty-five and sixty-four respectively. Bob's father, George Halbert, who was also in banking, died the year after. A native of Ayrshire, he came to Campbeltown in 1949 to manage the Clydesdale Bank and held that post until his retirement in 1968.[3]

Largiebaan, 1967

I forget how my interest in Largiebaan was stimulated. Did I hear about the place from someone? Until 2013, when I looked in the jotter that mice almost destroyed, I'd believed that my first trip to Largiebaan had been in 1980, but an account dated 20 August 1967, tells me that I reached Largiebaan caves that day. The account doesn't say that I set off for Largiebaan, only that I reached there, so I can't be certain that the destination was premeditated, but it probably was. I was with Iain Campbell, and we cycled off at about 2 p.m. with chopped egg sandwiches in our saddlebags, which we supplemented with fruit pies and 'orangeade' from the shop on Ralston Road, then owned by Jack and Jess McRobert and now owned by Michael McGeachy (p 29). Our route was down the main road to Southend, then through Glen Breackerie and 'onto the rocky Glenahantie Rd'.

> Eventually we reached Largybaan Farm & progressed from there on foot on a very pleasant stroll across the moors, foll[ow]ing a burn down to Dun Ban Cove where we saw mountain goats and three caves. Day was beautiful and the sun shone on the sea and cliffs. On way back to top of cliffs sighted 3 trawlers in N. Channel. Arrived home very happy about 9.30 pm and had bath.

The sighting of the trawlers would certainly have been a highlight of my day, because for years I had been obsessed with fishing, and that very summer, having left school at fifteen, I had joined the crew of the ring-netter *Westering Home* as 'cook'. I would have supposed that the trawlers were Fleetwood-based, because, as an avid listener to the 'trawler band' on the wireless set at home, in certain atmospheric conditions I could tune in to their skippers' banter as they towed back and forth in the deep water between Kintyre and the Antrim coast. When it came to swearing, these men were certainly in a league of their own! I knew some of the boats and skippers by name and followed their fortunes in commercial fishing publications.

Of all the journals I bought and kept, only a copy of *World Fishing* survives. It is dated December 1966 and the reason I kept that one is that it contains a letter of mine condemning industrial fishing and appealing for 'international agreement over conservation'. It also contains a page on 'Top Boats of the Month', and under 'Fleetwood' I notice familiar names:

Near Water (Irish Sea)
(1) *Fairy Cove*, R. Evans, Hazel, 160 kits, £1,533, Nov. 2, 14 [days at sea].
(2) *Fairy Cove*, R. Evans, Hazel, 127 kits, £1,254, Oct 19, 14.
(3) *Loch Lorgan*, W. L. Phillips, Colne, 151 kits, £1,254, Oct. 19, 13.

Largiebaan, 1980

My next trip to Largiebaan was on 29 June 1980 with a nephew from Drumchapel, Donald Docherty, and John MacDonald. We stopped for lunch at the spruce plantation mid-way down the glen, and I noted in my journal: 'A tiny burn gurgles by us and the sun is now warm in a clear sky.' Shortly after we resumed our walk to the cliffs, we encountered a ram with one of its massive horns caught in a wire fence. Donald and I worked the horn free, but the ram, once released, fell over. We pulled it to its feet and held it steady until it recovered and began grazing. Having descended to the shore, we explored the caves and added our names to the numerous others – some dating back to the late nineteenth century – on the lime-coated walls of the biggest cave.

We found a notice-board washed ashore and wedged it at head height in the cave. The warning on the board read: 'Layde Church/This structure is DANGEROUS/Please Keep Off.' I should have recognised the name, but didn't. It appears in Knocklayd, which is the most distinctive feature in County Antrim as seen from Kintyre. The hill is close to 1700 feet in height and is long and sloping, not unlike, I have often thought, our own smaller Slate as seen from town. In Irish it is *Cnoc Leithid*, 'Broad Mountain'.

11. On Largiebaan shore, with Layde Church notice-board held up for the camera, summer of 1980. The happy group, L-R, is: David Wallace; Willie Colville, Peter Kelly, Calum Macphail and Robert 'Bob' Ballantyne. Photograph by Teddy Lafferty.

I wrote a letter to the *Campbeltown Courier* noting the discovery of the notice-board and appealing for information on its origin. Re-reading that letter, which was published on 4 July 1980, I was amused by my description of Largiebaan as 'that magnificent western shore' – I had clearly fallen under its spell! My appeal elicited two replies, one of which (11 July), from Terence Nelson in Ahoghill, Ballymena, answered the question. The notice had been erected in Layd Church graveyard – in the townland of Moneyvart, County Antrim – which had been the subject of a closure order on 26 May 1980, and Mr Nelson suggested that it could have been thrown into the sea at Port Obe. The old church is on the coast opposite the Mull, so the board didn't have far to float before reaching land.

There was a further letter published in the *Courier* (18 July) and accompanied by a photograph of five men and boys grouped around the board on Largiebaan shore. The party was named as David Wallace, Willie Colville, Peter Kelly, Calum Macphail, and Robert Ballantyne. There was a footnote to that letter, which will later move the narrative on to matters ornithological: 'They spotted a rare bird during their meanderings in the hills ... a chough (pronounced "chuff") flitting in and out of a cave in the hill behind them here.'

The photographer was not credited in the *Courier*, but I was sure that Teddy Lafferty had taken the picture, and when I visited him in September, he confirmed it, and showed me a copy in one of his albums. He also told me that the express purpose of the outing was to see choughs. He had never seen one until that day, nor, he thought, had anyone else in the party (though I suspect Willie Colville could have been the exception). He was enthralled watching the birds, which would 'dive like a bomb straight down and then dart into the cave'. That cave was the middle one.

Teddy recalled an amusing incident during the party's descent to the shore. When they were about to cross the burn, Peter looked at Teddy and remarked to the two boys:

'Watch what this fella does – he does a lot of climbing.' After Teddy had advised the boys on safety considerations, the party proceeded to cross the burn. When everyone was safely on the other side, Teddy himself set off and promptly slipped on a rock and ended up in the burn with the water half-way to his knees! When Peter looked round and saw what had happened, he held up his hands in disbelief and joked to Teddy that he would have to report the mishap to their fellow-workers on the maintenance staff at RAF Machrihanish.

12. *Teddy Lafferty in mountaineering mode, Aonach Eagach, Glen Coe, c. 1975. The photographer's name is forgotten, but he was warden at Glencoe Youth Hostel at that time. From Teddy Lafferty's collection.*

David Wallace, one of the boys, is still in town, and I asked him how much he remembered of the outing. He had two outstanding memories. The first was of feeling 'petrified' on the last stage of the descent on to the shore at Largiebaan, when the narrow track crosses steep terrain. (Teddy Lafferty remembers suggesting that the party cross to the south side of the burn and follow it all the way to the shore, but he was overruled.) The second memory is of a meal of steak and onions fried over a driftwood fire on the shore, 'an outrageously brilliant feast' conjured up by the adults, who were 'equipped like Boy Scouts'. (Teddy, again, adds that the steaks had been in Peter Kelly's freezer at Machrihanish and had thawed by the time they reached Largiebaan.) I asked David how he came to be on that walk, and the explanation was Machrihanish Golf Club. Everyone on the outing, Teddy excepted, was a keen golfer, and Willie Colville was also greenkeeper at Machrihanish at the time. David's younger companion, Calum Macphail, would go on to become a club champion at Machrihanish, as his father Iain had been before him.

There is a sequel to David's story. In May 2013 he saw Largiebaan again. His brother-in-law, Rob Davies, had walked the Kintyre Way in stages and had only the latter part, Ballygroggan to Southend, left to do. He was keen to have company on that stretch and David agreed to walk it with him. As they crossed the cliff-tops at Largiebaan, David recounted his experiences there thirty-three years before, and, looking down, recognised the bit that had scared him as a thirteen-year-old. 'It still sends shivers down my spine,' he concluded.

Choughs

The red-billed chough, a member of the crow family, resembles a jackdaw, but is unmistakable with its red legs and red beak. That I saw the last of them which bred in Kintyre should, I suppose, be considered a privilege, but it's a privilege tinged with sadness. I still miss the birds, still look for them and still hope they'll come back. It could happen,

13. Donald Docherty on precipitous track on to Largiebaan shore, 24 July 1982. The main Largiebaan cave is visible close to top left-hand of picture. Photograph by the author.

if environmental conditions change in their favour, but looks increasingly unlikely, though there is a healthy population on Islay, from which Kintyre is no great distance away 'as the crow flies'. The species, which had also nested on the Learside, appears to have disappeared from Kintyre around 1940 and re-colonised the south-west coast in the early 1950s. I saw my first chough on 30 August 1981, while camping at the Inneans with Malcolm Docherty Jnr., who pointed it out as it flew over the bay, and my last at the Aignish on 1 May 1983. By the following year, they were gone.

On 8 July 1984, I was one of a party of ten, organised by Dr Eric Bignall – then of the Nature Conservancy Council – which walked the coast between Ballygroggan and Keil looking for choughs and checking traditional nesting caves of the species. Kintyre was then the last known breeding area in mainland Scotland.

14. *Chough hunters on Largiebaan shore, 8 July 1984. Welsh birders, with dog, on left, Rab Brown and Jimmy MacDonald, right. Photograph by the author.*

Rab Brown, young Jimmy MacDonald and I were given the coast from Largiebaan north to Ballygroggan to cover. I'd invited Teddy Lafferty along, but at that time his knees were beginning to cause him pain and his doctor had advised rest, so he declined. Rubha Dùn Bhàin south to the Mull was covered by two Welsh birders, while Eric Bignall himself, with the remainder of the group, which we didn't meet, walked from the Mull to Keil. Our two companions, from whom we parted on Largiebaan shore, collected us in town, and I remember a journey to Largiebaan in a Land Rover driven at alarming speeds, and a near-collision with a car on a bend of the Homeston road. (When I mentioned that incident to Jimmy in 2013, to my astonishment he remembered the car as a Ford Sierra.) We saw no choughs, nor did anyone else, and Eric Bignall's conclusion was that the chough was extinct as a breeding species in Kintyre.

I had met Eric two summers earlier, on 17 June 1982, in remarkable circumstances. A friend Ruari MacLean and I were at Largiebaan. He had gone north towards the caves to take photographs, while I headed south to Rubha Dùn Bhàin and sat briefly on the cliff-edge (fulmars nesting just ten feet below me). I was mid-way along the shore on my way to rejoin Ruari, when, to my surprise, I saw two men climbing down the rocks north of the caves. We approached them, and one of them, Eric Bignall, immediately asked if we had seen anything interesting. I replied that I had expected to see a chough in one of the caves, but hadn't, and at that point he declared that he was surveying the coast for a national census on choughs. He had looked in that cave, he said, and found no droppings. Before he and his companion disappeared up the scree slope to look at something, I promised them I'd have a pot of tea ready for their return.

The fire was tardy, but I finally had the tea brewed and poured them each a cup. To my consternation, Ruari dashed milk into their cups without enquiring if they wanted any – they hadn't! None the less, Eric and colleague – a botanist

– were decidedly 'chuffed' to be in that rocky wilderness sipping 'Earl Grey', and Eric had to photograph the odd ritual. I offered to accompany them to the south side of Rubha Dùn Bhàin and we all proceeded there. Ruari and I left them searching for plants, and two days later I had a letter from Eric, reporting that they had discovered 'a very uncommon plant – a Broomrape – a new record for S. Argyll', and had heard a chough call 'in the main valley from Largiebaan'.

Ruari and I climbed around the point past the caves – the very bit that would 'freak me out' thirty years later (p 39) – almost treading on gull chicks which had jammed themselves into rock crevices. We had a tough climb on to the Aignish and descended from there into the Inneans, where we spent an hour and a half with campers from Drumlemble, the late Duncan Brown, his wife Jean and son Don.

On 5 June, four companions and I had watched a herring gull in the bay swoop on, kill and then swallow a young rabbit whole, and Duncan reported that the hunter was still active and had killed at least one ringed plover chick. The gull had also cleaned out a 'cruban' (edible crab) shell from which Duncan had removed the boiled meat. A Drumlemble creel-fisherman, Tommy Paterson, had come into the bay in his boat and left three lobsters and the crab for Duncan.

Close to the end of the hike, we noticed a lamb stuck at the top of the big waterfall at Craigaig. I climbed up to it, caught it and lifted it clear. It was dazed and unsteady on its legs – hunger symptoms, I surmised – and I 'phoned Ballygroggan Farm from the call box at Machrihanish to report its location and condition. By then, we had missed the 10.30 bus home.

1983 and 2013

My first trip of 2013 to the cliffs was by bicycle, on 29 April. When I set off about 2 p.m., Hope not Certainty was my companion, and a couple of times en route I briefly contemplated abandoning the plan and settling for a less ambitious effort. I'd only ever cycled out there twice before, almost thirty years earlier, and I wondered if, at sixty-one years, I had the stamina to do the cycle, walk to the cliffs and then get myself back to town.

On that first trip – 10 July 1983 – John MacDonald was with me. The road journey from town to Glenahanty, where we left the bikes, took us two hours. It was 'yet another intensely warm day', and we found Teddy Lafferty camping at the Inneans. He had walked out the day before, and with the great weight of his pack had almost collapsed with heat exhaustion. Teddy told us he'd had visitors for a couple of hours, and we looked and saw Jan Mohamed and Eddie Brown ascending into the distance, on their way back to Machrihanish. After a cup of tea, I cooled myself in the sea for half-an-hour while John disappeared with an improvised fishing-rod to try his luck on the big tidal rock at the south end of the bay. Teddy and I amused ourselves throwing a frisbee – we reached thirty-odd catches in one spell – and then drank another cup of tea. By then – almost 7.30 – John had moved further south and out of sight, but it was time for us to leave and I had to go and fetch him. Teddy remembers the frisbee-throwing that day, but I don't – a notebook informed me of it – probably because it was a novelty to him. During the 1980s and into the '90s, a frisbee washed ashore wasn't an exceptional find; they were lost on one beach and found on another.

Looking back now to those days in the '80s, I am struck by how frequently one could meet fellow-hikers and campers at the Inneans; and it seldom happened that they were strangers, though, on occasion, a few enquiries might be necessary to establish who some of them were. More often than not, one would meet them again. The Inneans definitely held a small band of disciples in its thrall, but few of those whom I remember meeting there are fit to return now.

On my second bicycle trip, a week later, John was with me again, and also a friend of his, Michael Claffey. Our destination that day was Largiebaan. We cycled as far as Glenahanty – Michael feared that his tyres wouldn't survive the stony Bruach Dearg – and left the bikes in the old steading. I still have a photograph of the boys with their bikes in the cool gloom of the old Mathieson house, which had a tin roof on it then and barn owls in seasonal occupancy. We walked out to the cliffs, then down on to the shore and explored the biggest of the caves with a candle. Our fire on the shore to boil the tea-kettle was novel – instead of driftwood we had peats, collected from the road near Lochorodale. I surmised that Robert McInnes had been taking his peats home to Stewarton, and, when we passed within sight of his bank, I saw that it had indeed been cleared. Thirty years on, there is a forest there.

I don't suppose that Robert's peat-cutting was motivated by economic necessity. He was continuing a family and an occupational tradition, and when I began helping him I was consciously tapping into that tradition. Of course, I wrote about peat-cutting, a chapter in *Kintyre Country Life*, and much of what I recorded and described came from my times with Robert. After his appalling death in a car accident in 1987, I wrote a poem in his memory, and set it at the peat-bank, where I most remembered him (*The Song of the Quern*, p 15).

Almost thirty years on from the day I stopped and lifted the fallen peat blocks and stuck them into my rucksack, I was cycling that road again. Near the top of the brae past Lochorodale, I noticed an inviting knoll a few minutes' walk from the road, and decided I'd eat a late lunch on it. I left my bike in a lay-by and crossed a strip of moor to the knoll. While seated there, I was surprised to see a police patrol car pass by, heading north. I regretted not having waved to the officers, who must have seen me on the skyline. What did they take me for? Did I appear suspicious to them or merely the harmless traveller I was? Perhaps a mental note was made in case a criminal incident was reported later from that area. I doubt if they'd have seen another person on that

15. Michael Claffey (L) and John MacDonald with bikes in old steading at Glenahanty, 17 July 1983, before setting off for Largiebaan. Photograph by the author.

entire stretch of road. With the exception of a van, which earlier passed me going in the same direction as the patrol car, I saw no other traffic; which is why I judged belatedly that I should have waved to them – a friendly gesture in remoteness. The policemen were the last humans I saw that day until I rejoined the main Southend road in near-darkness and met a few cars, occupants unknown.

16. At the Lochorodale peat-bank, summer of 1986: L-R: Robert McInnes, Angus Martin and John MacDonald. Photograph by Judy Martin.

From Glenahanty I wheeled my bike up the steep track, but a locked gate just before Largiebaan steading persuaded me to take the bike no further and I left it chained there and walked out to the cliffs. The cliffs are usually windy and that day was no exception, so I dropped below the edge and headed directly for a 'dell' which Jimmy MacDonald occasionally favours for bird-watching (quaint 'dell' is his word). I have had a special attachment to that spot since Jimmy took my daughter Amelia and me to it on 15 May 2012. His preferred natural observatory under the cliffs had been too windy for comfort, so we descended further and settled ourselves on the northern slope of the hollow, a feature of which, an inviting table-shaped rock, was reluctantly rejected since it was over-exposed to wind. I hadn't been back in that hollow for almost a year, but my memories of it were fresh, and of course I found Amelia there, even in her absence.

On my approach to the spot, I noticed a raven alight on Binnein Fithich. Minutes later, it flew straight to where I had settled myself and swooped over me for a closer inspection. I remembered how Jimmy had fed a pair of ravens at Largiebaan during December 2010, experiences which he put into an article, 'Observations on Ravens', published in *Kintyre Magazine* No. 69. Was this one of the pair, recalling cast bread?

Binnein Fithich

While writing *Kintyre Places and Place-Names* in 2012, I agonised over the place-name Binnein Fithich. To be precise, the generic was the problem. Gaelic *binnein* is a diminutive of *beinn*, which the great Gaelic place-names scholar W. J. Watson said meant 'horn' in 'old Gaelic' before turning into 'peak'. There are merely three *binnein* place-names recorded in Kintyre and I'm not certain where, precisely, one of them, Binnein Buidhe, is, so have never knowingly seen it. Binnein dà Néill at Carskey I looked for in August 2102 and decided I'd identified as a 'perfectly rounded hillock'. Hills named *beinn* in Kintyre are not characteristically peaked and the generic is best translated simply as 'hill'. Had *binnein*, too, in Kintyre, lost its peak?

The sample of *binnein* place-names is so small, I should have left the problem alone, or, rather, avoided creating it. Graham McKinlay, retired farmer at Whitestone, whom I

59

tape-recorded in 1977, interpreted Binnein Buidhe as 'the small yellow ben', and he had enough Gaelic to know what he was talking about. But the interpretation doesn't define *binnein* with exactitude. The officers of the Ordnance Survey, who mapped Kintyre in 1866 and '67, didn't know about that one, but were told about Binnein dà Néill and Binnein Fithich.

The translation they were given for the former, by local Gaelic speakers, was 'Hillock of the two Neils', and for the latter 'Raven's Peak'. Their informants for the latter – which is the one that has bothered me most since the book's publication – were Donald Mathieson, Glenahanty, and Duncan Ferguson, Dalbuie. If they said 'peak', should I have been seeing a peak? I thought I should be, but wasn't … until the final proofs of *Kintyre Places and Place-Names* were with me and I suddenly realised that the photograph I'd included to illustrate *binnein* – Jimmy Macdonald standing on top of Beinnin Fithich with his dog Kosi – more represented a peak than a hillock, which had been my preferred interpretation.

I felt obliged to rewrite my reference to Binnein Fithich, but at that end-stage had merely three existing lines to work with, and, as with most late revisions, my intentions were frustrated. I'd taken the photograph on 15 May 2012, when Jimmy, Amelia and I regained the cliff-top by a transverse north to Binnein Fithich. Jimmy was on top of the feature and I was below it; but prominent landmarks, such as Binnein Fithich, are seldom, if ever, named from obscure proximities, and I felt that I had unwittingly distorted my case with that photograph.

I had first noticed Binnein Fithich in May 2009, when Jimmy pointed it out from the coast north of the Inneans, as we looked back into the south; except, 'it' is strictly 'them', because there are two features on the skyline, which I decided resembled knuckles. So, which one is the *binnein*? The higher, presumably.

Just to the south of the two grass-covered knolls of Binnein Fithich, and also right on the edge of the cliff, there is another knoll, which is also visible from the coast to the north, but I didn't notice it until after I'd become acquainted with it in the summer of 2013. Since I hadn't noticed it, it didn't exist for me, but now I notice it all the time. I am reminded of John Constable's maxim, 'We see nothing till we truly understand it'. I shan't claim to 'understand' that bump of grass-covered rock, but I can at least claim to know it. It is the highest point of the cliff line and overlooks Binnein Fithich.

I 'found' the spot on 5 June, a very warm day in that warm summer. If I hadn't known the kind of day it was, I could have guessed, when, shortly after alighting from the bus at Machrihanish, I recognised Francis and Madge McWhirter sitting on a bench at the roadside, watching oyster-catchers. I spoke briefly to them, noticing that Francis had the dome of his head covered quaintly with a knotted handkerchief.

Butterflies

Before I reached Ballygroggan that day, I had already seen hundreds of green-veined white butterflies, most of them swarming over cuckoo flowers in marshy ground. I was compiling butterfly records to pass on to Agnes Stewart, but that was the one species she told me to disregard – its numbers were too vast to log. In numbers and variety of butterflies, the summer of 2013 was the most spectacular I can recall. Certainly, my interest in these gentle insects is of years' rather than decades' duration, but the impression remains that 2013 was an exceptional summer (later confirmed by national records).

Butterflies were my beautiful companions on all my walks that summer; they were also, at times, an irritation, because in 2013, for the first time, I had set myself the challenge of identifying every butterfly I encountered, an aim which brought with it occasional frustration. There were individuals I simply could not name with confidence because they disappeared in rapid flight beyond me. At first, when binoculars failed to find them, or, having found them, failed to yield the information I required, I'd throw off my rucksack and try to track them, but that strategy never once worked and in the end I simply gave up on these fast-flying reds and browns. Since they didn't know what they were, was it important that I should? Well, yes, it was, in those moments of helplessness in the first weeks, when I vexed myself with thoughts of rarities which might have eluded me; but, logic protested, the walk itself was the primary motive, and I learned to let the butterflies go and to keep myself going.

When I look back on that summer's butterflies, certain images and moods recur. The strongest is also the vaguest. I am crossing Ballygroggan moor, the air is still, the sun is bright in a blue sky, and there are butterflies flitting all around me. None of them is identifiable, which doesn't matter any more since they are dead now. All that matters is that they shared that day with me, were my companions even if they cared nothing for me and never registered my passing.

Another memory is more specific but almost as dream-like. It is late afternoon on 12 July and on my way to Largiebaan cliff-top I lose the thread of the Kintyre Way and decide to head straight for the Aignish. As I cross the ridge to Binnein Fithich, I look down on to its southern face and notice a slight movement over a grassy ledge. It's a butterfly, but I can't make out the species, and since I don't see many butterflies around the cliffs, identifying this one assumes a special importance. As it moves, I move with it, pausing to train my binoculars on it. Minutes pass – perhaps five, perhaps ten – and finally I am satisfied that it's a common blue, a species I could watch elsewhere by the dozen. But this is the Aignish, and that tiny scrap of living blue flitting around an immense amphitheatre of rock delights me.

There were three butterfly species I saw – or identified, rather – for the first time ever in 2013. The first was a green hairstreak beside the Killypole track on 6 June.

The second was a ringlet on 7 July near the foot of Polliwilline Brae. Judy and I had hiked down the Learside to spend a night at our caravan. We'd been noting butterflies all the way, and at 8.25, by which time we didn't expect to see any more, I noticed a movement at the roadside. It was a butterfly, which I believe I disturbed at rest. It flew merely a couple of yards and settled again on a whin bush. We examined it, and, from the light circles on its dark wings, identified it as a ringlet. It was an exciting moment, but before that summer was over we'd see hundreds of them!

The third new species was grayling, several of which I logged on 25 July between the Wee Holm and the Castles, Polliwilline, all of them resting on sun-warmed rocks.

That day, on the foreshore north of the Wee Holm, I stood for around ten minutes and counted nine species. That's how remarkable a summer for butterflies 2013 was. Or so a convert believes. Butterflies haven't, however, disappeared from my life; but they have, in a sense, disappeared from their own lives. Small tortoiseshells are hibernating on the ceiling of the outside stair of my house. We see a few there most years, but this year's residents present a most unusual appearance. Instead of attaching themselves independently to the ceiling, as they normally do, no fewer than ten of them have formed a tight cluster above the stairwell window. When I noticed the formation in early September, I assumed it, at first glance, to be a fungal growth (that part of the ceiling admits rain). Naturalist Mark Cocker, in *A Tiger in the Sand* (p 46), noted a cluster of six in his bathroom. They were there for many weeks, but all of them 'misjudged the moment for awakening' and either 'fluttered out into a hostile world' or exhausted themselves fatally against the closed window. I await, with interest, the fate of my fragile lodgers.

It is easy to overlook the fact that butterflies are insects, just like midges, ants, clegs, ticks, wasps and all the other species which frighten and annoy world-ruler *Homo sapiens*; but butterflies are pretty, gentle, graceful and harmless, so they are immune from persecution. Most beetles are just as harmless to humans and their interests, but I have seen them killed on sight. Why? They are 'creepie-crawlies' and are perceived to be ugly and useless. Revulsion has many triggers, some of them subliminal.

I camped at the Inneans with an American in the early 1980s. He was intelligent, educated and stimulating company, but on our way out through the glen I noticed him stop, look at the ground and raise the tip of his walking stick. I guessed at once what he was up to and checked him. 'What are you doing?' – 'It's a bug.' (Not a word in my spoken vocabulary and I remember it.) I asked him to consider the fact that the 'bug' – which was a glossy-blue dung beetle – had been born in that glen and would live out its life there, whereas we were mere guests in its country. He accepted graciously my little impromptu lecture and let the beetle go on its way.

His response to the beetle's appearance was governed by conditioning and facilitated by ignorance. Had he taken time to observe the beetle there and then, or had he earlier informed himself of its life history, I doubt if he'd have wished it dead. But let's face a general truth – any species which can amuse itself in the torture, murder and mutilation of its own kind, babies and all, isn't likely to respect the life of an insect. Is there a model of social responsibility I could suggest from the insect world which we humans might profitably study in the interest of improving our moral conduct? There are thousands, but I'll recommend the butterfly, any butterfly.

High point at Largiebaan

I'm back in 5 June 2013, and that day I decided to leave the Kintyre Way – which would have taken me down the Inneans Glen to the sheep-fank and then up on to the Largiebaan cliffs by a steep, winding path – and choose a more direct route which would save me time and effort. That was the theory, but it failed. I left the Kintyre Way where Gleneadardacrock meets the Inneans Glen and crossed the burn on to Cnoc Moy. Then I began climbing the rough hillside and climbed and climbed. I reached a gate I didn't recognise and wrote my name and the date on one of the spars. I may never see that pencilled record again because I was in a place I shouldn't have been and may never need to be again in whatever future is left to me. I had gone too high on Kintyre's second highest hill, and instead of angling coastward, towards the cliffs, had let myself be directed, by the contours of the hill, towards the summit itself. Cnoc Moy has a big physical presence, but is short on distinctive features, and I had been climbing confidently, but, as it transpired, aimlessly. (I was reminded, incidentally, of an article 'A Journey to Cnoc Moy', published in 1921 and reproduced as Appendix 3. The 'journey' was over-dramatised, but I recall one remark: 'It was like climbing a ladder, a ladder without end.')

When I was finally high enough to see beyond the hill itself, the view momentarily startled me. I was then at about 1200 feet and looking not west, but south: Sanda was there before me, and Ailsa Craig, and in the nearer distance Glenbreackerie, and, right below me, Largiebaan glen. I quickly got my bearings and hastened west across the moor-slope. About fifteen minutes' walking took me to the cliff, and mid-way there I congratulated myself on the blunder when I spotted and managed to photograph a drab-coloured dragonfly which I quickly identified as a four-spotted chaser, a species I had never before recognised. My consolation was short-lived, however, because I was to see dozens more of the species in the following weeks – 2013 was a year of abundance for dragonflies as well as butterflies.

When I arrived at the cliffs, I was higher than I would normally have gone, approaching, as I generally do, straight from Largiebaan steading. I was, in fact, close to the summit of the ridge, at 1200 feet, and I decided to stop there. Time was pressing – it was now 6.55, I had lost about half-an-hour by leaving the Way, and had a bus to catch at 10.35 at Machrihanish. I allowed myself an hour there and reached the bus terminus with five minutes to spare. But what an hour!

In that hour, I think, is contained the core of this book's sensibilities. If the notion of the book was conceived at Sròn Gharbh, its true genesis perhaps goes further back to that day at Largiebaan. My hasty notes at the time scarcely touch that core of spirituality, in part because such experiences tend to enlarge and illumine themselves in memory: 'Idyllic. The grass emerald-green & the rocks glittering in the sunlight; sun's path glittering; the gentle sough of the sea.' I am not sure now about 'emerald-green' grass, but it must have seemed so at the time, or else 'emerald-green' was all that I could come up with to intensify the colour. I have never had a definitive 'mystical' experience, never felt myself 'transported', but I have known interludes of great spiritual peace; or call it 'contentment'; or merely that species of happiness which best pleases me.

I took a photograph of Binnein Fithich and one of the hollow, below the cliffs, in which I first sat with Amelia and Jimmy. Since December 2012 I've had a small digital camera, an acquisition I'd resisted for years. But I had obviously spoken often enough about how useful a pocket-sized camera would be for Judy to buy me one as a Christmas present. I had wanted one, but, characteristically, was reluctant to take the trouble of learning how to work it. I still prefer my SLR camera, with slide film in it, for quality of image, but that camera is bulky to carry and film seems expensive now, particularly when only about half of the photographs in a roll of film are ever worth keeping.

The small digital camera is therefore convenient and inexpensive, and, since I no longer have any pretensions to 'art' in my photography, that camera increasingly performs many of the functions formerly performed by notebooks. Instead of describing a flower or an insect on paper, I photograph it, if it can be photographed, and identify it from the image or else pass it on to others better qualified.

Had I been using the 'Canon' with slide-film, I might not have taken these two photographs. I might have reasoned that I didn't need them and would be better to conserve the remaining film for worthier subjects, in which case I would have denied myself two special reminders of my hour on the cliff-top. But photographic values are unpredictable. A casual snapshot of a place or person might, long after it was taken, acquire more emotional power than a book or album of technically superb images. The distinction is in the content and how one relates to it. I suspect that these two digital images from that day – each composed in seconds – will hold for me the pure essence of that summer.

17. *Binnein Fithich taken on 5 June 2013 with pocket digital camera.*

Silence

All 'still' photographs are silent, but in these two the silence is not simply of the medium, but is historical, and I can recover it from the images themselves. The peace of that day, and especially of that hour at Largiebaan, is what made it so special to me. I was enveloped, physically and spiritually, in that profound stillness which one may find – but not always – in remote places and in the absence of other humans. Certain places have it and others don't. I can go to particular points on a landscape and find it unfailingly. Even with a wind blowing, that 'eternal Silence' of Wordsworth's may be heard, if one listens for it, beneath the turbulence of surfaces.

It lives for me in moorland places, especially. East of the shoulders of Ben Gullion there is a little peak which I have called 'Conical Hill' (p 177). If I sit on its heathery summit and look north, I see the town and loch below me; I see Davaar Island and the Arran mountains and the sweep of the forested Kintyre hills extending into the distance, with Cowal and the Arrochar summits poking beyond on a clear day. But if I turn and face south, I have moorland before me, with its freight of silence. This is no 'mystical' fancy. I can take in that silence, as though breathing the air of that altitude, and feel my spirit – 'mind', should that be preferred – heightened and lightened. These places are hard to leave, yet one must leave them, but always in the knowledge that one may return. They never change and are always there; it is we who change, and vanish, ultimately, in the corridor of Time.

Malcolm

For me, one of the characteristic impressions of Largiebaan is ocean glitter, and it was striking on that June day. The effect, of course, is enhanced by elevation. At a thousand feet, and more, there's a lot of sea to survey; and the sun is always in the west when I am there. From Auchenhoan Head or the Bastard, on the Learside, similar effects could be experienced from the morning sun over Ayrshire; but I am not a morning person and cannot attest to having seen the sea glittering in the east, except from boats. Largiebaan is generally the scene of my observations, which I put into a poem 'Always Boats and Men', of which this is the final verse:

> images in memory
> like sunlight on the sea
> which is a wholeness but
> broken millionfold within.

There was an image in my memory that day, but it was no image from a poem. It was of my brother-in-law, Malcolm Docherty, on the cliffs at Largiebaan, a silhouette with sparkling sea behind him. I am over-fond of dates, I admit, but in that case I wasn't certain even of the year, because I couldn't find the slide when I looked for it and I suspected it might have been discarded on grounds of quality. I could remember the outlines of the composition and also a mysterious stone – like a miniature monolith – tilting from the ground near Malcolm.

I found the slide in the end, but it is too dark for reproduction. When I examined it, I discovered that, as usual, my memory had failed me in several details. Jimmy MacDonald is also in the photo, standing beside Malcolm, whose left arm is around him. There were actually three stones together, the upright one I remembered, a small boulder and a smaller horizontal slab. A bit of a fence visible near the cliff-edge ought to have clarified the location, but I remain uncertain, though Rubha Dùn Bhàin, where we ended up, seems likely, and if an opportunity arises I'll search there for the strange rocks. Jimmy's presence, however, allows me to date the photograph to 6 May 1984.

We had set off late for Largiebaan and met John Martin, his son-in-law Gordon McDougall, John Robertson, and

Hector Gatt, returning from the shore with a quantity of gull eggs for a woman in Campbeltown who would use them in baking. The first Sunday in May was the usual day for these expeditions to rocky coasts and islands to gather seabird eggs, but the custom seems to have died out, and a good thing, too, I say with my naturalist's hat on.

The sparkling sea had brought that day, and Malcolm, into my memory, because he was dying of cancer and would succumb on 19 June, just about the time I stepped off the 1 o' clock bus at Machrihanish on my way to the Inneans. I stopped in at my sister Barbara's house at Drumlemble on my way home that night to ask how he was and was told he was gone. I'd 'seen' him, back on the cliffs at Largiebaan, with the sea and the sun behind him, and I'll see him there again 'if I'm spared'.

He was brought up on a croft at Killeonan, born to the land and obedient to its seasons, almost to the end. Even when he and Barbara moved to Glasgow, where they spent most of their lives and raised their family, Malcolm never lost contact with the soil. He had two allotments in Maryhill, which he cultivated energetically, and when, in retirement, he and Barbara returned to Kintyre, he brought with him some raspberry canes from one of his plots. Initially, he and Barbara were in temporary housing, so Malcolm planted his canes in my back garden. He never got around to reclaiming them, and they are still there and bearing fruit.

Weather factors

I was deeply contented in that hour at Largiebaan. In part, it was physical relief (I'd been walking steadily since my late lunch on the northern edge of Ballygroggan moor and was glad of the rest) and in part the delightful weather (warm and dehydrating, but a joy to be out in). At times I try to convince myself that bad weather needn't spoil an outing, as long as one remains cheerful, but really there's nothing more dispiriting than trudging, soaked to the arse, for miles across sodden moorland, and I'd rather not do that ever again. The remarkable feature of this summer, which is passing as I write, is that for weeks on end one could set off on an outing, any day, without packing extra clothing. Yes, weather makes a difference. On a fine day in the hills, I'll feel fine. Here, however, is my daughter Amelia's pronouncement on the subject, noted on Knock Scalbert on 5 August 1998, when she was nine years old: 'I actually like walking in the rain because it's more like a Scottish walk.'

Before instant internet weather forecasting, one tended to assess immediate conditions and reach an intuitive decision. This approach was very much 'hit or miss' and sometimes resulted in aborting a hike if the morning was wet and setting off if it was dry; but a wet morning might give way to sunshine and a bright morning to heavy rainfall, so fine afternoons were lost and miserable ones endured.

One walk with Jimmy MacDonald, on 3 June 1990, illustrates the point. It took us from Ballygroggan to the Inneans, Largiebaan, and High Glenadale, and ended at Glenbreackerie schoolhouse where Judy was camping with a group of Campbeltown Girl Guides. But it almost didn't happen. I had arranged a lift to High Lossit from Judy's father, Alec Honeyman (p 107), and from Glenbreackerie we got a lift back into town, by which time rain had come. The following journal entry was written in the Inneans Bay.

> There was heavy rain last night & grey overcast skies this morning. I was definitely swithering, & had the decision been entirely mine I'd have stayed at home. But Jimmy, as of old, wouldn't hear of cancelling – this at 9.30, when I 'phoned him. By 9.45 there was heavy drizzle & it wasn't looking like easing even when Alec appeared at 10.05. The sky was full of cloud & Ben Gullion was swimming in mist. I tried once more to reason with Jimmy when we called for him, but he was still adamant, despite having only a pair of

trainers on his feet and no waterproofs of any kind. But his determination has triumphed. There has been no rain since we crossed off High Lossit ground and on to Ballygroggan ...

Crossing the moorland behind Craigaig, we startled a fox at pretty close range. It was, in fact, Jimmy's first close encounter with a fox, & a shaggy, disreputable-looking beast it was. We hoped to sight it again, but didn't. It probably swung round towards the coast & got in among rocks and gullies. Jimmy sighted a skylark perched on the Lossit/Ballygroggan march wall with flies in its beak. Here we saw hoodies – three – turning away a raven over Beinn na Faire.

Largiebaan, 17 June 2013

I didn't particularly examine that highest point on 5 June – I just sat on it for the first time – but I would look closely at it on subsequent visits. On that day, it appealed to me mostly because there was a little cooling breeze blowing over it, a 'saar' in Kintyre. Largiebaan – or any high ground, for that matter – is generally windy, and the immediate question on arrival tends to be: where can we sit to escape the wind and still enjoy a decent view?

The views from there were spectacular; but views from any point on the cliffs are spectacular. The nature of the place is simply – and here's that currently overworked adjective – awesome. In both *By Hill and Shore in South Kintyre* (pp. 47-50) and *Kintyre Places and Place-Names* (pp. 25-27), I discussed how Largiebaan and its caves became a 'visitor attraction'. In 1861, the 8th Duke of Argyll, George Douglas Campbell, visited the caves; in the following year, a party 'procured a guide at Largieban' – doubtless one of the shepherds there – and was led down to the caves (Appendix 2); by 1884, day-trippers were sailing to Largiebaan Caves in the Royal Mail Steamer *Kinloch*. Why the great interest? Scenic grandeur aside, the explanation is that these caves contained amazing specimens of stalactites and stalagmites, described in one report as rivalling 'visions of fairyland'. But that natural spectacle was ultimately destroyed, presumably by souvenir-hunters who plundered the caves of their millennia-old lime formations.

The caves appear to have contained other desirable natural accretions. Visiting Hugh McShannon in 1981 to interview him about the Mull of Kintyre hand-line fishery, in which he participated as a boy, I noted the following: 'went round to Largybaan caves to collect bird droppings – at it all spring for farmers – last century – guano.' That is all that the notebook contains, and I regret not having probed for more information. But his testimony seems quite clear. I presume that the droppings were from rock doves, which were probably more abundant in the nineteenth century. The rest is also conjecture. Presumably the guano was carried away by boat. There must have been a lot of it to have kept the labourers 'at it all spring', and the resource must have been rapidly depleted. Perhaps some reader knows more.

I remember camping at the Inneans in September 1981 with young John MacDonald and an American friend of my late brother Donald's, John Hathway. The American John had arrived in Kintyre from a tour of Ireland – his mother was of Irish immigrant stock – and had visited the famous Cliffs of Moher, but when I showed him the Largiebaan cliffs he at once volunteered the opinion that the Kintyre spectacle was decidedly the more impressive. Perhaps he desired to please his Scottish host, but I believe the praise was genuine.

Never having seen the Cliffs of Moher, except in photographs, I cannot comment. At their highest point they reach merely 702 feet, and I was sitting at 1200 feet, but I have been rather misleading the reader in some respects. Largiebaan has big cliffs, but it isn't all cliff. The south-north ridge between the burn and the east-west ridge of Aignish drops off to a scree slope, most of it quite accessible. The true cliffs – sheer and bare – rise above the caves and on the south side of Rubha Dùn Bhàin. The Cliffs of Moher appear to be all cliff; Largiebaan is cliff and scree, but all of it reaching to greater heights. A little internet research informs me that the Cliffs of Moher annually attract almost a million visitors, who are served by the 'Cliffs of Moher Visitor Experience', built into a hillside at a cost of €32 million. Admittance is €6 (children free).

There is nothing at Largiebaan, not even a hut to shelter in, but I'm certainly not complaining. Largiebaan's relative freedom from human disturbance is part of its appeal to me, and to others of my acquaintance. Of course, the reason the cliffs are little visited is that there's no road there. If you go there, you'll be on foot. There was a proposal, in the Argyllshire Road Act of 1800, to upgrade the old coastal tracks and make a ten-feet-broad road from Glemanuill to the Mull Lighthouse and thence to Kilkivan, near Machrihanish, but nothing came of it. By then, sheep were moving in and people moving out, and the coastal farming townships, which the original tracks served, were already falling into ruination.

The definition of 'wilderness' offered by Ben Gadd, referring to the Canadian Rockies, is apt for Largiebaan, indeed for that whole coast between Ballygroggan and the Mull: 'Where there are no buildings, no roads and no motors, there you will find wilderness. It's really as simple as that.'[4] Kintyre, of course, has nothing remotely on the scale of the Rockies, but what we have on the precious unspoilt margins is worth preserving from further coniferous afforestation and from the unrelenting threat of subsidised wind-farms. I have heard it remarked that if Largiebaan were on the Antrim coast, there would be a stepped path all the way down to the caves for the convenience of visitors.

Since August 2006 there has been the Kintyre Way, which has opened up the south-west corner of the peninsula to visitors. However, it's no easy way to see Largiebaan, which is mid-way between Machrihanish and the Mull. Once there, you have to return by the way you came, continue on the Kintyre Way to Southend village, or take some other route out (my preference being via Glenahanty and the Homeston road, which, in reverse, and by car, is a quicker way in).

The Way follows the line of the cliffs from the Aignish down, until it turns abruptly inland towards Largiebaan steading, which it bypasses with a turn south. The route understandably avoids the actual cliff-edge, and I suspect that few walkers actually deviate from the track to take a peek at what lies to seaward. I have sat under the top and heard the approach of walkers and watched them pass. Each time, they were unaware of my and my companions' presence. They were pushing on, and who could blame them considering the distance still to cover from Largiebaan? So, the Kintyre Way has brought more visitors to Largiebaan, but they are transient in the extreme. Owing to the distance of that final stage, Campbeltown to Southend, walkers tend to start out early, while I am still asleep, so I seldom see them.

18. Three walking companions who feature individually in this book, photographed together at Largiebaan, 21 March 2012. L-R: Amelia Martin, Murdo MacDonald and Dr Sandy McMillan. Photograph by the author.

I thought I had encountered a late starter on 17 June, but I was mistaken. She was aboard the same bus to Machrihanish at 1 p.m. and was conspicuously dressed for business, with shorts and rucksack. She disembarked in the village, while I continued to Lossit Gate, so I was ahead of her. She overtook me on the Way, past Ballygroggan steading, and I greeted her and asked her where she was heading. She didn't break stride, but replied in passing, 'clutching an O.S. map as though it were the Bible', that she would stop at a certain point and turn back to catch the 6 o' clock bus.

I was seated at my customary late lunch spot, on the edge of the moorland plain, when I saw her returning, a distant figure, 'half-running and still clutching map'. I decided to 'keep my head in this book' – my journal, in which I was describing her approach, with cynical amusement – and ignore her as she passed; but I squinted at her when she'd gone by and saw her glance behind at me. My final judgement, from the journal: 'She sounded and looked like a rather driven, obsessive type [hey – that's me too!] I didn't want her company; still, most walkers would have chatted a while and maybe learned something.' She was the last human I'd see that day until the bus arrived at Lossit Gate at 10.35. From my rock perch, after she had gone, I noted that 'the heat-shimmer on the bog cotton made the air appear alive'.

I was on my way to Largiebaan, and this time I stayed on the Kintyre Way. I found the uphill stretch from Innean Mòr a slog, but at least there were no burns to cross and gullies to negotiate, and I reached the highest point of the cliffs at 5.30. On my approach, I had been observing keenly my destination, and noted in my journal when I got there: 'This summit looks like a miniature dun from the south; and from the north, as one approaches on the Kintyre Way, the rock overhang beneath resembles an inverted shark's fin on a tilted horizon.' Mmmm ... quite!

A sheep below the Aignish

The rapture of my earlier visit would not be repeated. I didn't expect it to be – no experience ever exactly can be – but neither did I expect that my mind would be troubled all the time I was there. Almost immediately, I'd noticed a sheep on a steep grassy slope below the Aignish, and I feared that she was trapped. Sheep sometimes jump down on to a tempting patch of grazing but can't make the leap back up to where the adventure started. If they don't find another route on to the cliff-top, they either starve or fall.

The wild goats, too, sometimes – though less often – find themselves in precarious places. There were two, in the summer of 1982, which were stuck for months on a steep face south of Rubha Dùn Bhàin. One could tell exactly what their grazing range was – every bit of accessible vegetation had been cropped, leaving a yellow, sun-parched expanse. A nephew, Donald Docherty, and I tried to climb to them from the shore, but I suffered a nasty fall and in the end we found our line of ascent blocked by a vertical rock face. Even had we reached the goats, they would probably have killed themselves in escaping from our (to them) inexplicable designs. I presume they died there, anyway. I didn't want to know at the time. That story is told in full in *Kintyre: The Hidden Past* (pp. 161-62).

Anyway, all the time I was on the cliff-top I couldn't stop myself checking on the sheep's position. As I noted in my journal, 'compulsive viewing'. When I'd scan the slope with binoculars and fail to find her, I'd assume she had already fallen to her death. I even imagined I saw her corpse under the cliffs, but finally identified a gleaming rock. Then, to my momentary relief, I'd see her again; but she would begin baaing plaintively and I'd convince myself that 'she knows she's in trouble'. To complete the disturbing scene, there were four young hooded crows flying and calling around the cliffs. My conclusion: 'No idyll this time.' A raven – that astute attendant on the distressed and dying – would have completed the macabre scene I was already sketching in imagination. And midges were biting.

I e-mailed Jimmy MacDonald about the sheep when I returned home that night and his response was reassuring. I knew he'd seen a sheep on that same slope several years before, and that he'd been concerned for her safety, but he replied that he was certain she had got herself back on to the Aignish; and he had seen sheep there since. To reassure himself, he had checked the foot of the cliff and found no remains of fallen animals.

The Aignish

The shape of Binnein Fithich continued to vex my conscience, and I noted before starting homeward at 6.30: 'Northernmost "knuckle" is a pinnacle – from south as from beneath.' I had also been looking closely at the Aignish, not surprisingly since the sheep which had marred my contentment was under the ridge. It is a Norse name and I have wondered at its presence out there. Indeed, I have for years been pondering Kintyre Norse place-names in general.

The name owes its survival, as many place-names do, to the Ordnance Survey, which was active in south Kintyre in 1866. There was a local newspaper going at that time, the *Argyllshire Herald*, but its staff appears not to have noticed the military gentlemen measuring the landscape and scribbling place-names and (too seldom) their meanings into notebooks. Would the name have survived without its appearance on the first O.S. map of Kintyre? A few shepherds might have kept it alive, but I wouldn't have bet on that, since many shepherds in the nineteenth century were incomers from the Borders and elsewhere.

The Ordnance Survey's 'authorities', as they were described, for place-names north of the Mull were all natives and Gaelic-speaking: Donald Mathieson, Glenahanty; Duncan Ferguson, Dalbuie; Iain Campbell, Remuil; and Angus Campbell, High Glenadale.

The spelling in the O.S. 'name book' in 1866 was 'Eagnish', which is reproduced on the first map (sheet CCLXI) published in 1869. It was later changed to 'Aignish', but the difference is slight, and, in any case, both forms are phonetic and represent an oral legacy. The name does not survive in any written Norse form, and the local shepherd who pointed out the feature to the Army officers knew only its name as he had heard it spoken. Not surprisingly, then, the O.S. notebook contains no suggested interpretation, but it does contain a useful description: ' ... bold and precipitous range of rocks on the west base of Cnoc Moy.' When the Kintyre Antiquarian Society's place-names committee engaged with the name seventy years later, its description was: 'Cliff face near Largiebaan Caves.' But it isn't a cliff. It is what the '-nish' element declares it to be – a nose (*nes*) or point. The committee's interpretation was: 'Norse: Eggarnes: The nose of the ridge. See, however, MacBain's "Place Names of Highlands and Islands", p 101.' And here are the illustrious Dr Alexander Macbain's observations, from his chapter on 'Place-Names of the Hebrides':

> Aignish is called by the all-observant [Martin] Martin, 'Egginess'; and he remarks: – 'The shore of Egginess abounds with little smooth stones, prettily variegated with all sorts of colours. They are of a round form, which is probably occasioned by the tossing of the sea, which in those parts is very violent' (p. 10, West. Isles). In Captain [F. W. L.] Thomas's opinion also, Aignish was probably named from these egg-shaped pebbles, thus Aignis would stand for Eggia-ness, from Norse egg, an egg. But egg also means an edge, which equally well explains the name.

Perhaps, then, 'edge point' suits best – it certainly captures the nature of that entire coastal scoop at Largiebaan, which shepherds called 'the Corrie' and of which Aignish forms the northern rim. It is emphatically a place of edges. (The expression 'to egg on' – to incite – has nothing to do with the produce of hens, but is another survival of Norse *egg*, 'edge'.)

'Aignish' could be a thousand years old, more or less. There are, to be sure, much older names around, but it is still a huge historical shadow cast by a tiny name on a map, a name that's now 'at the back of beyond'. Between Ballygroggan in the north and Feorlin in the south, a twelve-mile stretch of coastline, more or less, there isn't a single occupied house. The Mull lighthouse and Largiebaan farm were the last places to empty in a population dispersal dating back to the late eighteenth century and the sheep invasion. Archaeology informs us that that coast was occupied by humans for thousands of years before the historical period, and archaeology will have further information to reveal out there should the sites which have slumbered unnoticed in their difficult remoteness be identified and investigated.

The nature of Scandinavian influence in Kintyre is still a subject of debate. Were there pockets of Norse-speaking settlement which were ultimately assimilated into the existing Gaelic population, or was the Norse presence more tenuous? Archaeologically, the record of Norse settlement in Kintyre is a complete blank, but that negative does not necessarily imply absence of evidence. Such evidence (if there is any) may simply not have been uncovered, and the debate will ultimately rest on place-names evidence, specifically on the proportion of Norse names which can be safely identified as signifying actual Norse settlement.

Earadale

I'll mention Earadale only in passing, having written in some detail about the place and name in *Kintyre Places and*

Place-Names (pp. 107-8). It lies directly to the south of Sròn Gharbh, and the name has survived by its attachment to 'Earadale Point', which, seen from the A83, is the furthest visible headland on Kintyre. Earadale, like Aignish, is Norse, and evidently means 'shingle-beach valley' (*eyrr* + *dalr*), but the description is quite impossible to relate to the landscape. There is another Earadale, on the east side of Kintyre, which was a settlement until the mid-nineteenth century and therefore spawned, in charters and leases, a variety of name-forms. The interpretation in that case is tenable if Glenahervie is considered to be the 'valley' and the shore at its foot the 'shingle beach'. There is a settlement, too, on the hillside north of Earadale Point, but it is prehistoric, possibly Middle Bronze Age, and its original name and the language of the name disappeared millennia ago. Looking south from Sròn Gharbh, it is evident that the land around the settlement huts has been cleared for cultivation, but the dominant impression remains one of stony bleakness. I still struggle to conceive of families settled and surviving there – my perception, however, is thousands of years out of date!

A visit to the Largieside

On 30 July I took the 11.30 Glasgow bus to Tayinloan and was met there by an old friend and fellow-antiquarian, Murdo MacDonald, who had driven down from his home at Balliemore, near Lochgilphead. Murdo, who retired as Argyll and Bute Council archivist in 2006, was born in 1939 at Tigh na Chladaich, the Killean and Kilchenzie parish manse at Muasdale. His father, also Murdo, and a native of Lewis, was minister there from 1932 until 1943. He was, remarkably, the fourth MacDonald incumbent, after Rev Donald (1799-1851), Rev Donald John (1880-1926), and Rev Donald (1926-1928), who died of a heart attack less than two years into his ministry. The MacDonald domination was interrupted only by a Macfarlane and a Macmillan incumbent; and the minister chosen by the congregation before Rev Murdo was also a Macdonald – William, a native of Islay – who declined the call in January 1932. If Murdo junior's 'calling' directed him away from the ministry, he none the less enjoys a deep interest in ecclesiastical history.

The main purpose of the meeting was to visit a rather obscure graveyard near Clachan, known both as 'Gartnagrenach', from the farm on which it is situated, and Cladh Mhìcheil. I'd never been there before, and Murdo had, so he was to be the guide that day. First, however, I wished to visit Killean churchyard and photograph several gravestones there. I had promised a friend in Perth, Archie Smith (p 239), that I'd send him photographs of his maternal grandmother Barbara Milloy's family stones. She was born at Claonaig and married into Tarbert, but the Milloys belonged to the Largieside and bore the magnificent Gaelic surname *Mac Gillie Mo-luaig*, 'Son of the servant of [Saint] Moluag', until such cumbersome constructions were deemed a liability, being difficult to spell and unwise to possess in the new social order in which English was the ascendant culture. (Coincidentally, I have a Barbara Milloy in my own ancestry, a paternal great-great-great-great grandmother, so Archie and I may be distantly related.)

I took the photographs for Archie and then photographed the grave of Norman Morrison, the Lewis-born naturalist whose reputation in his native island had recently been revived, and enhanced, by the discovery of a collection of his glass negatives, depicting islanders a century ago. We browsed among other stones – two inscribed in Gaelic were of particular interest as rare expressions of cultural loyalty – and then drove to Tayinloan Ferry for lunch in Big Jessie's Café, encountering there two ladies from Southend who were about to join the Kintyre Botany Group's outing to Rhunahaorine Point.

Achadh na Sìthe

Clachan was our next stop, and a revelation awaited me there. After Murdo had parked his car, he led me through a stone archway, inscribed *Achadh na Sìthe*, 'Field of Peace', towards a burial-ground of whose existence I hadn't known. This was the 'new' cemetery, an addition to the old churchyard, from which it is separated by a small field adjoining the village caravan site.

The gateway led us to an imposing bronze memorial to Lieut. Duncan Mackinnon of Ronachan, Scots Guards, who was killed in Flanders on 9 October 1917. He was the third son of Duncan Mackinnon of Loup and Balinakill, who was born in Campbeltown in 1844 and died in 1918. Mackinnon senior is buried at the high end of the graveyard under an 'Iona cross', which also commemorates his eldest son, Captain William Mackinnon, London Scottish, killed in action in France on 11 May 1917.

The bronze monument consists of two figures on a granite obelisk, Saint Michael and 'a mourning woman bestowing a laurel wreath'. It was designed by F. J. Wilcoxson, a London-based sculptor, and appears to have 'slipped the internet' because I could find nothing on it among all the items on its designer.

Oxford-educated Duncan Mackinnon was in India on business when the First World War broke out, but, in the now hollow-sounding words of the *Campbeltown Courier* (30/10/1920), '... the call of the Mother Country to her sons found him ready, and he did not hesitate to place his life at the service of the State'. The burial-ground had been gifted by him, and the dedication ceremony and unveiling of his memorial took place on 23 October 1920.

Compared with its elderly, disorderly neighbour, the cemetery was a vision of neatness and calm – a 'Field of Peace', indeed. While Murdo examined the memorial, I began browsing among the gravestones. Though none of them predates the early twentieth century, there were names and places which interested me, though I had known very few of the people. Near the far end of the graveyard, however, I read an inscription and then read it again with a frisson of recognition. The names and dates were: John McQuilkan, died 6 February 1934, aged 78; his wife Janet Campbell, died 6 January 1950, aged 83; grandson John McQuilkan, died 14 March 1977, aged 28; and son Duncan McQuilkan, died 22 June 1978, aged 71.

John McQuilkan

I could recall the bottom two, Duncan and John, father and son, whose deaths occurred in my adulthood. Duncan was a well-known bus driver and I remember him clearly, though if I ever had a conversation with him unconnected with travel, I've forgotten it. But I remember a conversation I had with John, and its strangeness has preserved it in my memory.

He was three years older than I, which, at school, is an almost unbridgeable gulf in social status, though the gap shrinks to nothing in later life; except, poor John didn't have much 'later life'. I remember him visiting me at 24 Crosshill Avenue. I knew who he was, but didn't know him as a person. By then he had graduated in History from the University of Edinburgh and qualified as a teacher, a career into which his sister Jean, who died at the age of fifty-five, followed him. I was writing my first book, *The Ring-Net Fishermen*, which I'd started in 1974. He knew about the book and that's mainly what we talked about.

One remark alone of his has lodged in my memory. He said to me how fortunate I was that I was writing a book and would leave something behind me in the world. The words may be inexact, but they represent his sentiments. I remember asking myself what was to stop him writing a book if that's how he himself would wish to be remembered.

I didn't know, and I don't recall his telling me, that he was dying of cancer.

He died in March 1977, by which time I was almost three years into my research. His visit, therefore, was probably in late '76 or early '77. I don't remember and have no means of checking, since I stopped keeping a diary a year or so after I began work on the book. I checked the *Campbeltown Courier* for an obituary, but there was none – only his death notice, which told that his life ended on 14 March in Addenbrooke General Hospital, Cambridge, and that the funeral service would be held in Lochend Church, Campbeltown, at 1.30 p.m. on Saturday 19 March, 'thereafter to Clachan Cemetery'. Lochend Church – demolished in 1990 and its site now a supermarket car-park – was the McQuilkan family church, and John's father, Duncan, was successively Elder, Clerk of Deacon's Court and Session Clerk there.

Since I hardly knew John, I asked William Crossan, whom I knew to be a contemporary of John's, if he could write a brief memoir for me. Willie, who recently retired as Rector of Campbeltown Grammar School, turned the appeal over to a group of his old school friends which meets occasionally to circulate news and to reminisce. One of the group, Jim Edgar, a retired teacher in Dunfermline, obliged at once and wrote the following piece, for which I am most grateful. Its effect on me was not just to bring John McQuilkan out of the shadows a little, but to bring my own past out of those same shadows, which obscure the late '60s and early '70s, a period of my life which was characterised by emotional insecurity and reckless behaviour.

> I'm not surprised our memories of John are perhaps a bit confusing after forty-odd years without him.
>
> I suppose I became aware of him as a distant figure from the top end of Limecraigs when I lived at the bottom end. It's a bit like 'blue remembered hills'. If we wandered too far up the hill and across the fields to what we called Roy Watson's, kids, John among them, would chase us back. If we went the

other way along Limecraigs Road we eventually arrived at Ralston Road where a different lot of kids would intimidate us. Some of them were girls, which was really scary.

The Grammar School was when we first got to know each other properly. The important affliction we had in common was our parents. We were both children of teachers who taught in the school we were attending as pupils. Not just any old teachers, but teachers people in their eighties still talk about in Campbeltown today – not all with a cheery smile.

Apart from that we had little in common and that was why we enjoyed each other's company. We would wander along Kilkerran Road to the bottom of the Cutting, and politics was the main talking point. I fancied myself as a Marxist and anti the war in Vietnam. He by that time was a right winger. I always felt he found me amusing. He always had a smile on his face. Was he teasing me? Was he really a Tory or was that his way of winding me up?

I remember his ambition was to be an officer in the British Army. I also remember us hiding in the shrubbery at Limecraigs House and shooting the heads off what I think were tulips with his rather impressive .22 air rifle. His other impressive possession at that time was an original copy of an album by Jimi Hendrix called *Electric Ladyland*. I can't remember much about the music but the cover consisted of a group of naked women in provocative poses.

I suppose we lost touch for a year or two. After a miserable time working in an accountant's office, I went to Dundee, and he went to Edinburgh. Occasionally we met during college breaks.

Finally I met him one night in the Ardshiel. I was married and was with my wife. He seemed like the same old 'Quelch'. He chuffed away on his silly pipe and captivated Helen with his nonsense. He had his History degree from Edinburgh. Was he still toying with the idea of the army?

It was then he told me he was ill. He had an open wound on his back which had to be kept open to drain fluid, and he had what I think was a pacemaker in his chest. He opened his shirt and let me press my ear to his chest. He was ticking like a clock.

I suppose it was a few months later somebody from Campbeltown told me the sad news. The army wouldn't have taken him, on health grounds, anyway, but he would have been a great sniper and he had immense courage.

Psychedelia

I remember that Jimi Hendrix double album, *Electric Ladyland*, but it was by no means as rare as Jim suggests. I certainly bought a copy soon after its appearance in November 1968. With Cream's *Disraeli Gears* (November 1967) and the Beatles' *Sgt. Pepper's Lonely Hearts Club Band* (June 1967), it was a classic of the 'psychedelic' era. I had the beads and the shoulder-length hair, but the 'free love' rather eluded me. Perhaps I was in the wrong place or perhaps my disguise was too transparent.

I was invited, one Saturday in the early '70s, to a party in Campbeltown, and was asked to bring some of my LPs. The girl's parents had gone on holiday, hence the party, but when I left the gathering, I left without my albums, and when they were finally returned to me, some were missing. One of these was *Electric Ladyland*, with its female nudes spread across the covers. Since the girl's father was a prominent member of the morally rigorous 'Wee Free' Church, I assumed that he had seen the album and destroyed it. I replaced it easily enough, but failed to replace one of the other missing albums, Pink Floyd's *More* (the soundtrack to a Barbet Schroeder film). Perhaps I didn't try hard enough at the time, but a recent internet search disclosed that I could have a digitally re-mastered version on CD for less than £10, and, forty-odd years on, I replaced it. The decision was a mistake, as many nostalgia-motivated decisions are, and when I played the disc I rediscovered its essential blandness.

I haven't looked at the *Electric Ladyland* cover in years, but I can clearly visualise two of the girls' faces, as though in

19. *The author disguised as a hippie in 1973. Photograph by Gordon Hunter, Campbeltown, for* The Scotsman.

that earlier life I had really known them. I have no recollection – a favourite test – of where I was when J. F. Kennedy was shot, or Martin Luther King, or John Lennon; but I do remember where I learned of Hendrix's death (on 18 September 1970). I was in Larne, County Down, hung-over, as Hendrix would have been had he survived that night.

But Cream was my greatest musical love in the late '60s, and I clearly recall where I was when I first heard 'Wrapping Paper', the band's first single – outside Wallace Cottages, Southend, delivering Sunday newspapers with Alistair McEachran and his son, David, in October 1966. The song was on the car radio, and as soon as its few minutes were over I decided I must have it. Cream's second single, 'I Feel Free' (December 1966), had an even greater impact on me. I was lying in a bath on a Saturday morning when Ginger Baker's drum introduction thudded out from the transistor radio propped at the end of the tub.

Jack Bruce, Cream's Glasgow-born bassist, lead singer and principal song-writer, bought Sanda Island in 1969; £32,000 sticks in my memory as the price. I was reporter on the *Campbeltown Courier* at the time, and the purchase, as well as being local news, was personally exciting. The editor Colin Macaulay and I were to have crossed to Sanda with Bruce on Sunday 24 August 1969, but he postponed the trip until the following day, when neither Colin nor I could go. My diary conclusion, 'I'm not terribly disappointed', seems scarcely credible.

An 'exclusive interview' with Bruce finally appeared in the *Courier* on 24 December 1970. With Colin Macaulay's departure in November 1969, I had taken over as editor, and was apparently still in the job when the interview was published. Much of the detail in that unsigned piece – e.g. Bruce's recent collaboration with American musician Carla Bley, in her 'jazz opera' *Escalator Over the Hill*, his earlier collaboration with lyricist Pete Brown, whom he thought would 'probably be recognised as a great poet after his death' (wrong there, Jack!) – suggests that I wrote it, yet I cannot recall having met Bruce. Bizarre! Can any reader resolve the authorship question?

My musical interests were to expand hugely in the early 1970s. I can't put a date, or even a year, to the shift, but I remember the circumstances. I was in the crew of a fishing boat which put into Rothesay one day. I knew that my friend Jim Macmaster's father had moved there – the *Courier* of 17 June 1971 reported that Archie Macmaster, a native of Tobermory, was leaving, after twenty-five years in Campbeltown, to become Royal Bank of Scotland manager in Rothesay – and I resolved to find the Macmaster house. I succeeded, and Jim was at home. While we were chatting in his bedroom, there was an album playing in the background; but before long Jim was in the background. The album – a double, with one twenty-minute composition per side – was Soft Machine's *Third*, released in 1970. I had discovered 'jazz fusion' (or call it what you will, if you have any opinion) and unknowingly embarked on a musical journey which would lead me through Miles Davis, Weather Report, and Passport to Nils Petter Molvaer, Esbjorn Svensson, Jan Garbarek and a clutch of other super-talented Scandinavians at meeting-points of genres. Yet, my loyalty to that hypnotic album, *Three*, remains absolute to this day.

There was a more immediate sequel to that party in Campbeltown. I returned home very drunk and very hungry, and, finding a cooked chicken in the fridge, retired to bed with it. I was wakened later that day by my mother, enquiring after the Sunday dinner, the bones of which we soon discovered in bed with me.

The 'Ardshiel', to which Jim Edgar refers, is an hotel on Kilkerran Road. At that time, it had a very genteel reputation, and the bar-room and back room were known as 'The Whispering Rooms'. I was there one evening, probably around 1969, and probably with David Cameron. He and Jim Edgar, in conference, decided it was time a social outrage was committed in the bar. They were sitting together on the window seat when a 'fight' broke out between them, with grabbing and slapping. It was simulated, lasted only seconds, and I may be the only one who remembers it, but it impressed me at the time as a superlative ploy in that citadel of bourgeois restraint.

Duncan and earlier McQuilkans

With the passage of time, Duncan, like John, has come to mean more to me than he did in life. I perceive him, now, not as Duncan the bus driver – an ignorant simplification, anyway – but as Duncan the Gaelic speaker, and one of that last generation of true natives who lived among the rest of us without our necessarily being aware of their cultural distinction. By then – the 1950s and '60s – they were, of course, fully assimilated and spoke much like the rest of us; indeed, those of them – probably the majority – for whom English was a second language, learned in school, could speak with greater grammatical precision and clearer enunciation. When, in 1978, I began tape-recording native Gaelic speakers in Kintyre, I concentrated my efforts on finding subjects in the rural parts – chiefly the Largieside – where I was told the last of them were. I overlooked Duncan, who lived in town, and he died in the summer of that very year. Perhaps, had he lived a year or two longer, I'd have reached him too with my tape-recorder. I now greatly regret that I missed him, and the same could be said of several other men and women in whose lives I discovered an interest years after they had died.

Duncan, however, was accorded an obituary in the *Campbeltown Courier* (30 June 1978), unlike his son, who hadn't lived long enough to earn one. Duncan was born in Clachan, the only child of John McQuilkan who ran the coaching inn there for thirty years and afterwards farmed Lagalgarve. Duncan, as a boy, assisted his father with the changing of the horses. The mail coach service ended in 1913, but from 1931 until his (partial) retirement in 1974, Duncan himself would be running mail between Campbeltown and Tarbert, in a bus. He joined Craig Brothers in 1928, and, according to his anonymous obituary-writer, was instrumental in 'laying the foundations of' West Coast Motor Services Co., epitomising, with his partner William Craig, 'the rural bus drivers of the day who were known to everyone on the route and who carried out a variety of errands and obligements in addition to their normal duties'.

I can attest to that, having sat in a parked bus after Duncan disappeared with a newspaper, and other messages, into a roadside cottage on the Largieside. He was absent long enough to provoke a buzz of consternation and speculation among the passengers, and returned, pipe in mouth, to resume the journey. I guessed at the time that he'd been blethering to some acquaintance, perhaps in Gaelic, for all I knew then. His obituary described him as a 'fluent Gaelic speaker' and noted that he was president of the Campbeltown branch of An Comunn Gàidhealach, 'The Gaelic Society', which continues to flourish, but not in Kintyre.

McQuilkan was once a very common name in North Kintyre, but the few remaining McQuilkans now live in Campbeltown. The old pronunciation 'MacCoolkin' – represented in such spellings as 'McCulkyn' and 'McCulkyne' in seventeenth century records[5] – can still occasionally be heard among older folk. The name represents *Mac Cuilcein*, 'Son of Wilkin', a diminutive or pet form of 'William'. In Largieside the name hardly mutated, but on the opposite side of the peninsula, from Skipness down to Grogport, 'Wilkie' was the preferred form by the mid-nineteenth century.

I have already touched on the Anglicising (or, at the least, de-Gaelicising) of native Kintyre surnames, a subject which has fascinated me for most of my life. My definitive treatment of the subject is in *Kintyre: The Hidden Past*, first published in 1984, but I have returned to it in subsequent books and keep returning as new insights emerge. Later, I'll look at Loynachan/Lang, but here is MacIlhattan/Hattan ... and something extra besides!

In January 2014, I had a letter from Mr David Martin in Lewiston, U.S.A., enquiring about his great-great grandparents, Donald Martin and Rachel Hutton, who emigrated from Campbeltown to Canada in 1836. The name 'Hutton', by which Rachel was known throughout her life in Ontario, seemed to me impossible to connect with Kintyre until Judy suggested that it might represent 'Hattan'. Sure enough, when she checked the Old Parish Registers she found her as 'Rachael Macilchattan', born on 1 July 1810 in Campbeltown Parish. Needless to say, without an awareness of local surname mutations, Rachel's true identity might never have been uncovered. That identity is *Mac Gille Chatain*, 'Son of the Servant of Saint Catan', an interesting and rather rare Kintyre surname which was chiefly of Largieside provenance and is now extinct in Kintyre. In a Largieside whisky-smuggling case in 1829, two brothers, identified as James and Duncan MacIlchattan, were questioned, and each signed his statement 'Hattan', nicely demonstrating a surname in transition.[6]

Duncan McQuilkan's grandmother, Sarah McBride, was also the bearer of a rare Kintyre surname. It, too, was of ecclesiastical origin – Gaelic *Mac Gille Brighde*, 'Son of the servant of [Saint] Bridget' – and it too is extinct. There is certainly Miss Margaret McBride in Carradale, but her grandfather came over to Kintyre from Arran in the nineteenth century. There were also Irish McBrides came to Kintyre in the nineteenth century, and Irish Hattans, and Irish McQuilkans, and Irish Martins, and on and on. Where do the connections begin and end?

Sarah McBride was born in Skipness and so was her husband, Duncan McQuilkan. When the 1861 census of Kilcalmonell was taken, they were in 'Tallavtoll' with three children, Duncan's young brother Alexander, a sixteen-year-old domestic servant, Mary Gilchrist, and an elderly visitor, Alexander Duncan, against whose name, for occupation and parish of birth, 'NK', for 'Not Known', was noted. These omissions are curious, but I suggest that the old man had landed on them from Skipness, where the surname Duncan was abundant at that time. It represents MacConnachie (*Mac Dhonnchaidh*, 'Son of Duncan'), but there's more – these Kintyre MacConnachies were originally Campbells, and some of them used both surnames simultaneously.

Duncan had an unusually long spell as shepherd in *Talamh toll* ('Land in the hole'), which stands a ruin now to the south-west of Loch Ciaran. He was there, of course, in 1861, and still there in 1891, when nominally retired, so around forty years would be a fair estimate of his occupancy. His wife Sarah was with him in 1891, two sons, Donald and John – both now tending the sheep stock – and his youngest daughter, Helen. He died on 28 December 1900, aged seventy-eight, at Lagnagortan, Clachan, as the consequence of a serious fall – the cause of death is recorded as a fractured neck and femur.

By the 1901 Census, an Ayrshire-born shepherd, William Weir, is in 'Talavtoll', and John McQuilkan is proprietor of Ronachan Inn, Clachan, and still unmarried at the age of forty-four. Helen is with him as a domestic servant, assisted by nineteen-year-old Mary Ann Leitch from Islay. John McQuilkan and Janet Campbell, whom he subsequently married, lived in retirement at 32 Saddell Street, Campbeltown, just up the road where I live. His obituary described him as a 'good Gaelic scholar' and a 'staunch supporter of the activities of the local branch of An Comunn Gàidhealach',[7] as his son Duncan would be after him. A family commitment to the Gaelic cause may be inferred from this, though the description 'Gaelic scholar', which recurs in nineteenth and early twentieth century obituaries, should not be interpreted as meaning anything more than a degree of familiarity with the written language, otherwise there would have been as many linguistic experts in Kintyre as in the rest of Scotland! He died in Saddell Street on 6 February 1934, and his death was registered by his son, Duncan.

McIntyre family

Duncan's wife, Catherine, had a similar background, but without the Gaelic fluency. She was a daughter of Duncan McIntyre, who lived at Cruachan, near Tayinloan. She taught English and History in Campbeltown Grammar School, and I remember her as firm but fair.

Catherine's brother, Allan, was also a teacher of English. He taught first in Dunfermline, then Bathgate, was appointed Rector of Linlithgow Academy in 1951, and of Bo'ness Academy two years later. He died in 1957 at the age of fifty-five. His library, or part of it, must have found its way to Campbeltown. The McQuilkans lived in Limecraigs House, where Catherine's sister Mary, a nurse, later lived with her in retirement. There was an outbreak of fire in the house in May 1981,[8] and the sisters moved temporarily to 181 Ralston Road. A house-clearance must have taken place at some time, and a quantity of books was donated to Campbeltown Public Library. These turned up later in a sale of unwanted stock, but they had clearly never been incorporated into the library.

I bought a number of these books at very modest prices. At the time, I guessed the source of the books, because some of them were university texts with John McQuilkan's name on them, but I wasn't, until many years later, able to link Allan McIntyre's books to that clearance. One of them, which I still have, is a first edition of Norman MacCaig's *The Sinai Sort*, published in 1957 and signed by the author with the date 'June 1957'; but Allan didn't have it for long, because he died later that year. An inscription on the inside front cover has been blackened over with a felt-tipped pen, but most of it is legible:

> To Allan MacIntyre
> a true, leal Scot
> [illegible]
> From Bo'ness Rebels

Literary Society
[illegible]
July 1957

Allan's widow, Mary, subsequently moved to Carradale, where yet another McIntyre sibling, Christina ('Chryssie') was a teacher. She married, in 1934, a Carradale fisherman, Donald McIntosh, owner and skipper of the ring-netter *Paragon*. They lived at Ardgowan, and she was known to her pupils, some of whom she conducted in the Carradale Junior Gaelic Choir, as 'Mrs Donnie'. She died on 13 November 1983, aged eighty-three, at Cruachan, the home of her daughter and only child, Alaine, who herself married a Carradale fisherman and boat-owner, Colin Campbell.

Cladh Mhìcheil

Murdo and I finished our day at Cladh Mhìcheil, a cemetery without a chapel. The name translates as 'Burial-ground of [Saint] Michael', and the dedication is puzzling. Since none of the gravestones is earlier than the eighteenth century – in other words, post-Reformation – in what circumstances, and when, was the burial-ground named after a saint? Records are sparse, and the Royal Commission on the Ancient and Historical Monuments of Scotland's *Inventory of the Ancient Monuments* for Kintyre (p 110) devotes merely four lines to Cladh Mhìcheil. Its present status also puzzled us. It clearly wasn't a private graveyard, unless the humble corpses there had all been employees of Gartnagrenach Estate or relatives of employees, yet it appears not to be a public graveyard either and evidently isn't maintained by Argyll and Bute Council, though the old County Council tended it (p 99). It is overgrown inside and virtually surrounded by outreaching lime trees, described in 1853 as 'about thirty feet in height'. Murdo and I had a final cup of coffee and then began exploring the little graveyard.

20. Murdo MacDonald in Cladh Mhìcheil, 30 July 2013. Photograph by the author.

Most of the interesting burials are of Campbells. In one of the enclosures there are three memorials to the Campbells of Kintarbert, who owned Gartnagrenach estate. 1. Isobel Campbell, daughter of Archibald Campbell Esq. of Melford and wife of Duncan Campbell of Kintarbert, died 4 February 1778, 'aged about 40 years'. 2. Dugald Campbell Esq. of Kintarbert, died 1 January 1788, aged 69. 3. Lieutenant General Robert Campbell of Kintarbert, died 13 May 1837, aged 74. Then there is a James Campbell, 'who was killed in China by pirates in 1847 in the 29th year of his age', and, finally, the noted benefactress Miss Lucy Campbell.

Miss Lucy Campbell

The inscription to her is probably as lengthy as I have seen devoted to any individual in any graveyard in Kintyre – 134 words, by my count. She was born in Ardchattan in 1760, daughter of Donald Campbell of Ballimore and Ann Campbell, lived for nine years at Leamnamuic near Clachan, then in Gowanbank (now Stronvaar) Campbeltown, which she built and in which she died on 23 January 1843. She founded two schools in Dalintober and left £4,600 for their endowment; she benefited Campbeltown with £600 for the Female School of Industry, £300 for the support of a parochial missionary and the same for Sabbath schools, £500 for the poor of the parish and £600 for the Female Benevolent Society. Those sums of money, converted into present values, are big. She also left money for the poor of Ardchattan and Kilcalmonell parishes and 'for the support of charitable institutions in Edinburgh and Glasgow'.

From the researches of Colonel Charles Mactaggart, Campbeltown, Lucy was orphaned at an early age and was 'very poor', her home at Leamnamuic being 'a little thatched cot'. This is the story of her elevation to wealth and status, as retold in 1932:

> Eventually she inherited what was for those days a large fortune, and the facts connected with her getting possession of it are remarkable. At that time a Mr Sinclair, the father of Mr Dugald Sinclair, who was one of the best known men in Kintyre about sixty years ago, was tacksman of the part of Stonefield estate which lay in Kintyre, and one day when looking through a newspaper he saw an advertisement calling for information as to the heir of a gentleman who had died intestate and whose money was in Chancery. He came to the conclusion that Miss Lucy was the missing heir, and he supplied her with money and legal assistance through which eventually she made good her claim to the fortune. Her inheritance consisted mainly of West Indian estates,

and the story goes that as soon as she took possession she gave orders to free the slaves, but that action was prohibited by the laws of the colony.[9]

An anonymous account of a brief stay at Kilchamaig House, 'the delightful residence of D. Sinclair, Esq.', published in the *Campbeltown Journal* of 31 March 1853, includes the following over-egged description of the finding of Lucy's tomb:

> The honeysuckle and blue-bells hung in mournful dew-drops large and sparkling, distilled from the womb of night; the little rill that rimpled by gurgled in doleful strains, and only at intervals did the tune of the distant chorister break up the quiescence that slumbered in the gloomy booth. Whilst looking at and reading the inscriptions on the various tombstones, I was attracted by one which reared its vase and hid it in the thick clothed branches of the lime trees. I advanced and found it to point out the resting-place of worthy Miss Lucy Campbell, Gowan Bank. Whilst reading the inscription which narrates her benevolent acts in erecting institutions, her christian graces and pious life, a radiant sunbeam flashed through the dense foliage and brightened up the marble plate with its roseate hues, as if to say – 'Mark the christian's grave.'

In 1932, Argyll County Council, in recognition of 'the considerable endowments that had acured (*sic*) to them from Miss Lucy Campbell's benefactions to education, etc.', agreed to fund the maintenance of her grave and tombstone 'in perpetuity'. To that effect, 'the man who cut the grass at Gartnagrenach' for £1 per annum was granted 10s extra. That 'special attention'[10] has evidently ceased.

Killypole

I was at Killypole more often in 2013 than in any previous year of my life, not by design – it just happened that way.

Killypole is a ruined shepherd's house above Drumlemble, but it hasn't been ruined for all that long. The roof was certainly still on it in the mid-1980s. I wasn't often there afterwards, and one time, when I returned, I found the roof collapsing. It was a shame, because Killypole is in a lovely situation, though spoiled by a coniferous plantation at its back. It looks, from an elevated position, out to Campbeltown, Davaar Island and the Arran mountains. Many a magnificent sunrise must have been observed by shepherds setting out for the hills after the customary bowl of porridge. I know people – my wife among them – who dreamt of buying Killypole and renovating it, but it would have taken a great deal of money to make habitable again, even if the owner had been prepared to sell.

21. Killypole with the roof still on it in 1986. Photograph by the author.

There are two roads to Killypole. The old one – more a track, really – leads uphill from Drumlemble village to High

Tirfergus and thence to Killypole Loch. The other, which is much more popular now, because easier walked, is a forestry road which runs out to Killypole from the top of Lossit Brae. George McSporran, Benjie and I occasionally, as a change from Ben Gullion, would walk to Killypole by night on that road, an outing I wouldn't care to risk on the other one. The loch at Killypole – dammed around 1770 to power the water-pumps in Drumlemble coal-mine – is lovely and worth a visit in its own right.

In the summer of 2013, I was going to Killypole when I felt like a short walk, and a couple of times, when slogging up Lossit Brae in the heat, heading for the Inneans or Largiebaan, I decided I just didn't have the energy for these destinations and took the left turn for Killypole. Before the Slate was planted with conifers, there was a route to the Inneans which passed Killypole. It suited the Drumlemble folk, and it also briefly suited me, but a time came when that route round the foot of the Slate wasn't worth the bother. The afforestation forced one so far towards Ballygroggan ground that it made more sense to start from Ballygroggan.

I was already complaining in 1981. On 28 June, having left Killypole, 'I had to follow the forestry fence right to its end, which took me to the edge of Ballygroggan ground and increased the length of the hike'. In 1983: 'The hike from Killypole was very hard-going – I made the mistake of trying to cross the forestry plantation.' That was on 20 June, 'a marvellously clear and warm day', as I described it in my journal. I cycled to Drumlemble and left my bike at James McPhee's house in Rhudal Cottages. John MacDonald was already there, having arrived in Hamish Jackson's car, a lift I had arranged. The bay was busy that day. Willie McMillan was already on his way out, having set off from town at 6 a.m., and Allister and Agnes Stewart, young Peter Strang from Gobagrennan (who died in England in 2013) and Betty Kerr (a policewoman who lived in Machrihanish) were there as a group and had a bathe before John and I too braved the chill Atlantic.

I photographed John on our way to the Inneans. He is stripped to the waist in the heat of the day and chewing a stalk of bog cotton. We must have been below the tank on the Slate which, combined with a second tank on Ranachan Hill, supplied RAF Machrihanish with its water. At upper right of the photograph may be seen a section of the pipeline which carried the water down to Drumlemble and under the main road there to the base itself, where it entered a holding-tank.

Teddy Lafferty, when employed by the Department of the Environment at RAF Machrihanish, would assist plumber Morris McSporran in periodically cleaning out the Slate tank and checking the pipeline for leaks. I remember sitting one day in the Galdrans in my mail van, having lunch, when Teddy and Morris appeared on the shore. They had been at the Killypole tank and were heading I don't know where by a long route on a pleasant day. The year was 1991, which I know because the conversation somehow turned to the seaweed *Laminaria digitata*, whose stalk, topped by a bunch of long fronds, resembles a donkey's tail, the name they used for it; so 'donkey's tail' duly found itself in a file on local dialect, with the date of the record attached.

For a succession of summers in the late 1970s and early '80s, George McSporran would spend a day on the Slate gathering blaeberries with John Kelly, a neighbour of his wife Margaret's parents, Arthur and Jenny Thomson, in Machrihanish. They would always go during the first fortnight in August, and always to the same spot, which John had selected. It was above the water-tank and easily reached from the Killypole track. The conifers planted on the hill were tiny at that time and the blaeberry spot was clear of trees. John's sister Dorothy – with whom he lived at 6 Isleview until his death in 1998 at the age of seventy-eight – made jelly with the fruit.

22. *John MacDonald with bog cotton below the Slate, 20 June 1983. Photograph by the author.*

Graffiti

Killypole steading was, and remains, a popular place for leaving one's mark, the plastered interior walls being ideal for writing on. Since the roof's collapse, however, most of the plaster has weathered, cracked and fallen off in lumps, leaving the bare rubble walls. The south-west gable contained the greatest concentration of names and dates, but the bulk of these are now on the floor. I had my own space for years on that gable and kept adding dates and comments to it. They are all gone, but, by good fortune, Steve Walker, in April 1996, photographed my contribution to the social history of Killypole and sent me a print. I have it before me now and will first transcribe my own writings chronologically:

ANGUS MARTIN 24 SEPT 1967
A DARK AND RAINY DAY

ANGUS MARTIN 28 JUNE 1981
EN ROUTE TO THE INANS

18 JUNE 1983 – EN ROUTE TO THE INANS

22 MAY 1986

14 SEPT 1986

9/9/89

Below these inscriptions there is a comment of mine: *'NOT NECESSARILY CORRECT – THE ONLY CORRECT FORM IS THE GAELIC FORM. A.M. SO THERE!'* Nothing visible in the photograph explains these testy remarks, but I remember them as a reply to a message left on the wall questioning my use of the spelling 'Inans'. I later, as a matter of fact, adopted the spelling 'Eenans', and still later settled on 'Inneans'. My point, however, remains valid. In *Kintyre*

Places and Place-Names (pp. 181-82), I list no fewer than thirty-six different spellings taken from historical sources. One of them is *innean*, which is the correct Gaelic form.

23. Billy McTaggart in the Inneans Bay. His shadow, cast to the west, indicates a morning photograph, so 2 July 1985. Photograph by the author.

My linguistic adversary was William McTaggart – namesake of Kintyre's greatest artist – whose name first appeared on the wall on 25 June 1986. His comments – faded by 1996 – belonged to that day. At that time I didn't know him at all well, but had met him once, in the Inneans Bay, on 1 July 1985. My wife Judy, her son Allan, Jimmy MacDonald and I had arrived that evening for a two-night stay, and found Billy – on his first ever visit – already there, his little tent pitched at the north end of the bay. He had heard about the Inneans from an uncle, Malcolm 'Tiger' Hamilton, who was a regular out there (p 23); Malcolm's wife, Margaret Anderson, was a sister of Billy's mother, Laura. We spoke to Billy at his tent, and he confessed to being rather uneasy, therefore glad to see us, because the date on the Sailor's Grave, 16 May [1917], was coincidentally his date of birth in 1958. He joined us in our tent for beer and whisky before returning to his solitary pitch, close to the cross with its 'eerie date', as he put it. The next two days were scorchers, and both Allan and I suffered from our exposure to the sun. He was absent from school for two days, and my legs were so swollen I could hardly walk, though I went to work anyway.

Judy's name was also on the wall, with the dates 22 MAY 1986, 14 SEPT '86, 2 APRIL '89 and 9 SEPT '89. Our first daughter is next to her, in my writing, since she was still a baby: SARAH CAMPBELL MARTIN 2/4/89 and 9/9/89. I see also Robert Kelly (Machrihanish) 10 AUGUST 1987 and J HARVEY, 59 LIMECRAIGS, CAMPBELTOWN, undated.

My middle daughter, Amelia, born in 1989, doesn't appear by name in the photograph, but I notice in a journal entry that she was at Killypole on 19 January 1992, and that I added her name, which must have gone on to some other part of the wall. The whole family had gone there with Robert Pollock and Mary Butler, both archaeologists, who lived at 1 Front Row, Drumlemble, prior to emigrating to New Zealand. Before setting off up the hill, we enjoyed Robert's pancakes – his maternal grandfather was a master baker – and home-made ice cream. Sarah walked the whole way there, which I considered good going for a four-year-old. We heard a crashing in bracken and then saw a fox on the opposite side of the gorge our track followed, but the main nature sighting of the day was a short-eared owl over the forest west of Killypole Loch, 'seeing off a buzzard', as I noted, and, on the loch itself, three whooper swans, 'dipping to feed'.

Alec

Amelia and I had a walk to Killypole by the Lossit track on 8 August. She was home for the funeral of her grandfather, Alexander Macintosh Honeyman, who had died on the 3rd, aged ninety-three. On that day I had walked with Jan Hynd and her daughter Iona from Glenahanty road-end to High Glenadale, the roofless shepherd's cottage where Jan's father Robert McInnes (p 56) was born in 1917 and spent his childhood.

I hadn't seen Jan's husband Bob for many years, and didn't need much persuading when invited into their house for a post-hike dram. After Bob had poured me a glass of malt, I asked if I could telephone Judy to let her know where I was and when to expect me home. Her voice sounded strange when she answered the 'phone, and she had unexpected news for me when she managed to deliver it.

Alec, as I knew, had been admitted to Campbeltown Hospital with a minor infection. That afternoon, when Judy went to visit him, she couldn't waken him. He'd had a shower, eaten lunch, lay down for a rest and died from heart failure. His must have been an enviably peaceful end, for no one, fellow-patients and nursing staff alike, knew of it until Judy discovered him lifeless. I drank the whisky with guilty haste, then Jan ran me home to Judy and her inner turmoil. Once again, I'd been in the hills when a family death occurred. The summer of 2013 would be memorable for more than its weather.

24. Alec Honeyman on the Old Road beside reservoir with Judy and Sarah Martin, 20/8/1991. Photograph by the author.

Alec was born and raised in Hamilton, the elder son of Allan J. K. Honeyman, a metallurgist, and Margaret Macintosh, whose family origins were in Dores, Inverness-shire. His geology studies at Glasgow University were interrupted by the Second World War, from which he returned with the army rank of Captain. He completed his studies at the university, remaining in the Geology Department until 1952, when he took up a lecturing post in the Geology Department at Nottingham University. He retired in 1982, and soon afterwards he and his wife, Winifred Keith, who was born in Dundee, returned to Scotland, settling first in Carradale and then in Campbeltown after Judy moved there.

Golf, ever since Judy remembers, was Alec's main sporting interest, but he was a keen climber during his student years, and one of half-a-dozen students who were active from 1937 to

'39, calling themselves 'Glasgow University Mountaineering Club' before that organisation was formally constituted. While going through Alec's papers after his death, Judy came across an article, 'A Winter Adventure in Glencoe', which she hadn't known he'd written. Between Christmas 1939 and the New Year, he and two companions, Gordon Graham and Patrick Hamilton, cycled from Glasgow to Glen Coe for a few days' camping and climbing. I found the narrative both well-crafted and interesting, and since it matches the character of this book – albeit his adventures were rather more daring than mine! – I reproduce it (Appendix 4) as a reminder of the Alec we hardly knew.

I'll mention a local link – quirky though it is – which predates Alec's first visit to Kintyre (a family holiday in Carradale in 1960). His article appeared, in April 1940, in *Colvilles Magazine*, which was published by the company which employed his father. That company was founded by a Kintyre man, David Colville, and by 1904, as David Colville & Sons, was the largest steel-manufacturing business in Scotland.

Amelia and I had a browse inside Killypole ruin, but there is now so much of the roof lying on the floor, and fallen plaster with it, that we were constantly watching our feet. I examined one likely-looking slab of plaster, imagining it might bear my name, but there was no writing on it, and, rather than further disturb the resident insect population, I left the rest of the slabs unturned. Noticing the name of one of Amelia's school friends, Naomi Angus, near the doorway, I suggested that Amelia too leave her name. She selected an untouched cement surface under a window and scratched her name and the date with the point of my knife. I photographed the inscription and told her that I'd think of her whenever I returned.

Later, on our way to High Tirfergus, we were discussing (if I remember correctly) the selectivity of memory, and how certain experiences acquire their allure retrospectively, while others are recognised as significant at the time, or, as Amelia put it, and as I recorded in my journal, to her amusement: 'It feels like a memorable day when it's happening.' I was reminded of a similar remark in Richard Burton's diaries. On an evening in May 1966, in Italy, he and Elizabeth Taylor stopped to eat at a rustic café, and at dusk found themselves listening to mass in a chapel on a nearby hill, the voices of the choir drifting on the air 'like an invisible mist'. He noted: 'It was one of those moments which are nostalgic before they are over.'

25. *Amelia Martin at Killypole steading, 8 August 2013. Photograph by the author.*

Snow on the moors

Killypole features in a day I recall without the least nostalgia. When I wrote an account of that day from memory in 2007, there was a lot wrong with it. I published it privately in *Memories of the Inans, Largybaan and Craigaig: 1980-85* (p 44), tagged on to five years of edited journal transcripts. I remembered that 'it was an Easter and my companions were all children, the Macaulays from Penicuik', but stated that I had 'no written account' of the day. I had, but had failed to find it, or, having found it, to recognise it. Here is the transcript, dated 22 April 1981 at the Inneans:

> With Christina, Henrietta, & Niall Macaulay, & Niall's friend Peter [Arkle]. Left at 9.45 & were dropped at the junction of the Dalsmirran & Glenahanty roads. Climbed up through the glen, avoiding farms, & made a stop at Gleneadardacnoc, & then into the bay. Got a fire going & quickly boiled the kettle. The day is fairly warm, but the sun has so far failed to break through with any consistency. Rathlin & the Irish coast are remarkably 'close' today, dull though it is.

The entry was signed by all four of my companions, with two fictitious names added in disguised handwriting, 'Pete Banks' and 'Fearless Frog' – the latter a private joke between Niall and me – and 'squashed fly' beside a speck on the opposite page. I remember Christina remarking to me, as she wrote her name, that I should stop using pencil for filling in my journal and change to ink, which would fade less quickly. I eventually took her advice, but thirty-three years on, that first hiking journal, all in pencil, is still entirely legible. Christina, the oldest of the Macaulay siblings, became a freelance television producer and director, and I notice from her entry in *Who's Who in Scotland* for 2000 (p 328) that she was born in Glasgow on 16 March 1964, so she was hardly a 'child' in 1981.

The Macaulays were in Campbeltown with their mother, Margaret, who belongs to the town, and I had agreed to take them out to the Inneans. Margaret's father, John McDougall, who had a joinery business in Campbeltown, probably drove us to our starting point; he certainly collected us at the finishing point, High Tirfergus. I remember a warm morning and my companions attired in the lightest of clothing.

The journal entry for that day ended with these bogus signatures, because a blizzard swept in on us soon afterwards. We got moving right away, but warm clothing was lacking and the moorland crossing was an anxious time for me. To keep morale up, I kept reminding my companions that we'd stop at Killypole for tea. As Niall, the youngest of the three Macaulays, never tired of reminding me, he was sustained in his imagination by the vision of a cosy farmhouse kitchen and the farmer's wife handing round freshly baked scones and pancakes. In reality, the tea was merely the dregs of a flask and Killypole a ruin.

26. *The Wee'uss, or Weigh-house, at head of Old Quay, Campbeltown, with Royal Hotel in background, c. 1970. Photograph by Teddy Lafferty.*

The Weigh-Hoose Folk Club and Dick Gaughan

I ended my account in 2007 with an appeal: 'If anyone can tell me the date of Dick Gaughan's "gig" in the Royal Hotel, that was the evening of the same day, and I was mighty relieved to be relaxing in the audience.' My memory, once again, was at fault. When I finally got around to searching back issues of the *Campbeltown Courier*, I found that Gaughan had played in Campbeltown on Thursday 23 April 1981, the day after the hike. Having secured that date, I then checked my 1981 hiking journal and found the entry for the 22nd.

Since Gaughan – a luminary of the Scottish folk scene – was booked to return to Campbeltown on 12 April 2014 as part of the *Ceòl** programme, my interest in that first engagement, thirty-three years earlier, was stimulated. I vaguely remembered that a local folk club had functioned that year, and, when I researched the *Courier* files, found the date of its genesis. In the issue of 30 January 1981, an announcement appeared that the Weigh-Hoose Folk Club would be launched in the Royal Hotel on 12 February at 8 p.m. (The club was named after the building at the Old Quay Head, opposite the hotel, where ships' cargoes were weighed. It was a popular gathering place for fishermen and 'worthies', and its demolition c. 1974 was bitterly lamented by sentimentalists, myself included.)

* *Ceòl* is a series of diverse and dynamic musical events organised in Campbeltown since mid-2013 by local musician Les Oman in association with the management of the Ardshiel and Seafield Hotels, Flora Grant and Marion MacKinnon. I was at the Gaughan performance in the Seafield Hotel on 12 April, the evening before this book went off to the publisher, and asked Les to mention, in his introductory remarks, that first Campbeltown engagement in 1981 and to enquire how many of the audience had been there. Hands were raised, my own included, and the total came to six.

The club, which met every Thursday evening, was founded by two local musicians, Campbell McMillan and Niall McManus, who were joined by other 'regular performers', Archie Stewart, David Bissett, Robert Lang, Georgina Anderson and Davie Robertson. Membership was £2, with members paying 30p admittance and non-members 60p. The club was featured in a *Courier* report of 6 March, accompanied by three photographs of a lively concert in progress. It was stated that the club intended to use its funds to invite well-known folk singers to Campbeltown, and that the organisers were in contact with 'the well known authority on Folk music, Gordon MacCaulay [Gordon MacAulay, himself a Campbeltonian] to get Campbeltown established on the folk singers' circuit'.

Sure enough, in the *Courier* of 10 April the Weigh-Hoose Folk Club advertised a 'special guest', Dick Gaughan, for 23 April in the Royal Hotel, tickets £1.50. Gaughan's actual visit – which was preceded five days earlier by Gaberlunzie in the Argyll Arms Hotel, tickets £2 – wasn't reported in the *Courier*, but I remember the upstairs function room of the Royal Hotel as being well-filled. Which wasn't the case when Archie Fisher – 'one of Scotland's foremost Folksingers and Guitarists', as the advertisement proclaimed him – appeared on 28 May, tickets £2. He certainly fulfilled the promise of his billing, but the audience was woefully sparse. I attended the event with Iain Campbell, himself an accomplished guitarist, and remember him enthusing over Fisher's performance.

The folk scene in Argyll appears to have been thriving at the time, because Fisher appeared two days later in Ardrishaig, with Battlefield Band, as part of the three-day Argyll Folk Festival, which also drew Jock Tamson's Bairns and the Whistlebinkies. But, for the Weigh-Hoose Folk Club, unfortunately, the best was over, and it soon afterwards slipped into oblivion.

27. Georgina Anderson on tin whistle and Davie Robertson on guitar during a session at the Weigh-Hoose Folk Club in the Royal Hotel, 1981. Photograph from D. Robertson, but photographer unknown.

Hamish Henderson

After Amelia and I had stepped out of Killypole ruin and back into the evening air, I told her about the night poet and songwriter Hamish Henderson spent there in 1940. I had read his account, related to Adam McNaughtan and published in *Tocher* No. 43, and found it so interesting that I obtained permission to reproduce it in *Kintyre Magazine* No. 62.

Henderson, later of the School of Scottish Studies and a pioneering collector of traditional music, had arrived in Kintyre to acquaint himself with an unfamiliar part of Scotland. He was about to be called up for Army service, but was captured, on suspicion of being an enemy spy, by the Southend Home Guard, of which author Angus MacVicar was a member before he too went off to the real war. But I have reached the end of Henderson's story of his holiday in Kintyre without explaining how Killypole features in it!

He arrived in a lorry, having hitch-hiked south, and was deposited at Machrihanish. The name so appealed to him, he said, that he wanted to see the place. From there he headed into the hills with his 'bivvy', and had settled in for the night, writing poetry, when rain came on. The summer had been 'gorgeous' – much, I imagine, as the summer of 2013 was – and he hadn't paid much attention to the rigging of his makeshift shelter. As the rain fell harder, it was lashing into his space, and he decided that he'd be as well to 'walk through the night' than lie in the bivvy and catch his 'death o cauld'. So, he packed up and moved on, and, seeing the light of a house in the distance, headed towards it, uncertain of the reception that might await him. It was a shepherd's cottage – Killypole, in fact, though Henderson did not identify it by name – and the shepherd was Jamie McShannon.

By an amazing chance, Henderson had arrived at the door of one of Kintyre's foremost traditional singers, who at once recognised the wanderer's plight and invited him in. The two 'sang practically all night', and Henderson was treated, from McShannon's repertoire, to such local classics as 'Flory Loynachan', 'Machrihanish Bright and Bonnie' and 'Donald 'Clean'. As Henderson later reasoned, the rain had done him 'a good turn'. From Killypole he crossed the hills – unforested then – to the Mull and spent the day there. His Kintyre visit would end in his farcical arrest at Keil, but he survived active service, when it came, and returned to Kintyre after the war to tape-record not only Jamie McShannon, his host that night at Killypole, but also Jamie's brothers, Jock and Alec, who shared his song traditions.

Hamish didn't mention her, but Jamie's wife 'Polly' must also have been there. Jamie had been widowed, and Polly – whose real name was Mary Colville – went to Killypole to keep house for him. He was fifty-four years old and she was forty when they married on 2 November 1938 at the Highland Parish Church manse. Agnes Stewart's father, Willie Mitchell, who had close ties to Drumlemble, was at the wedding and wrote a poem to mark the occasion (Appendix 5). As Agnes concedes, 'It's extremely sexist, but that's how things were then'. As a Kintyre singer, songwriter and collector of songs, it was only a matter of time before Hamish Henderson reached Willie too. I asked Agnes for her memories of Henderson and she obliged with the following.

> It was in the early 1950s that Hamish first got in touch with my father. As Hamish himself tells in the article about my father in *Tocher* 31, he first heard about Willie Mitchell from J. S. Woolley of the Linguistic Survey of Scotland, who had earlier recorded some material from my father.
>
> Hamish, who had first visited Kintyre in 1940, and had his now famous meeting and ceilidh with Jamie McShannon, decided that another visit to Kintyre was a must, and visit he did in early December 1956. That visit culminated in the ceilidh at my family home in Smith Drive, when numerous songs were recorded from my parents, helped along by me, and from the McShannon brothers, James, John and Alec.
>
> I have clearer memories of the visit Hamish made in May 1979, when he collected material for the above-mentioned article in *Tocher*, and when there was another ceilidh in Smith Drive. On that occasion Hamish had with him Tim Neate, who took several photographs.
>
> There was, as I said, another ceilidh in Smith Drive, in the course of which the subject of practice verses used for Scottish Psalm tunes was discussed at length, and many of these nonsense verses were sung.
>
> I will never forget Hamish acting the part of precentor and leading the family in the slow version of the tune 'Martyrdom', sung to the ridiculous words: 'There was a man that had twa

sons, and thae twa sons were brithers, Jehosophat was the name o' yin, an' Balthaeus was the ither. Noo Balthaeus was a wicked man, we'll ne'er see him no more, he stole his faither's coffin lid tae mak' a hen-hoose door.' Hamish did it all so solemnly, despite the words; we all used very solemn four-part harmony; and to me it was completely hilarious and singularly memorable.

As far as I know, Hamish's last visit to Kintyre was in 1986, when he attended my father's funeral. He stayed with us at Lagavurich the night before the funeral, and in the course of the evening he demolished a fair proportion of a bottle of Glenfiddich. Dad always said that Hamish had hollow legs as far as drinking whisky was concerned, for he could consume a huge amount and still remain far more sensible than most people could. After the funeral, he got a lift back to Glasgow with my cousin Billy McMillan, who by then was a Church of Scotland minister in Erskine, and from whom Hamish certainly wouldn't get ANY whisky!

28-30. Ceilidh with Hamish Henderson in the Mitchell house at Smith Drive, Campbeltown, 1956. 1. (opposite) Henderson putting reel into tape-recorder. 2. Willie Mitchell recording Jock and Alec McShannon. 3. A celebratory drink, L-R: Willie Mitchell, Jock McShannon, Mrs Mitchell (Agnes Morrison), Alec McShannon, and Hamish Henderson (back). Photographs by Agnes Stewart.

I saw Hamish Henderson, who died in 2002, only once, in the 1970s, when Jim Macmaster (p 90) pointed him out to me in Sandy Bell's, an Edinburgh pub much frequented at the time by the folk fraternity. The name 'Hamish Henderson' is one that won't be found on the walls of Killypole, but each time I stop there I think of him and Jamie singing lustily within its walls on that wet night in Kintyre as France fell to invasion.

Auchenhoan

On 21 June – Summer Solstice – my sister Barbara and her twin daughters, Barbara and Christine, ate with Judy and me in the evening. Barbara's husband Malcolm had died two days earlier (p 69). I had been walking recently out to Largiebaan from Machrihanish and thinking about days shared there with Malcolm in the early 1980s. I remembered photographing him, his son Donald and a neighbour in Drumchapel, Robert McMullen, on an outing which took us on to the shore below the Aignish in May 1983. I was keen to view these slides again and suggested that I set up my projector in the living-room. Everyone agreed, and the projector, unused in years, was pulled out of storage. I wasn't certain that it would still work, but it did, and the show lasted more than an hour as I selected slide after slide, most of them of family members.

One of them, which I'd forgotten I had, was of my daughter Sarah standing on a boulder on the top of a hill overlooking the Second Waters. It was, and remains, a hill where horse mushrooms may be gathered in late summer and autumn. The date on the slide is 4 September 1991, when Sarah was four years old. I decided there and then that I'd like to revisit that boulder. Until the moment of rediscovering the image, the stone had been just an object in the landscape, without any remembered associations.

31. *On the rocks below the Largiebaan cliffs, 1 May 1983, L-R: Robert McMullen, Donald Docherty and Malcolm Docherty. Photograph by the author.*

In *By Hill and Shore in South Kintyre* (p 18), there is a photograph, taken on the same evening, of Sarah and Sandy McSporran examining horse mushrooms on that hill. Sandy's father, George, and the family dog, Trudy, were also in the picture, as silhouettes on the eastern skyline, but were cropped out in its published form. There was no journal entry for that brief expedition in George's car, but I remember a delightfully warm autumnal evening, as the photograph suggests – both are in shorts and Sandy is stripped to the waist.

On 19 August 2012, Judy and I had a walk around the hill, hoping to find mushrooms, but without any real expectation. There was one, cap unopened, and when we went to pick it we found another close by, emerging dome-like from the earth. We left that one and could have returned for it days later but didn't. The one we did take was perfect – dense in the flesh and maggot-free – and I sliced it and fried it in butter that evening. We hoped there might be more in the usual spots and continued around the hill until we reached the top field where I'd photographed Sandy and Sarah in 1991.

I stood for a few minutes near the spot, transporting myself in memory to that other time, and 'seeing' once again my daughter and her companion as the camera saw them twenty-one years before. Both are now in Glasgow, but I brought them back to Auchenhoan and returned them momentarily to the immemorial earth.

Then I saw, over the ridge to the south – which Jimmy MacDonald habitually scans from Balnabraid, on the other side of the hill – a raptor which I took to be a buzzard, but which became, as I watched it through binoculars, a golden eagle. It disappeared below the skyline, and Judy and I waited and watched, hoping it would reappear. It didn't, but minutes later a second bird, a hen harrier, passed over the same ridge, and I remarked to Judy that many a visiting birder would be thrilled to log two such relative rarities in the space of five minutes.

I returned in 2013 to the hill to revisit the boulder and to assess its rediscovered place in memory. I should attempt

– and here is as good a place as any – to rationalise this recurring gravitation to particular landscape features which matter in my history. The roots of the fascination are fed, I believe, by aloneness. My children are grown up and pursue their lives elsewhere; friends too are less accessible, some of them dead, which is inaccessibility in its most extreme form. If I cannot have their companionship in present reality, then I can recreate it, from memory and from devices such as photographs, which both inspire and sustain remembrance. Sad admissions, perhaps, but the human spirit must nourish itself on whatever scraps it finds; and increasingly, as I age, I inhabit my own history.

That tendency, of course, is hardly peculiar to me. Places sanctified in memory abound in world literature and folklore. I shall offer just one example, which impressed me deeply when I read it in W. R. Rodgers's *Irish Literary Portraits* (p 184). A few days before his death, the thoughts of the poet F. R. Higgins returned to the County Meath of his forefathers, and he said to Brinsley Macnamara, who was with him: 'Mac, when you go down to Laracor again, put your arms round the land for me.' Higgins was buried in the graveyard at Laracor, beside the church where Jonathan Swift was once vicar.

A walk through any Kintyre graveyard will reveal the strength of attachment to place. Many inscriptions reveal that farmers, and others of the 'ordinary' class, wished to be identified in death with the places they occupied in life. This identification is valuable to genealogists and also, from the often idiosyncratic spellings, to students of place-names; but these expressions would have come at a cost – many farm names are lengthy, particularly those with a division added, e.g. 'Laigh' (Low) – and must have substantially increased the sculptor's bill.

I returned to the hill on 31 July and performed the usual circuit, checking for mushrooms in the usual spots – patches of old arable which have escaped, so far, the encroachment of rushes and bracken – but I was too early and there were no mushrooms. As I approached the boulder, I noticed its alignment with Ailsa Craig on the horizon and that it resembled a miniature Craig. I had never before noticed that resemblance – but then I've never written this book before! I sat where Sarah had stood, on the top of the boulder, and ate a late lunch.

I was looking into the Second Waters, and experienced a curious pang of nostalgia for my winter trips there by bicycle in search of driftwood. I keep an old rucksack for carrying wood and use it only in winter. A small bush-saw fits neatly into it, and rucksack and saw are my constant companions until spring arrives and I revert to the main rucksack, which contains bird and flower identification books, a 'Leatherman' knife, rudimentary first aid kit, bottle-opener, sugar container, spare bootlaces, bunches of net-twine lifted from the shore, and other paraphernalia which have cluttered – and weighted – the rucksack, and its predecessors, for decades. It also contains broken and redundant objects which sentimental attachment prevents me from throwing away. For example, deep within one of the side-pouches there is a strange-looking blob of plastic which was once a compass. It melted one night when the rucksack, drying after an outing in heavy rain, was propped at the fireside too close to the heat. I don't miss it, though, because I never learned how to use it properly!

Boulders and scares

The boulder I was seated on had clearly been positioned there by human hands. As with most such boulders, its base had been packed with smaller rocks and earth to hold it firmly in place, but generations of sheep and cattle, circling the rock to rub themselves against it and relieve itching, had eroded the base, and the stones around it had been exposed. Some of these boulders, isolated in fields or close to old steadings, may have been designed to serve as rubbing-stones for livestock, but most of them, I suspect, are boundary markers from the time before surveying equipment existed for the mapping of estates. The boundaries between farms were then delineated by a succession of immoveable, recognisable and named features on the landscape.

32. *Boulder marking the boundary of Lossit and Ballygroggan, looking south, 6 June 2013. Photograph by the author.*

Whenever possible, and for obvious reasons, these boundary-defining features would be natural – streams and hillocks and crags – but, where natural features were absent, existing man-made features – such as dykes and drains – would be incorporated, and, if need be, the necessary markers would be specially created, which is how many boulders and cairns appeared on the landscape. These boundaries were preserved by oral tradition, and the elders in a community would be called upon to 'walk the marches' in the event of a dispute involving trespass by neighbouring tenants or their livestock. In my *Kintyre Places and Place-Names*, under the generics *clach* ('stone') and *càrn* ('stone-heap'), I looked at these landscape features and their importance before estate maps appeared in the late eighteenth century.

That boulder I was sitting on could have been a boundary stone – certainly, it is close to an existing wire fence – but I have begun truly noticing boulders only in the past few years, and I have a lot to learn about their significance in the landscape.

I logged one more on 6 June, when I happened to sit close to it. I was heading for Killypole, decided to stop for lunch close to the radio masts at the top of the hill, and cut through a ride to the edge of Lossit forest, where I could enjoy an unobstructed view out over the Ballygroggan moors to the enticing hills in the south-west. I was also interested in identifying an old crossing-point on to Ballygroggan ground, favoured when a past owner of Ballygroggan was hostile to walkers starting out from his steading. I didn't find the crossing-point, but found the boulder, planted in isolation and quite clearly an import. It sat just a few feet back from the boundary fence of Lossit and Ballygroggan, and its significance seemed obvious.

I have a photograph of what I described, on 8 November 1981, as 'a curious stone beside a turf dyke' near Glenmurril, on the south side of Balnabraid Glen. Looking at that photograph now, I see a rounded boulder very similar to

33. John MacDonald at boulder near Glenmurril, 8 November 1981. Photograph by the author.

the one at Auchenhoan, but smaller, with Balnabraid and its clump of trees visible across the glen. A young John MacDonald is standing beside the boulder, so the scale is clear. I haven't seen that stone again, but it is doubtless still there. At Glenmurril, that day, I also photographed John beside an old clipping-stool, which likewise I never saw again. That winter walk took us from Kilkerran graveyard on to Ben Gullion 'and round the highest tops into Glenramskill, thence over a short moor and down into Balnabraid Glen, stopping at Glenmurril ...' We ended up on the coast, in Queen Esther's Bay, heating soup in a little black pot and jumping every time one of the sandstone rocks, which formed the fire-place, heated up and shattered.

In 1977, Calum Bannatyne and Sandy Helm, retired shepherds, discussed with me a stone with a big iron ring in it at the head of Glen Murril. They suggested it might have been for tethering ponies, but it was in 'a funny place ... right in the open'. If it still exists, I reckon it's somewhere in the direction of Ru Stafnish radio station, but I have yet to find it. It was certainly a familiar sight to them, and they debated whether the ring had been fixed in the stone with sulphur or with lead.

Craigaig, an old coastal township south of Machrihanish, represents Gaelic *Creagag*, 'Rocky place', and a more fitting name would be hard to find. I examined the settlement and its history in *Kintyre Places and Place-Names* (pp. 89-90), so will confine my attention here to a particular rock among many. It's north of the township ruins and was undoubtedly placed there for a purpose, but what purpose? Was it a rubbing-stone, a tethering-stone, or was its significance more obscure? In a different location – remote from an historical settlement – I'd assume it to be a small standing stone.

The photograph of that stone was taken by Hartwig Schutz on 14 August 2011. He, his wife Elisabeth, my daughter Amelia, and I walked out to Craigaig from Ballygroggan, but went no further. Hartwig recalled it as one of the 'most

34. The author beside boulder at Craigaig township, looking north, 14 August 2011. Photograph by Hartwig Schutz.

beautiful' of all his walks in Kintyre. He also remembered that Amelia distributed slices of birthday cake as we sat at the corn-kiln; she had turned twenty-two three days earlier. Coincidentally, when I opened my journal of 2011 to find that day and recover its events, midnight had just gone and the date was 6 February 2014, my own sixty-second birthday. Pressed between the pages, I found a sprig of bog myrtle, an unintended gift to myself, I imagined. We'd looked for and found clumps of that supremely fragrant shrub beside Craigaig Water. I didn't need the journal to remind me that we were joined that afternoon at Craigaig by two women revisiting their native Kintyre, Fiona MacAllister and Alison Sutherland, who ascended mysteriously from the bay and chatted with us for a while. I'd never met them before, but by discreet probing uncovered their identity, as they did mine. Such chance encounters in the hills are seldom forgotten, and afterwards acquire in memory – mine, at any rate –a special aura which similar encounters in towns and cities seldom do.

At the risk of being condemned as an obsessive bore, I'll return to an uncanny experience I had more than twenty years ago near Greenland. The full account appeared in *By Hill and Shore in South Kintyre* (pp. 122-24) and was followed by a summary in *Kintyre Places and Place-Names* (p 75). The main reason for returning to it yet again is that I have a friend's testimony to add to it. On 15 February 1992, a grey sleety day, I was heading alone to Greenland from Auchalochy when I noticed for the first time a boulder on a knoll to the east. I turned off my route to look at it, and when I approached close to it I seemed to fall under a kind of transfixion. My heart began palpitating madly and my breathing became constricted as though I were suffocating. After some minutes of fighting what seemed to me to be a demonic force emanating from the boulder, I broke away and resumed my journey. I was badly shaken and, enquiring later about the origin of the mysterious rock, discovered that it had been uncovered during drainage operations nearby and set up on the knoll as a rubbing-stone for livestock.

While sorting through personal papers in 2013, I discovered a letter from Hector L. Mackenzie, Rector of Campbeltown Grammar School while I was a pupil there. Hector and his wife Margaret later became friends and 'Scrabble' adversaries of mine, and after they left Campbeltown we kept in touch by letters and occasional visits. His letter, dated 1 March 1992, was sent from 15 Grosvenor Crescent, Edinburgh, and referred to the Greenland experience, which I had obviously related to him. If the poem he refers to was ever written, I don't remember it.

Dear Angus,
I had an experience once (and only once) similar to yours. I was seized by an inexplicable terror in a copse near Edinburgh about 40 years ago, and had to take my courage in both hands and run past the spot. I remember the extraordinary heaving and panting afterwards. I therefore sympathise with your experience and look forward to reading your poem about it.

I had another disturbing experience, on Ben Gullion, almost nine years after the Greenland incident. The date was 12 February 2002, and again (aside from Benjie) I was alone. I sat at a rock outcrop for the first time, though I'd passed it many times and occasionally sat close by it. Nothing obvious happened at the rock to frighten me, but the longer I sat there the more uneasy I became. It was as though the atmosphere was turning increasingly hostile to my presence, so I moved ... and quickly! While seated there, I had described a bright and starry night, with the sound of water tumbling through a ravine, and predicted that 'I'll be here more often'. I never returned. Further down the hill, in scribbled notes, I tried to explain the experience, and attributed it to a nearby wooden 'voodoo cross' which some boys had planted years before amid trees:

> cross: how even the most infantile of gestures can define a place – returning from a hike in dark is somehow comfortable, but going up the hill in the dark can be scary – maybe the enclosing trees and the sounds – Benjie also nervous which doesn't help – OK lower on hill.

Some friends and acquaintances consider night walking in the hills a crazy pursuit, but it seldom bothered me. There was the above occasion, and the following, on 19 November 2007. On my way to Ben Gullion, I met a fellow dog-walker on Kilkerran Road and stopped for a chat. 'Where are you heading?' he asked, and when I replied 'Up the loch', he flashed me an incredulous look and said that he would never go there in the dark. His remark preoccupied me all the way to the spot I chose to sit at, and I immediately began exploring the subject in a poem which I titled 'Fear of the Dark'. By the time I finished the poem, I had unintentionally induced in myself the very state of fear I was analysing. This is the last verse:

> Still, as I write, this forest refuge
> conspires to waken a latent fear
> and as I listen to east wind thrash the treetops
> and water crash through an unseen void
> and watch the dog pressed to my legs
> glancing uneasily this way and that
> I begin to imagine the sudden pressure
> of huge hairy hands at my throat.

In early spring of 1978, a nephew, Malcolm Docherty, a student at Glasgow School of Art, was researching a Liberal Studies dissertation on Kintyre townships. While drawing and taking photographs at Balnatunie and Balnabraid, he decided to visit the south side of Balnabraid Glen, where, he had heard, there was the site of an illicit whisky still. While exploring the ruins of Glenmurril, he recognised a corn-kiln and decided to explore it. He was rummaging around in the bottom when 'something snapped' under his feet and he was 'overcome with a terrible inexplicable fear'. Sensing that someone was staring at him, he looked out over the rim of the kiln. There was no one to be seen, but he was suddenly 'overwhelmed with terror' and just as suddenly yanked bodily out of the kiln. He remembers catching hold of the stonework on the edge of the kiln as he hit the ground, then getting to his feet and running to the township ruins. But his camera was still at the kiln. The final words are his own: 'I called to the evil spirit that I was coming back, but only to pick up the camera, and did so. I spent the next few hours in fear, taking some time to calm myself. Over the next few days, I often thought that over the friendly face of Ben Gullion and down to Balnabraid Glen was that fearful place. I feared that the malevolent spirit could translate itself over the moor and grasp me again.'

A significant feature of such experiences is that they almost invariably happen when the witness is alone. My final example wasn't frightening, only puzzling; but then it happened in daylight. I was sitting at Smerby Castle on Friday 13 September 2013, hearing what sounded like a shotgun somewhere to the north. When one of the reports seemed uncomfortably close, I started for the top of the castle knoll to have a look around. Half-way there, I heard voices from the south side of the promontory – 'a distorted babble of words, but with an English accent', as I described it in the journal. My first thought was of a shooter there talking into a hand-held radio. The burst of voices certainly wasn't a product of imagination, because several seals, hauled out on rocks and ignoring my presence, instantly plunged into the sea. I searched the promontory and saw no one. Later, I noticed a couple of naval ships a mile or two offshore and wondered whether I had overheard, by some freak of atmospheric conditions, a minute's worth of inter-ship communication. And might the gunfire also have originated offshore?

My final boulder overlooks the Inneans Bay from Beinn na Faire (p 14), and it too has been discussed, and illustrated, in *Kintyre Places and Place-Names* (p 75). As I explained there, I first noticed the boulder not in the landscape, but in a photograph which Jimmy MacDonald took, on Hogmanay 2008, of a golden eagle about to land on the rock, with two agitated ravens in close attendance. I have since deduced that the boulder marks the corner of the old road which runs down the north side of the Inneans Glen past Innean Beag, before turning north towards Earadale. Since acquainting myself with the boulder and the track it marks, I now make directly for that marker when leaving the bay to walk back

35. Road-marker boulder near Innean Beag, 15 May 2012. Photograph by the author.

to Machrihanish by the coast. The climb up to it is quite stiff, but, once on that track, about thirty minutes takes one to Sròn Gharbh, remarkable going compared with all the other routes I've tried. The grassy slope below the boulder has become a favourite resting-place on days when I choose not to go into the bay, but just look into it. Amelia, Judy, Jimmy MacDonald and Murdo MacDonald have all sat there with me; and, yes, even when alone I can bring them back in memory.

There are no human signs on these boulders I have described, or on any others I have seen in Kintyre, apart from those with cup and ring marks cut into them, but that's a complex subject, best left to specialists. During my visits to Germany, when left to my own devices I would invariably head for the Black Forest, a mere field away from the Schutz family home in Engelsbrand. The forest there is intersected by many clearly marked tracks and can be safely explored.

During my meanderings, I repeatedly encountered boundary stones with dates and symbols carved on them, and the sense of history imparted by these monuments was palpable, even though their precise purpose was obscure to me. I asked Hartwig Schutz what they signified, and he explained that they marked the old 200-mile boundary between the Grand duchy of Baden and the Kingdom of Wurttemberg. On one side of the stones is carved the coat-of-arms of Baden (a red diagonal stripe on a yellow ground) and on the other side that of Wurttemberg (three stags, represented by antlers). Some stones are of nineteenth century origin, but others – as in the illustration – were erected in the sixteenth century. Hartwig concluded: 'Since 1952, the above-mentioned federal states have been united and called Baden-Wurttemberg. Many Badenians take a sceptical stance with respect to Wurttemberg and its capital Stuttgart because they feel disadvantaged. Can this relationship be compared to the Scottish and English relationship?'

36. Sketch by Wiebke Schutz of Baden-Wurttemberg boundary stone in Black Forest, showing Wurttemberg coat-of-arms and the date '1569'.

Balnatunie

I was back on the hill at Auchenhoan on 15 August, but merely glanced at the boulder, having already taken from it as much of its 'energy' as I desired. I was again looking for mushrooms, and found sufficient for that evening's meal. The first two had attracted slugs and were eaten right through, so that the holes in the white caps resembled nothing less than eye sockets in skulls. I was desperate for produce and dropped the remains into a bag, anyway, anticipating that I might not find more, but I did, on a hillside near Balnatunie.

The sky was dense with cloud, and promised rain. So far I had only been spat on, but I should have heeded the warning and started back home. Balnatunie, however, was close, and since I hadn't visited the ruins for a few years, I decided to pay a 'courtesy call'. Balnatunie is one of a cluster of old mid-Learside farms, which also includes Balnabraid, Glenmurril, Corphin and Auchenhoan, which alone is still inhabited (though no longer by a shepherd).

I passed half-an-hour at the ruins, examining the site. I haven't been there often in the past thirty or so years, compared with its neighbour, Balnabraid, which appeals more to me for a host of reasons, not the least of which is a family connection (p 250). Balnatunie has been more a place I might arrive at during mushroom-gathering outings, and, consequently, I have few memories of it.

The first memory relies on photographs I took there on 29 January 1984. Jimmy MacDonald stands in the old stackyard with the ruins behind him and, further in the north, a snow-mottled hill-slope. In the other photograph, he stands in the fire-place, his head occupying a gap in the lintel, which has since collapsed. On a narrow sandstone block above the lintel, the initials 'MD' are clearly visible. These were carved, five years earlier, by Malcolm Docherty (p 132), and, though slowly eroding, can still be seen.

137

37. *Jimmy MacDonald standing in the fire-place of Balnatunie ruin, 29 January 1984. Photograph by the author.*

When I looked in my journals for that winter's day in 1984, I found that Jimmy – I believe it was his first ever walk with me – and I had set off late, about 12.45, and had missed the sunniest part of the day. We met Teddy Lafferty's father, Edward Senior, in town, and heard from him that Teddy was on the coast. Indeed, we met him later in the Bloody Bay, south of Auchenhoan Head. He was preparing to leave, 'in advance of impending rain', as I noted, but was persuaded to stay and share a cup of tea with us, after which we all returned by the shore. Not a scrap of the above information remained accessible to my memory thirty years on. Without the slides and the journal, the day was lost to me. Not, however, that it was exactly packed with incidents ...

I do remember a subsequent visit for an element of mystery. George McSporran, Benjie and I were sitting near the ruins when we heard voices and two men passed by, their appearance so surprising that neither George nor I thought to acknowledge them; nor did my ever-vigilant dog react in the slightest. In the space of a minute, the strangers had disappeared downhill, oblivious, I am certain, to our presence. We could only guess at the reasons for their being on the hill that day. I had no idea of when the incident might have occurred, but, since Benjie was there, it had to be within his lifetime. I had a look through my pile of journals and selected, first, the one marked '2005-6'. I found the entry within minutes, and the date was 13 October 2005. We had been mushroom-gathering and found only one, 'most of it maggot riddled, but the remainder edible'.

My third memory of Balnatunie is preserved in *By Hill and Shore in South Kintyre* (p 283). George and I were mushroom-gathering on 2 August 2010 and sat above the ruins, 'hoping for a breeze to counter the midge threat'. It was an evening of astonishing clarity. Ailsa Craig was 'shining like a jewel', and the distant coastline, from Ayr south to the Mull of Galloway, lay before us 'in sharp definition'. We could even see, with the naked eye, two cross-channel ferries manoeuvring at the mouth of Stranraer Loch.

Two days after my visit to Balnatunie in 2013, I mentioned to George that I was writing about the place, and he produced a further memory, which he had good reason to retain. He was there on an August evening and climbed to the top of the hill which separates Balnatunie from Balnabraid. From there he saw the Irish ferry, *Claymore*, heading north to Campbeltown. That too was a clear, still evening, with light fading and an emergent moon. A lovely scene, and he captured it on film with the video camera he'd taken with him. But months later he accidentally erased the film, and, when he realised what he had done, was so angry with himself that he never again used the camera. A year for that evening? He suggested I might find it in a journal, and I was bemused until he assured me that I too had been there. I remembered nothing, having, unlike George, little reason to remember, but I agreed to check my notebooks. That time-span was simply 1997-99, the three years that the ferry service ran, but I found no entry, and the evening seemed to belong to George alone, until I discovered by chance that I had written it up, without journal notes, for the *Kintyre Magazine*. The date was 15 August 1997, and the account is reproduced in *By Hill and Shore in South Kintyre* (p 99).

Of course, in the centuries of its existence as a human settlement, Balnatunie must have been the scene of a million incidents more interesting than the feeble few which form my memories – marriages, births, deaths, quarrels, cattle raids, political alarms, dreams, nightmares, laughter, sorrow, harvest celebrations, ceilidhs, wakes ... the list could be extended indefinitely. Equally, of course, almost nothing is known of what actually did go on there, though much could be safely reconstructed around the seasonal cycle of the farming community.

Langlands and Lang

It is known, however, that in 1811 eight-year-old Catherine Loynachan, with a younger brother, children of Lachlan Loynachan in Balnatunie, was herding cattle on the shore when she saw a 'mermaid', with a child's face, 'rubbing or washing its breast with one hand'.[11] It is also known that in 1830 ten-year-old Agnes Langlands, daughter of Matthew Langlands in Balnatunie, was sexually assaulted on the Learside road by a young Irish-born farm-servant, John McQuin, who was later sentenced to seven years' transportation.[12]

I believe that the Loynachan and Langlands families overlapped at Balnatunie. The first Langlands in Kintyre, George, was the 5th Duke of Argyll's land surveyor, and received the lease of Balnatunie in 1775 – the year that the Duke brought in the first of the northern English farmers to modernise agricultural practices in Kintyre – but he himself wasn't farming the land. In 1792 Langlands and his family were in Campbeltown, and Balnatunie was occupied by Donald Olynachan, his wife More McNaught and sons John, Alexander and Neill.

The lease of Balnatunie remained in the Langlands family right to the end, and the farm was latterly worked by Matthew, a son of George. He and his family were there when the 1851 census was taken in April, but he had already signed a lease for Dalabhraddan farm in Southend, and that same month no fewer than forty neighbours, old and new, turned out to contribute a day's ploughing at Dalabhraddan, 'to testify their respect'. The neighbourly spectacle moved a reporter to the *Campbeltown Journal* to remark: 'In the face of cheap markets, and the general uproar as to rack-rents and sterile soil, it was gratifying to notice that the display of horses and harness would scarcely be equalled in any of the far-famed high-farming districts – Ayr, Renfrew and Lanark'.[13] By the 1861 census, the place was deserted.

The Langlands family came to Kintyre from the north of England, where – in Chollerton, Northumberland – George the surveyor married Sarah Kitchen in 1764. The family integrated and thrived, and descendants were still here in the early part of the twentieth century. The name has now disappeared from Kintyre, as has Loynachan, in all its variants. Yet the Loynachans remain, disguised in the community as Langs; victims – as so many natives were – of a nineteenth century social improvement drive which strove to subvert all things Gaelic. It succeeded remarkably well, not least in its greatest undertaking – the eradication of the language itself.

I am reminded of a little anecdote I heard, from an uncle, Henry Martin, about Lachlan Lang, a boat-builder in Campbeltown. To provoke him into an outburst of anger, all that Henry and his young friends had to do was to shout after him: 'Lachie Loynachan!' That's who he really was, but by that time – the turn of the nineteenth century – the old form was officially buried in Campbeltown, and Lachie clearly wanted no reminders of it. He was of Balnatunie stock – his father, Duncan, was born there around 1808. Genealogy, in the wrong hands, can kill conversation and sink a book, so I'll keep Lachie's brief. His mother was Flora Reid, born in Carskey in 1819, and his paternal grandparents were Lachlan Loynachan, tailor, and Agnes MacPherson.[14]

Loynachan families were settled initially in Southend parish – the first of the name on record was at Feochaig in 1653 – and one might suppose that their origin was Ireland, but no certainty is possible, and the etymology of the name itself is rather obscure. I had long assumed that the surname disappeared completely, but I was mistaken. In 2009, I was contacted by an American who was planning a visit to Kintyre. His name was Jerry Loynachan, and he was descended from David Loynachan, who emigrated in 1836 from Eden farm in Southend to Washington State, Ohio, with his wife, Isabella Breackanridge, and their nine children. There are Loynachan descendants of David's in (at the last count I have) no fewer than fifteen states in the USA.[15]

Balnatunie ruins

I return to Balnatunie, which is obscure except for the first elements, *baile*, which is Gaelic for a farming township, and *na*, 'of'. Attempts have been made to fill in the blank – see *Kintyre Places and Place-Names*, p 4 – but these have not been conclusive. The name's first written appearance is in a charter of 1502, as 'Ballenatoyn', but the settlement, and its name, no doubt pre-date that appearance.

There are two sets of ruins there, the 'modern' one, which is aligned roughly north-south, and the earlier one, aligned east-west. The latter ruins, narrowly built of drystone, are reduced to overgrown foundations, but the former, of rubble and mortar, are in better shape. The north-facing gable, in fact, is in a perfect state of preservation, without a stone out of place; and the rest of the structure diminishes from that perfection. In the caption of a photograph in my *Kintyre Country Life* (p 144), I dated the steading to the early nineteenth century, which remains a reasonable estimate. That caption is probably the longest I ever wrote, and provides a concise interpretation of what the structure's three compartments represent: byre at the north end, kitchen/living-room in the middle, with its fire-place, and, at the south end, the 'room', a parlour of sorts which might also serve as sleeping quarters.

The byre is windowless, and, where the door was, a rowan has taken hold. It has been there for as long as I can remember, and, as it thickens its trunk, pushing against the wall and sending its roots further through the lime mortar of the stonework, is slowly destroying the structure – a fair example of nature's patient reclamation of space which man enclosed in mere days. An iron hook embedded in the south wall of the byre, close to the doorway, is the only artefact remaining in the entire structure, unless there's more buried.

The living-room floor was overgrown with grasses, nettles, thistles and rushes, with here and there a late summer flower adding a touch of colour. The interior walls are tufted all around with spleenwort ferns, but the fire-place's only occupant was a spindly, trailing herb robert whose initiative and endurance I admired. There are two well-proportioned windows in the east-facing wall, looking out to Ayrshire, and one in the west, with a 'press', or cupboard, set into that wall, where a fourth window might have gone had the need been felt. Compared with the earlier houses – unmortared, draughty, with tiny windows and a fire-place in the middle of an earthen floor, its smoke swirling all ways – that room suggested radical improvement: well illumined by daylight, relatively cosy, and the smoke from the fire directed up a chimney. Directly south of the steading, a square turf-walled enclosure – choked with rushes now – suggests a past garden.

A little stream flows past the north-facing gable, not, as one might expect, at a distance from it, but against the base of the wall. Had that been the farm's water supply? It would appear so. At the eastern end of the gable, a pool collects water. If it wasn't a 'well' in centuries past, it certainly could be now, with a little deepening and cleaning and maintenance.

At the western corner of the gable, I picked up a shard of coarse white crockery and one of black bottle-glass, suggesting that the steading's midden-heap might have lain there or thereabouts. As I was handling these broken bits of the past, my hearing began tuning into a curious, repetitive ticking sound. It was the voice of the little stream as it rippled over a ledge and through a rock channel. Doubtless it has other voices for other days.

A roadside spring

I headed downhill to return to the road, and my bicycle, which I had chained to a fence at the top of the twisting hill down into the Second Waters. I cut off the Balnatunie track, to save a few minutes' walking, and gained the road opposite the coniferous plantation. There is a spring at the roadside there and I wanted to check its flow. The previous time I was on that road, there was only a trickle emerging from the pipe – a sign of that dry summer – and I had to forego a drink. Now the flow was adequate and I rinsed out my tea flask and filled it with water to take home with me.

I had lost my knowledge of that spring and had been looking for it for years, though not with any urgency or I'd doubtless have found it. It was known, in the first place, to George McSporran, and I'd watched him fill bottles there either side of the millennium; but in recent years he hadn't spoken of it. Earlier in the year, when we were on the Learside, I asked him where the spring was and he showed it to me. It was still running, from a blue plastic drainage pipe (I later uncovered an earlier white plastic pipe); but it had been in use long before the invention of plastic, because George's mother told him about it. She was related to the Clarks who farmed Feochaig, and, in fact, the day that George pointed out the spring to me was just three weeks past the centenary (7 February 2013) of the death of little Mary Clark on that road and almost within sight of Feochaig. The dog-cart her father Robert was driving home from market in Campbeltown ran over a sack of animal feed, which had fallen off a cart ahead, overturned, and threw Mary on to the road.[16]

Campbell Macarthur

George recalled that he and Campbell Fraser Macarthur, his boyhood friend, used to stop at the spring for refreshment when cycling on the Learside. Campbell died of cancer in 1970 at the age of twenty-one. I hardly knew him, but I have one memory of him, and it is in that category of memories which are apparently trivial, yet somehow deeply embedded. Both of us are sitting with a group of contemporaries at a table in the back room of the Locarno Café, and that's all there is to it. Campbell wasn't a friend of mine, yet I 'see' him, and him only, in the room.

Campbell and George were close in age – Campbell was born on 28 December 1948 and George on 2 January 1949 – and lived next door to each other at Glenramskill until George was seven and his family moved to Range Road in town. The friendship survived that move, however, and George would frequently cycle to Glenramskill and meet up with Campbell there. They explored the glen and fished the burn for trout, and, when older, would cycle the Learside, exploring the coast as far south as Feochaig. They also took their bikes on to the Old Road and spent many hours rafting on the little reservoir beside that road.

When the NATO jetty and fuel-tanks were built at Glenramskill between 1962 and '65, an 'adventure playground', as George put it, opened up for them. There was even a little shop for the workers, set up in a field beside the farm track and managed by the late Tommy Kennedy; George and Campbell would buy sweets there when they had money. George was keen on sports, football in particular, but Campbell's interests were of a more practical nature; in fact, in 1966, when in his fifth year at Campbeltown Grammar School, he came first in Technical Subjects.[17]

One interest which George and Campbell did share was photography. While in the Grammar School, they were both members of a photography club which was supervised by one of the teachers, Robert Crerar, whom I remember as a rather stern disciplinarian in French classes. Once, at a club meeting, while Mr Crerar was out the room, a fellow-pupil was shut in a cupboard for a laugh. George remembers Campbell suddenly sounding the warning, 'Quick – Bob's coming, Bob's coming!', to which, quietly, but with an edge of menace, came the immediate response: 'Bob's here, Campbell.'

George remembers one exploit of Campbell's which greatly impressed him. They were constructing a hut beside Glenramskill Burn, and Campbell had devised a system –

basically a bicycle wheel with paddles attached – to generate electricity from an adjacent waterfall. A length of copper wire was necessary, so he cut what he needed from a telephone line which had been run from the jetty to the pump-station at the burn, then connected the snipped ends to a wire fence, which appears to have successfully restored communications. Ironically, perhaps, after leaving school Campbell became a telephone engineer with the General Post Office, as it then was.

He and George shared a twenty-first birthday party in the Mayfair Restaurant, Campbeltown. George hadn't realised the gravity of his friend's illness, and when Campbell died later that year in the Cottage Hospital, he was deeply shocked.

In January 2014, George and I visited Campbell's sister Mhairi, who lives around the corner from me in Lady Mary Row, and I listened to them share reminiscences of Campbell. The conversation was concentrated on memories of Glenramskill, and Mhairi, naturally, was able to supplement George's stock of memories.

For several Easters in succession, she and Campbell would accompany the MacDougall family – in Glenramskill farm at the time – on egg-rolling excursions to a hillock they knew as 'The Wee Green Hill'. Their mother, Seonaid, would boil and decorate eggs for them, and they would meet up with the MacDougall children on the farm-track. Mrs MacDougall would be there, too, with picnic provisions. Once, Campbell's boiled egg hit a rock at speed and disintegrated, the yolk flying off in one direction and the rest of the egg in another, a mishap which upset him. Even more upsetting, perhaps – 'The Wee Green Hill' was obliterated when the NATO tanks were constructed, and the very site disappeared behind a security fence.

They would also sit on top of the 'Look-Oot' – a vantage point at the Rocky Burn – and direct clods of earth on to the road below when walkers were passing. The object of the sport was to create a spot of alarm, not to hit anyone – they were too well-behaved for that – but in 1913 the *Argyllshire*

Herald reported youths, stationed at the 'Look Out' on Sundays, showering passers-by with stones and turf.[18]

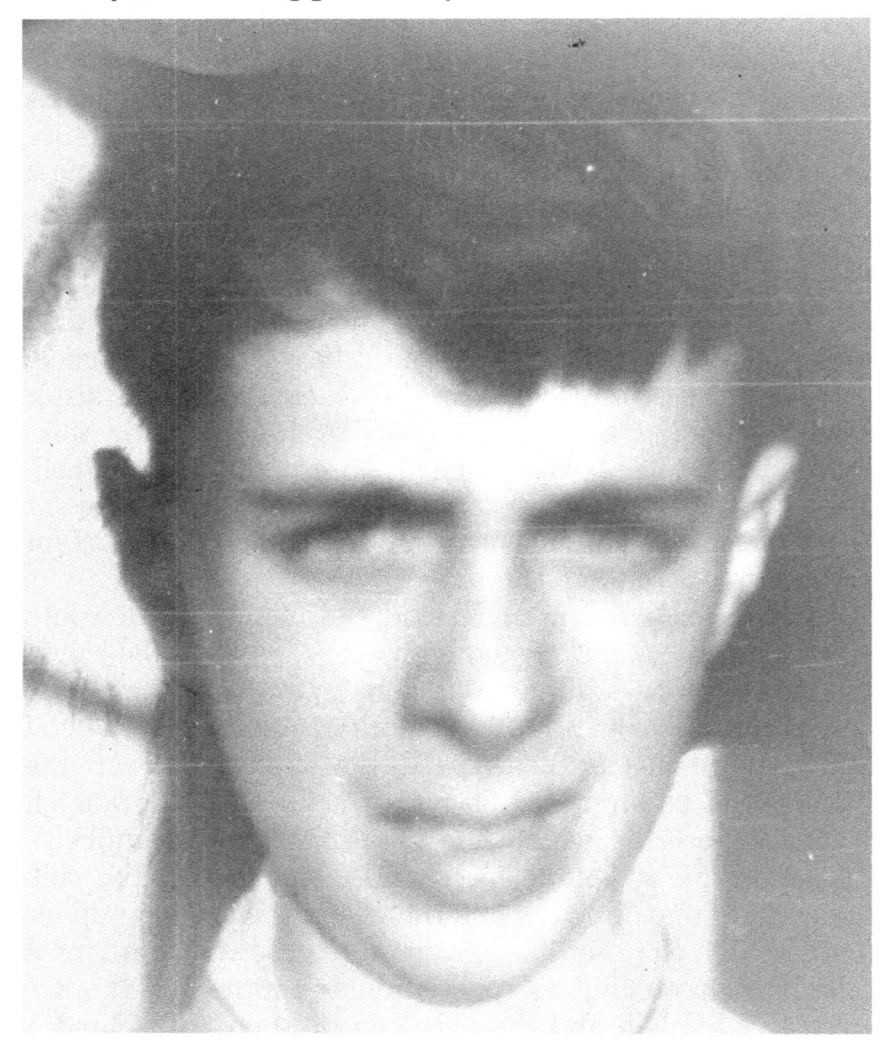

38. Campbell Macarthur, self-portrait, c. 1965. From Mhairi Reid, Campbeltown.

Mhairi recalled a 'bogie' which Campbell and George constructed from wooden fish-boxes collected from the lochside. These home-made vehicles were popular among boys at the time, but this one was of exceptional dimensions, 'built like a tank', as George recalled. It had four wheels, a steering apparatus, and was six boxes high. There was even a door in it, and George remembers clambering inside at the onset of a squall and listening to hailstones battering off the roof. Mhairi, being younger than the boys – and a girl, moreover! – was excluded from bogie games, except for one dubious privilege – she was allowed to push the boys in it!

When Campbell left school to find work, his technical teacher, James Edgar, was dismayed; but Campbell had resolved to 'start at the bottom', and reasoned that a university education could wait. He almost got that education. The Post Office agreed that he should enhance his qualifications, and would pay him while he studied. He was already enrolled at a university, with a starting date in October 1970, when he took ill in April of that year. He was working in Motherwell at the time, and the doctor he consulted there advised him to return home for referral to the Southern General Hospital in Glasgow. He was operated on there and subsequently underwent a course of chemotherapy. When he returned to Campbeltown, he appeared to have recovered and had six weeks of deceptive 'normality'; but the cancer had not been arrested, as a final x-ray examination in Glasgow revealed.

On the evening before Campbell's death, Mhairi and a friend went to the Picture House to see *Ring of Bright Water* (Bill Travers and Virginia McKenna in an adaptation of the Gavin Maxwell book, showing twice on the evening of 29 July, at 5.30 and 8.50).[19] By then, the Macarthur family had moved from Glenramskill to a new bungalow in Peninver, Coul na Mara, and Mhairi's father was to collect her after the film. When he appeared with a neighbour in the neighbour's car, she sensed that something was wrong. Sure enough, he told her that Campbell was in a coma. Cancer, at that time, she said, was a taboo subject, and Campbell's illness had not been openly discussed within the family. She had been entirely unaware of the gravity of his condition and was entirely unprepared for his death. She has never felt able to watch *Ring of Bright Water* again – the film itself has enough sadness in it, but its personal associations have too much.

The Macarthur family

Campbell's family was long established and well respected in the business community of Campbeltown. Its progenitor was a shoemaker, Neil Macarthur, who was born in Tiree in 1795. He married Catherine Mitchell in Glasgow in 1819 and they came to Campbeltown, where their six children were born. One of the sons, James, a rope-spinner and later a butcher, was Campbell's great-great grandfather. He married Catherine Hawthorn, a surname which at first sight appears incongruous in Kintyre, but is actually a pseudo-translation of *Ó Dreáin*, which probably arrived in Kintyre by migration from Ulster and was popularly and mistakenly identified with Gaelic *droigheann*, the hawthorn.[20]

Campbell's great-grandfather, Robert McFarlane Macarthur, was an 'offal merchant' in town. A notice in the *Argyllshire Herald* of 4 January 1890, dramatically headed 'TRIPE! TRIPE! TRIPE!', announced the opening of his new shop at 92 Longrow, where 'carefully cleansed' puddings, sausages and tripe would be offered for sale, with 'poultry always on hand'. Robert's first wife's surname, McCuaig, subsequently ran through the whole family. His address, when he died in 1935, was appropriately Arthur's Seat, Dalaruan, a now forgotten property.

Campbell's grandfather, Neil, was apprenticed as a baker to John Kerr in Longrow, and worked for him – while also acting as secretary of the local branch of the Bakery Workers' Union – until 1935, when he took over the business, which he expanded in 1946 to Port Ellen, Islay. Neil died in 1950, and the business, Messrs. Neil Macarthur & Sons, was continued by his sons

Robert (Campbell's father), Fraser and Neil, and daughters Elma (Mrs Alexander Mackinnon, Islay) and Melba.[21]

One of the many curious local stories which emerged during the Second World War was the meeting of Robert Macarthur and his brother Fraser in India in 1943. They had joined the army at different times and were posted abroad, but they both 'landed in India and arranged to hold a family reunion'. The news item appeared in the *Campbeltown Courier* of 15 May 1943, accompanied by a photograph of the brothers together in uniform.

39. Private Fraser Macarthur (L) and D/M Robert Macarthur together in India, 1943. From Campbeltown Courier, *15/5/1943.*

In the following year, their parents – 'of the Campbeltown firm of bakers and purveyors' – organised a whist drive and dance in the Town Hall to raise money for 'Salute the Soldiers Week'. Whist-players were asked to bring their own packs of cards, owing to 'the playing card shortage', and the Macarthurs' catering staff gave their services free at the event, which, at 5s a ticket, 'including tea', raised £115 15s.[22]

On the fortieth anniversary of Campbell's death, 30 July 2010, George and I together visited his grave in Kilkerran. We cycled there in the evening, rather guiltily passing the Picture House, outside which a queue had already formed for the premiere of Jan Nimmo's video history of Argyll Colliery, *The Road to Drumleman*. We both felt we ought to be supporting the launch, but, as we later heard, the cinema was packed and our presence was unnecessary.

During March, I cleaned out the bit of ditch the spring ran into, and scooped out a shallow basin, which I lined with 'chuckie' (quartz) pebbles and bits of white cockle shells, collected from the shore during wood-gathering excursions. Near Queen Esther's Bay, I had noticed a rock fall which had laid a trail of sandstone slabs on to the foreshore. I brought several of these slabs, one at a time, from the shore, and placed them in the ditch as a platform for water-filling duties. By July, however, neither spring nor platform was visible through the mass of vegetation which had sprung up, and the only indication of the spring's existence was its sound ... until that too disappeared with the water flow which gave it a voice.

While I was walking back to my bicycle, after the visit to Balnatunie, heavy rain started. The road was covered in flying ants – mid-August is the time of their emergence to breed and, in the males' case, having mated, to die – but the rain didn't appear to trouble them. At Sweetie Bella's Quarry, above the First Waters, I decided to shelter, and backed under a canopy of overhanging bushes, a tactic which works only until the leaves begin shedding their weight of droplets. I didn't stay there long enough to suffer the deferred penalty, but while there my vision fixed on two shags standing on a distant offshore rock. There were no other creatures to be seen through the rain, which explains, I suppose, why I focused on the 'scarts', black and immobile on their sea-washed perch, until they began to resemble tiny people.

Sweetie Bella's Quarry

The quarry must have been a source of rock for the roadmen who maintained the Learside road, a full-time job on all public highways. Piles of rock would be left at the roadside, where needed, and then broken by a 'stone-knapper' with a double-headed hammer and wire-meshed goggles to protect his eyes from flying chips. The quarry took its name not from any roadman's ironic nick-name, but from a winkle-gatherer who was in the habit of leaving her bags of 'wilks' there for collection. So I was told by the late Iain McIntyre in Glenahervie, who gave me the name.

I love those names which are attached to otherwise insignificant little places, but their hold is often tenuous and they have to be helped if they are to survive. Towards the end of their lives, those names may be known to only a few local folk, usually elderly; and once these individuals die, the names also die, unless they have been recorded. Sometimes, even then, they die in reality, because books, and all artificial media, operate in varying states of detachment from their subjects. Try identifying, from an Ordnance Survey map, a small feature on the actual ground, without an intimate knowledge of its physical character, when, on paper, the name could relate to several similar features close together. Often, no tradition survives to a explain a place-name, which is sad, because the value of a name, like that of an old photograph, is diminished when it can no longer be interpreted. The same applies with ancestry research – the further back in time one reaches, the more one is dealing merely with names, of people who once had lives; but there is nothing left of their lives.

In the case of 'Sweetie Bella', I was fortunate, even if poor Bella wasn't. On 20 January 1902, at the age of forty-five, she was admitted to Campbeltown Poor House. She was registered as Isabella McMillan McMillan, and there can be no doubting her identity, because her nick-name, too, was registered. She was born in Bolgam Street, on 5 February 1856, to Peter McMillan, fisherman, and Jane McKay. On 11 February 1878, at 41 Shore Street, she married Duncan C. McMillan, who was also born in Bolgam Street, in 1859, to Hector McMillan, carter, and Mary Ann Coffield. Bella's marriage to Duncan was childless and they separated after six years. He began 'cohabiting' with Elizabeth Ferguson, who bore him seven children. Bella died in the Poorhouse Hospital, in her native Campbeltown, on 22 August 1920.[23] Since she appears to have been a local 'character', I checked the *Campbeltown Courier* in the hope of finding a notice of her passing, but there was nothing. Nor have I noticed a memorial to her in Kilkerran – a pauper's grave may have been the final service to her performed by the parish.

Her nick-name was a puzzle to me – many nick-names are! – and I'd given up on finding an explanation, when, in the *Argyllshire Herald* of 13 January 1894, I chanced on a court report headed 'A SWEET-TOOTHED THIEF'. On the last Saturday of 1893, Isabella McMillan, an 'outdoor worker who has frequently been in the hands of Campbeltown police for various crimes', paid a visit to the shop of Mrs Graham in Kirk Street. Mrs Graham 'had had her suspicions of the mission of McMillan in visiting her shop', and, when Bella left without buying anything, she pursued her and got hold of her, when bottle of caraway and a jar of jelly fell on to the street. Bella was jailed for thirty days.

When the rain eased, I got back on the road and found that all the ants were off it – the multitude must have flown to shelter. I collected my bicycle, and, since the rain had temporarily stopped, I searched the blaeberry bushes near Sweetie Bella's Quarry and collected enough berries to provide a sweet, with whipped cream, for Judy and me that evening. It followed the mushrooms on to the table, and, soaked though I was by the time I reached home, I judged the afternoon a success.

Ben Gullion

On 18 August, a Sunday, I decided to head for the top of Ben Gullion. I'd been on the hill several times earlier in the summer, picking blaeberries in evenings, but now I wanted to reach the highest point visible from town, a pinnacle east of the shoulders (*guillean*) from which the hill was named, and close to the march with High Glenramskill. My own name for the feature is 'Conical Hill'; it deserves better, but to have contrived a Gaelic name for it would have been dishonest, because I am not a Gaelic speaker and there are no native Gaelic speakers left in Kintyre. I am in no doubt, however, that it had a Gaelic name – possibly corresponding to my own descriptive effort – but the name, whatever it was, is lost.

The Ordnance Survey, when it covered South Kintyre in 1866, did a great disservice to the place-names record of Campbeltown Parish. The yield was feeble, and what there was contained few insights into the meanings of the names. My complaints will be found in *Kintyre Places and Place-Names* (pp. 173-74). One of them was that the O.S. 'consulted the wrong people'. I left it at that, but will elaborate here. Campbeltown burgh (the town and environs) at that time had a big population from which the O.S. officers could select their few 'authorities' on local place-names and their meanings – over 6000 people.

The men they picked, from that large body of people, to guide and advise them, clearly had no knowledge of specifics in the landscape, and Ben Gullion proves the point. The name is all there is, and it's erroneously placed. Ben Gullion is a big hill, by Kintyre standards, and it stands over an historic settlement. Were there no other names that could be attached to it? I am certain there were, and equally certain that if a shepherd whose beat was on the hill had accompanied the surveyors, the first six-inch map would have shown burns, knolls and crags with names.

For comparison, take a look at south-west Kintyre on the O.S. 'Explorer' map, tracing names from the Mull north to Cnoc Moy and out to the line of Glenbreackerie. That geographical area, even then, was thinly populated, but the place-names coverage is impressive. Why the greater density of named natural features there, when the names on the landscape around Campbeltown are mostly of habitations (easily collected), with natural features largely represented by the biggest hills and lochs and streams? The explanation is that, in remoter parts, the O.S. would have been directed straight to the popularly acknowledged custodians of local lore, the Mathiesons and Campbells and others who were native to the area, and knew it, or their own bits of it, intimately. None of them was a 'scholar' of Gaelic – these were few anywhere in Kintyre in the mid-nineteenth century, and the methodical study of place-names had scarcely stirred into existence anywhere in Scotland – but they knew the names, from long hereditary usage, and interpreted them as best they could. Ben Gullion is a hill with few names, but George McSporran and I have filled in some of the blanks, to equip our minds with tools of reference and recognition.

Litter and vandalism

So, I was heading for 'Conical Hill'. I walked over Cross Hill and down on to the dam of the reservoir which took its name, Crosshill Loch, from the hill. The north end of the dam was strewn with litter, which was no surprise to me. I'd noticed, from the top of the Ben Gullion trail the previous week, a gathering of teenagers there, and assumed they'd leave a mess. Here is an inventory of that mess: carrier bags, crisp packets, sweet papers, drink cans, bottle tops, an emptied packet of 'Flocloxacillin' capsules, an orange-coloured towel, socks, a shoe, three pairs of boys' underpants and two pairs of girls' tights. (The last two sets of discards might be construed as evidence of a sexual orgy having taken place there, but the explanation is likely to be rather more mundane: a dip in the reservoir.)

Litter, and particularly its plastic elements, is a curse on the countryside and beaches. It vexes me, and I still gather it whenever practicable, but increasingly I try to ignore it, because the problem is unrelenting. There isn't much that I, or any individual, can do about it, and the problem isn't going to diminish any time soon.

The Ben Gullion trails – for walkers and cyclists – are constantly littered, particularly with empty plastic water-bottles. Consumption of 'plastic water', as I call it, is, to me, one of the most ridiculous of modern habits. That anyone would spend money on months- or years-old water from somewhere else in the world when there are safe local springs from which they could take as much fresh and free water as desired, is incomprehensible to me. I am no connoisseur of water, but I prefer mine straight from Mother Earth. (I suppose my daughter Bella must be a 'connoisseur', because she declines to drink the water from Miss Lloyd's Well, Baraskomel, in which she detects an 'earthy' taste.)

As a general rule, the further one goes from towns, the less litter there will be, and the explanation is that serious walkers generally take their social responsibilities seriously. On the sections of the Kintyre Way I have walked in recent years – and particularly that between Ballygroggan and Largiebaan – I can report no deliberate littering; but on 18 July, on the moor stretch past Ballygroggan, I thought I'd discovered the first offence, a cigarette packet on the path ahead of me. When I lifted it, however, I realised that it had been lost rather than discarded. It was a pack of ten 'Marlboro', and I counted nine cigarettes still in it (but initially missed number ten, which had been part-smoked and returned to the pack).

The circumstances of the loss were probably these: walker provisions himself (or herself) with pack, sets off early to attempt the Machrihanish-Southend section of the Way, lights up some time after completing the steep climb to Ballygroggan, enjoys several leisurely puffs while surveying the route ahead, nips the fag, sticks it back in the packet and carries on. Packet, whether in pocket or rucksack, then falls out. The addict's consternation at the next stop may be imagined. He feels and fumbles for the pack where he believes he placed it, but it isn't there and he begins searching elsewhere on his person and in his rucksack. Finally, when a thorough – and probably frantically repeated – search has failed to locate the pack, he realises to his chagrin that it is gone. He ponders his dilemma, briefly considers hurrying back along the trail to seek the delinquent pack, but decides – or is persuaded by companions – that the delay would be unconscionable, and resigns himself to a smokeless day (unless, of course, he has a spare pack, or a companion can help him out). So, on he goes, cursing his carelessness.

I put the pack into my rucksack and took it with me. As a dedicated pipe-smoker, the cigarettes were of no personal value to me, but the thought occurred to me that I might just encounter the distraught one later on in the day and restore his loss to him, failing which Jimmy MacDonald could be the recipient next time I met him. Weeks and months passed, however, without my meeting Jimmy, and I finally gave the cigarettes to someone else.

Late in the evening, near Glenrea, I had another find – a pair of 'Next' sun-glasses lying at the roadside. One of the lenses was missing, but I found it nearby, pressed it back into the frame and stuck the glasses into my rucksack along with the cigarettes. Retribution, however, was at hand. I stopped at Lochorodale bridge to drain my water bottle, and never saw it again. Since I don't smoke cigarettes and don't wear sun-glasses, these two finds certainly didn't cancel out the loss of that capacious plastic bottle, which several days later I searched for without success. Someone, clearly, had beaten me to it – a litter-lifter, perhaps!

Thanks to the Scottish Arts Council, in 1981 I acquired my first decent camera, a Pentax ME SUPER. I'd had it only a few weeks when, on 11 June, I left the lens-cap on the top of Cnoc Moy. I'd set off alone from Glenahanty for a night's camping at the Inneans, and, with my new camera in my rucksack, decided to climb Cnoc Moy and attempt some photographs. Whatever my technical failings, the mellow evening light enriched my efforts, and I still admire those slides, albeit through nostalgia's peep-hole. When I arrived on top of Cnoc Moy, I removed the lens-cap and put it in a pocket, but it fell out before I'd even taken the first photograph. 'I looked hopelessly for it,' I noted in my journal, 'and, sure enough, failed to find it.' I took the photographs, and, 'reconciled to the loss', headed down into the bay to set up camp. I have lost many objects over the years while hiking – jackets, money, pens, knives, pipes – and seldom recovered any of them, so I returned to Cnoc Moy next day without much expectation of seeing the cap again.

> I made the top of Cnoc Moy and in preparation for the search for my lens cap planted my stick in the ground. I made a start low down on the slope, but – inspirationally? – calculated that by some natural law or other I might find the cap close to where I had planted the stick, and, walking a short distance from it in a northerly direction, sure enough there it lay, glistening with dew.

Litter on Ben Gullion isn't confined to forest trails. These trails draw unwelcome visitors, some of whom will decide to explore beyond the routes designed for their convenience. Some are motivated by a spirit of adventure, but others just don't want to be observed doing whatever they are actually on the hill to do, which won't be botanising or bird-watching.

For many young folk, a day – or night – in the hills means partying unsupervised, with alcohol or drugs and usually a fire as well to add a flicker of atmosphere. These fires are often lit inside the forest and will involve damage to or destruction of trees ... and, after the fun has ended, litter as well, sometimes even the very camping equipment! I once saw a girl's soft toy lying amid an abandoned camp-site on Ben Gullion – rain in the night had driven the campers home – and my heart went out to it. 'Boys will be boys', of course, and girls nowadays will also 'be boys'. I worry about forest fires, but so far, by good fortune, none has burned so far out of control as to set stands of timber ablaze. These reckless campers – many of whom never repeat their experience of the outdoors – reveal their presence, anyway. A column of smoke inside the forest isn't a difficult sign to interpret, and anyone who knows Ben Gullion at all well can identify the exact location of the fire.

On occasion, however, litter will be found in a location so relatively remote or difficult of access as to be entirely unexpected. These evidences, which are usually small – a cigarette butt stubbed out on a rock, or an empty can – are the most disturbing, particularly in a favourite spot which one had imagined to be exclusive. It is like returning home and discovering that a stranger has been in the house. Nothing has been disturbed or removed, but he has left a nasty token of his intrusion.

When George McSporran and I, on the last day of June 2011, arrived at Conical Hill and found empty cans of 'Tyskie' lager shoved into the heather, we were bemused. Who would climb to that height and, having enjoyed the beauty there, decide not to carry the empties away with them? There is no simple answer to that question, but that the culprits had no intention of ever returning there is probably a safe deduction.

Returning to Knockbay by a 'secret' route through the forest from Fin Rock on 24 August 2014, George and I passed a curious sight – an old trainer suspended from a tree, and with an empty 'Carlsberg' bottle stuck in it. I have to admit that I'd tied the shoe by its laces to a branch a few years earlier. I was fond of the trainer – of the pair, actually – and their history persuaded me to hang one in the forest as a memorial to the many days I'd spent with it on my left foot and Benjie at my side. There was a further and more specific motivation. On the first evening I'd worn the trainers, 20 June 2007, Benjie and I had gone to Fin Rock by a marshy route which I now avoid. I blundered into a wet hole that evening and swamped the brand-new trainers, an accident which piqued me at the time. To my symbolic trash – a moss-invaded shoe – some unknown person had added his emptied beer bottle. I have told my little story, and made my confession, but his story will never be known, unless he reads this book and elects to confide in me. How likely is that?

Years before I hung the shoe on a tree, I'd hung a Breton cap on a tree beside another 'secret' forest route, leading to the Hawk's Peak on the opposite side of the hill. I'd bought the cap in 1991, in a local charity shop, and it fitted my head and suited my style to perfection. But Benjie, who appeared in my life in 1996, was prone to frenzies provoked by the sight or sound of other dogs, and during one of these outbursts he seized my cherished cap and tore the crown out of it. Since it wasn't fit to wear and I was fond of it, I gave it to a tree and the tree wore it until it mysteriously disappeared.

Tidal litter is a worse nuisance, since its origins can seldom be identified and its perpetrators, therefore, must remain immune from reproach, far less prosecution. Some of it demonstrably arrives on the coasts of Kintyre, and especially on the Atlantic coast, from thousands of miles away. Merchant seamen, fishermen, and yachtsmen are all to blame, though much of the litter in and around Campbeltown Loch – e.g. polystyrene take-away containers – has clearly been discarded from the harbourside. There is so much litter washed ashore now that it is effectively part of the scene – particularly on remote shores where collecting it is impractical – and I seldom now consciously register the nuisance. Sometimes, however, it announces its presence, as, when walking on overgrown foreshores, or even through adjacent fields, a hollow crunch underfoot signifies that one has tramped on a hidden plastic bottle or some other container which has blown inland.

Vandals and large scale litterers are usually one and the same. Ben Gullion, close to town and popular, is where I see most evidence of mischief – wilful fire-raising, wooden stiles and bridges sawn up for firewood, living trees hacked down. Again, 'Boys will be boys'. Youths with guns are thankfully rare in the hills now, and, when they know they are under observation, tend to exhibit signs of unease.

I was amused to read in a local newspaper from 1910, under the headline 'Hill-Climbing Danger', an outraged report of an incident on Ben Gullion that summer. A group of youths had 'unloosed a huge sharp-edged stone and set it rolling down the hillside', then gleefully fled the scene. When the 'huge missile' hurtled past groups of visitors out for a stroll, 'considerable consternation prevailed'.[24] I wonder if that rock still lies where it came to rest more than a century ago. I might even have sat on or near it once or twice!

Bush-burning has long been a sport of boys, and I know responsible walkers with a keen interest in nature who admit that, as boys, they enjoyed nothing more than heading for the hills with a box of matches. A favourite whin of mine, which grew on a knoll at the back of Crosshill Dam, was burned in 2004. It was in a very visible location, but I occasionally sat there during walks in winter with Benjie when I'd have the place to myself. I have intermingled memories of lingering there under clear nocturnal skies, looking at stars and watching for meteors.

The place had an additional significance, which I didn't at first realise. Judy and I had taken our daughters there on Easter Sunday 1993, to roll eggs and enjoy a picnic. The date was 11 April, which I know because it's written on a slide; but there's no mention of egg-rolling in the journal,

40. Egg-rolling at Knockbay, 11 April 1993. L-R: Amelia, Bella, Judy and Sarah Martin. Photograph by the author.

which records a sunny spring day with a cold east wind, and primrose, wood anemone and wood sorrel adorning the burn sides. I was dismayed by the destruction, but, noticing a few shoots which survived the fire, I reckoned the whin might regenerate. It did, and by 2009 it was again recognisably a bush; but in autumn 2013 it was mechanically mashed during scrub-clearing operations on Knockbay farmland. A few stalks survived, however, and once again I entertain optimism: See you later!

One of the most annoying acts of vandalism I witnessed was in the Inneans in 1982. I'd gone there on 25 July with young Niall Macaulay and his friend from Penicuik, Pete Arkle. During our approach from the north side of the glen, I'd noticed smoke drifting and announced to the boys that we could expect company, but as we neared the camp-site we saw it to be deserted ... and destroyed. Whoever had been there had left a pile of blazing debris. The planks which had served as benches, several logs, and two car wheels, dragged from the shore, had all been piled up and set alight. While our tea-kettle came to the boil in the smouldering remains, I photographed the damage. I had hoped to discover the identities of the perpetrators, but never did.

41. *The camp-site in the Inneans Bay burnt by vandals, 25 July 1982. Photograph by the author.*

Afforestation of Ben Gullion

The afforestation of Ben Gullion – a huge act of vandalism – was a controversial proposal from the day it emerged at a public meeting in the Victoria Hall in September 1977, and the issue ultimately split the community. Its main advocate was Tom Coulson, the Forestry Commission district officer, whose house on Low Askomil overlooked the hill. He argued that, although it would take twenty-five years before the forest 'would make any money', over a fifty-year rotation each acre would yield six tons of timber. The main opponents were Rear-Admiral Robin Mayo, whose house on High Askomil also overlooked the hill, and John O'Neill, a local dentist. 'In planting these 220 acres,' Rear-Admiral Mayo argued, the Forestry Commission would 'ravage the natural scenic beauty which is the backcloth to Campbeltown'.

Arguments and counter-arguments sizzled in the letters pages of the *Campbeltown Courier* for almost two years – even Paul McCartney, an opponent, had his say – but on 2 February 1979, Forestry Commission ploughs began tearing up the hill. Almost immediately, however, the ploughing was halted, when Swanney Farm Cheese Ltd., owners of Campbeltown Creamery, obtained an interim interdict in the Court of Session, claiming that the plantation would adversely affect the catchment of Crosshill Reservoir, which supplied the creamery annually with twenty million gallons of water, and also supplied the two local distilleries, Glen Scotia and Springbank. Meantime, 1,216 local folk signed a petition against the planting, but it was too late. The interdict was recalled, and the plantation – of 'landscaped' sitka spruce, lodgepole pine, Japanese or hybrid larch, and native broadleaves – proceeded.

As it turned out, the reservoir levels were unaffected, but no timber has ever been taken from the forest, and, ironically, even before the ploughs moved on to the hill Mr Coulson had taken up a new post in England. The project was a folly from the start, but one I have become comfortable with and wouldn't now reverse even if that were possible.

Largiebaan, 18 July 2013

In between finding the fags and losing my bottle, on 18 July, I had a delightful day ... but without my journal I wouldn't remember how delightful it was. It would be behind me, a day among days: sunshine, Largiebaan, the finds, the loss, and the rest of the day's memories merged with those of other days. That day was the second time I did the walk from Machrihanish to Auchencorvie. It was humid and misty, but by the time I reached Innean Mòr fank the mist was confined to the top of Cnoc Moy and there was a brisk, cooling breeze off the sea. Close to the fank, I noticed a flat rock, which I decided, and decided to note, 'I just know lots of people have sat on'.

I imagine some of them now, out there, seated on the rock, with the Atlantic swell running in below and the big skies of the west above – constants. But it's difficult to imagine faces, and they all end up recognisably from my own past, emerging from the shadows of memory, boys and girls who inhabited my own childhood, then dispersed into that big world beyond Kintyre which increasingly disturbs me. One fantasy entertains me – somewhere on that coast I meet a fellow-walker, around my own age, and when we stop to talk our identities emerge and we recognise each other as classmates fifty years back in a school of which only the playground walls remain standing.

I was hoping that day for a good picking of blaeberries during the slog up from the fank and on to the Aignish. When I'd done that part of the Kintyre Way the previous week, I'd eaten berries as I found them, and expected, by actively searching for them this time, to collect enough to take home with me; but I wasted time for a meagre take.

At Largiebaan, well over an hour later, I descended into the sentimental comfort of 'Jimmy's Dell', noting seven butterflies below the cliff-top. I had four ravens for company, in soaring flight at first, gull-like when the sun would catch the sheen of their wings, but finally alighting together on the highest point of the cliff-top, where I would myself have rested had the day been less breezy. When I arrived in the hollow, a one-horned ewe was standing alert on the most southerly visible rock outcrop, and she stared at me for ten minutes. I wondered, not for the first time when scrutinised by sheep, what she could be thinking, and noted: 'I was wishing I could have quizzed her about her most interesting experiences in life, but that was not to be – not in this world or, probably, in any other.'

The most inspired idea I have ever had for a book was to spend a full year living in one of the Largiebaan caves, and, at the end of it, to write a book on my experiences. My main interest at the time was the wild goat population of that coast, but there would have been many other subjects for study, among them raptors, seabirds, foxes, cetaceans, the botanical rarities of the cliffs ... and, not least, those humans who came my way.

Until my retirement in 2012, however, I couldn't have devoted a whole year to any project, and, now that I can, I suspect that the rigours of cave-dwelling would soon kill me! There would, of course, be contact with so-called civilisation – provisions and mail to collect, damaged or worn-out equipment to replace, visitors to be received, and so on – but it is now too late to consider such an undertaking; and, if I am honest with myself, I doubt if I would ever have attempted it, even had the time and resources been available to me.

I believe the notion gripped my imagination in the early 1980s when I was researching *Kintyre: The Hidden Past* and read about Alexander McMillan, who in 1907 disappeared for a fortnight to the Largiebaan caves and lived on shellfish and dulse. He was a fisherman to trade, but had obtained temporary work as a labourer at Killellan Quarry. He set out for the quarry from his home at Machrihanish at 6 a.m. on Monday 11 March, but failed to arrive.

> He dropped as completely out of the life of the community as if he had never been a member of it, and the search parties who scoured the district in quest of him failed to find him or learn any tidings of his whereabouts. Not only were moss and field, ditch and hollow, explored, but Kylipole Loch was dragged; and all the time the object of the search – the missing fisherman – was safe and sound ... McMillan returned to his home at ten o' clock on Saturday night, when no one was expecting him, and his homecoming, like his setting out, was practically unobserved. He was seen peering in at the window of his house, and on search being subsequently made he was found in the hen-house ...

An earlier newspaper report revealed that McMillan had been 'for a number of years an inmate of the Argyll and Bute Asylum', and had been 'dismissed no later than January last'. He would die there on 27 February 1921. He had been married in 1898 in Lossit House, where his Pitsligo-born wife, Annie Robb, was doubtless a servant. A note in his poor roll entry suggests that 'their marriage seems to have put both wrong'.[25]

To date, merely two caves in Kintyre have been archaeologically excavated, Saint Ciaran's (1924-25) and Keil (1933-35), but most of the remainder – those at Largiebaan included, I suggest – would have been occupied intermittently from prehistory until the twentieth century. Excavation of the Largiebaan caves would present unusual difficulties, owing to their remoteness, and I doubt if the effort will ever be made; but I would love to be there if the carpets of goat-dung on the floors of the caves are ever lifted and the human past methodically laid bare.

Mist

I mentioned there was mist on 18 July and that it cleared, but until it cleared I was preparing for the possibility of being caught in it on the high ground I was heading for. I have been lost several times in hills, and the experience was always unnerving, the two major uncertainties being: when will the mist lift and where will I be when it does? The most alarming experience of all happened on my way back to Glenahanty from the Inneans with Donald Docherty, John MacDonald and Michael Claffey. I quote from my journal of 26 March 1983.

> We had hardly got out of the Inans when mist closed in from the sea. We seemed to be going safely enough, but landmarks were obscured and such features as fences and drains were becoming more and more strange the longer we went. We finally saw a glow – an eerie big glow – near the brow of a ridge, and found ourselves at Largybaan steading. Had we been a little higher, then we should have missed the road entirely and most probably carried on right round Cnoc Moy.

Instead of passing low through Gleneadardacrock to join the road at Gartnacopaig, we had been steadily gaining height on Cnoc Moy without the least awareness of our error. With two schoolboys in tow and darkness approaching – this, remember, was March – the consequences of missing that light at Largiebaan would have been dreadful: our blundering around in darkness and mist among rocks and close to cliffs; the police alerted by the boys' anxious mothers; a search party despatched to find us (if anyone was actually aware of where we'd gone); the humiliation of newspaper reports on our disappearance.

Yet, in the long term, my memory of that day failed me, as I discovered when I consulted my journals. The sequel was that we returned to Donald's car and he drove to the

Keil Hotel, Southend, where he and I had a pint of beer and the boys had a glass of 'Coke', with 'crisps all round'. With the passage of time, that day had become confused with a later day in 1983, when John, Michael and I had cycled out to Glenahanty (p 55). To the dramatic events in the mist had been added a tense bicycle journey home in darkness, but it didn't happen that way, which demonstrates that memory alone is often not enough in reconstructing the past. The wooden shepherd's house at Largiebaan is nominally a Scottish Wildlife Trust warden's residence, but is effectively unoccupied, and no light shines there now for Blake's 'lost Travellers under the Hill' (excuse the omitted 'Dream').

There were other misadventures in mist on that coast, one of which I remember for the loss of a 'Thermos' flask which I'd filled with blaeberries. I also remember where I was when the mist engulfed me and that I got myself safely back to Machrihanish by finding Craigaig Water, but not much else. The homeward stages of a hike generally go unrecorded, unless I have time to stop and reasons for making notes. In this case, I found myself sitting in the bus shelter at Machrihanish waiting for the late bus, and I briefly set down my experiences in the mist. The date was 18 July 1991.

> Very, very still now, with mist over the Laggan – 3 photographs from the Lifeboathouse. I was caught in dense mist on the moors between the Inans and Craigaig. The fank [at Craigaig] was in sight, if distant, but I was intent on gathering blaeberries. And then the mist moved in. I'd seen curls around Cnoc Moy earlier on, but thought nothing of them. I got lost and must have been heading east, because I picked up Craigaig Water well inland. I wasn't certain of it, & had a qualm when at one point the landscape looked like the head of the Inneans Glen where Glean Eadar da Crock joins it. But I followed it & eventually, after much apprehension, came to the fank. I sat to eat the last of my rolls, & the mist cleared.

I'd set off in rain, which lasted all the way to the Inneans. It was so heavy that the insoles of a brand-new pair of Hogg's boots – of Czechoslovakian manufacture, and not as expensive as I should have been prepared to pay – didn't stand 'the test of the bogs' and were 'quite spoiled'. But the day undoubtedly had its compensations. While gathering blaeberries on the way out, I encountered a tiny fawn-coloured toad beside a moorland burn, and put it into a poem which was published seven years later in *The Song of the Quern* (p 48). Another poem, which has never been published, was inspired by a young fox which appeared while I was writing up my journal in the Inneans Bay.

> I was interrupted there by a little fox, which, when I happened to look up from my notes, was standing 6 or 7 yards away from me, looking curiously at me. I hadn't my camera with me, because I'd been sheltering under a nearby rock while I had my tea, so by the time I fetched the camera, the fox was on his way. But I got two distant photos & followed him among the shore rocks at the north end of the bay, surprising him again before he took off up the slope of Beinn na Faire. A curious incident, indeed.

The poem, which was written on the spot, lies unrevised in a file, but here is a small part of it in which I seek to explain the creature's fearlessness:

> Was I the first of Beast-with-Poison
> Beast-with-Snare and Beast-with-Gun
> the first embodiment of that
> most feared and ineradicable
> death symbol in your instinct's code
> that came before your eyes?

The final lines remark on my preoccupation with the photographic record:

> But what's my picture-box to you?
> Hardly worth a sniff!

There was one further natural history observation already in the notebook.

> I am sitting in the Inans. The rain is dying away, & my fire is going out. There are about 10 goats still sheltering under rock ledges on the cliffy parts above the Singing Rock. As soon as the rain started again, all the goats broke off from grazing and hurried for shelter. I looked to see what the sheep in the bay were doing, & they were just doing what they'd been doing before the rain came on: grazing and sitting around.

I wrote a third poem, after I'd arrived home, and titled it 'Mist'. Like 'Little Fox', it didn't satisfy my standards, but I have been re-reading it, twenty-odd years on, not as a poem, but as a document which offers insights into my state of mind in the mist that day. I admit in the poem that I had ignored the first 'trailing wisps' and 'boasted to myself', even as a 'pouring sea of it' advanced, 'that I would hold my line/ straight to the big sheep-fank and safety'.

> But I got lost, and suddenly
> all was strange and all a dim
> oneness of similarity
> with not a crag or burn
> I could locate in memory.

Later, after describing my increasing disorientation and my anxiety that 'shame at the least and death at worst' might follow on my folly, I admit that

> I was a wandered child again
> crying within for some familiar thing
> that I might cling to.

Did I, for dramatic effect, exaggerate my fears in the above lines? I cannot be certain now, but I'll trust my literary integrity.

Of the final experience in mist I wish to relate, I remember little, and the written record is scant. John MacDonald was with me that day, 16 May 1982, and the first part of the walk was documented.

> Uigle Burn. Unusually, in my own experience, built a fireplace and got a fire going inland; but the actual setting is not unlike a shore. John and I are seated, in warm sunshine, on a high and dry bank of the burn. We came upon this spot – which is a lovely little glen, scooped out by the burn – accidentally, as it were, when walking out from the Black Loch. We walked up to Crosshill Loch and round the back of Ben Gullion and are heading for Feochaig. Saw a curlew and photographed meadow pipit eggs in a nest a little out from the Black Loch.

The account was resumed a week later. We reached a ruin – which I later identified as Arinascavach – and found our way back to Ben Gullion from there.

> Last Sunday's misadventure with John ... We went too far south of the back of Ben Gullion, found ourselves in mist, took a forestry road and landed above Achnaglach. By the time we had extricated ourselves from the forest and were again on the moorland south of Ben Gullion, we were too late to find our way to the Coast.

The Hidden Crag

But I am back on Ben Gullion, on 18 August, and at the top of the trail I head up in a south-easterly direction, following the burn on its north side and gathering blaeberries as I go, until another burn joins it. I'll cross at that confluence and climb directly to Conical Hill, but not yet – it's time to eat beneath a canopy of spruce. I'm at the entrance to a short route into a tiny forest clearing which Sandy McSporran named 'The Hidden Crag'. He noticed the spot one day from The Hawk's Peak when we were sitting there. The clearing was visible and inviting then, but isn't now – it's completely hidden. Thus, a name which was loosely apt thirteen years ago has become entirely so. We decided, at the time, to find a way into it. The first attempt got us there, but not without difficulty, and at the second attempt we found the route which served us thereafter.

Our first visit was on 3 March 2000 and merited only a sentence: 'Sheltering in trees above Blaeberry Patch – a bit Sandy found – because wind is surprisingly brisk.' George, Sandy, Benjie and I were back on 29 March, when the name 'The Hidden Crag' appears in my journal, presumably newly minted. I describe 'a new clearing' with 'a fine view west', record two local deaths, and finally: 'Lot of birdsong. Hazy & darkness coming.'

Just over a year earlier, George and I had sat inside the entrance of the route to the Crag, without suspecting what lay deeper within. The date was 2 January 1999, and it was George's fiftieth birthday, which we celebrated by sharing a miniature bottle of 'Springbank' whisky. To further mark the occasion, George uncharacteristically wrote a few lines in my journal – 'My 50th birthday. Decided to join Angus in walk up the trail.' – and I took several photographs of him. On our way downhill, we noticed, and I noted, 'A figure atop Ben Gullion at 1630 in near-darkness'.

There's hardly any reason now for going to The Hidden Crag. Nothing can be seen from there except a wall of trees which now blocks what was once a fine view out over the Laggan. I'd have forgotten the expanse of the vista were it not for a photograph Sandy took of Benjie alert on a rock, head raised and tail cocked. It is quite the most evocative portrait of Benjie I have, and it hangs in the living-room, his old collar and tag looped over the frame. There is a clear view, into the north-west, of a hazy orange evening landscape. He stands on his rock, below which, at the very bottom of the picture, are visible the tips of the spruce which grew and grew until they closed the view.

On visits there, Benjie usually occupied that jutting rock, while I, and whoever was with me, sat further in, up close to the trees at our backs. No doubt his station gave him a sense of control of the space. There was little enough space there, but it provided excellent shelter on wet or windy days, and a private retreat – no one outwith the small circle of 'initiates' ever found a way in, or, if they did, they left no trace. Judy's first time at The Hidden Crag was entirely owing to Benjie's familiarity with the spot. They were on Ben Gullion together, and when he turned into the trees, she followed him, guessing that he'd take her to a place he'd been with me, and so it was that she found herself there.

The bone temple

I placed the corpse of a fledgling feral pigeon in one of the trees at The Hidden Crag on 20 August 2006, the day after his death ('his' sex was unknown, but 'its' seems too impersonal). He had been found with a mangled leg on Main Street and given to me at my workplace, and I carried him home in a box. Benjie's vet, Jon Hooper, suggested we care for him until he was strong enough to undergo an amputation. Judy faithfully fed Paddy, as I had named him, and he seemed to be recovering, but one afternoon I returned from work and found him dead, 'under a table, his wings outspread/that never once had flown'.

We had grown fond of him in his time with us, and his death hit me harder than I could have anticipated. Complex personal factors underlay my response, and I tried to rationalise these in a series of poems I wrote between 19th and 24th August. Three of them were written at the Crag, where I'd carried him, wrapped in a cloth, on the 20th. I laid the body across the branches of a spruce and tied the cloth to a branch, creating, as I put it in one of the poems, a 'tree shrine'. The poems have never been published and probably never will be. Perhaps their intensely personal nature led me into sentimental excess. Seven years on, however, they still affect me, and it is by words I shall remember Paddy, not by bones and a dangling rag. I shall remember too that 'place of cherished memory' and the three summer evenings I sat there, Benjie at my side, hearing distant fairground music from Kinloch Green and trying to direct a tide of emotions into the clear channel of a poem. These were the last lines I wrote on the last evening at the 'bone temple', before I set off downhill into darkness.

> Now look! – the sun's last shaft of mellow gold
> has struck your tree and you within it
> a momentary transformation
> that bathes you in a living glow.

On 28 July 2013, after a night in our caravan at Polliwilline, I walked up the Learside with Amelia, stopping for half-an-hour at the quarry overlooking the little reservoir beside the Old Road. It was a warm day and we were thirsty, so we decided to divert through the middle of town and buy ice-cream. In Main Street, I noticed a feral pigeon perched on the ledge of a shop window and looking helpless. It was attracting the benign interest of passers-by, but I was not tempted to 'rescue' it, and passed it by after a cursory, and guilty, inspection.

Conical Hill and harebells

The sub-title of this book might almost be 'Rocks I have known and loved', and I would revisit two before my day on Ben Gullion ended. The first of these, on Conical Hill, was where I first truly looked at harebells, on 14 August 1999. There were merely three flowers, and they were leaning out of a mossy crack in a rock. Harebells do not thrive on heathery ground, but will occupy rock outcrops on such terrain, if the merest accumulations of organic detritus exist to give the seeds a start. I had, of course, seen harebells before, but hadn't noticed them, a distinction which I increasingly recognise. The harebell, since that day, has been one of the flowers I most admire, and I love to look closely at its delicate, tremulous bell.

42. Conical Hill under snow, from west, February 1970. Photograph by George McSporran.

Botanical textbooks maintain that the harebell (*Campanula rotundifolia*) is known in Scotland as the 'bluebell', but in my childhood a bluebell was *Hyacinthoides non-scripta*, which is the bluebell of the textbooks. If there was a local name for the harebell, I still haven't heard it, and Latimer McInnes has nothing in his *Dialect of South Kintyre*, published in 1934. Geoffrey Grigson, in *The Englishman's Flora*, explains that the 'hare' in harebell is a 'witch animal' – the hare in Kintyre was the main supernatural disguise of witches – and, all in all, the innocuous-looking harebell, to judge by its various names throughout the British Isles, had dangerous associations. I have looked for a Kintyre Gaelic name for the flower, but that too is elusive. Two cuckoo-related names – *bròg-na-cubhaig*, 'the cuckoo's shoe', and *currac-cubhaige*, 'cuckoo's cap' – are likeliest, from the few clues I could find. In 'The Fell Sergeant', an early short story from the pen of Inveraray's Neil Munro, an old Mull woman, Aoraig, who is dying in Glen Aray, speaks of being courted long ago by a Glen Aray man named Macnicol, who brought her blue flowers all the way from mainland Argyll. These flowers, which Munro calls 'cuckoo brogues', were clearly harebells.

I returned to that rock to photograph the harebells once I had satisfied myself from books that I had seen on high ground a flower which I'd always associated with lower ground. My knowledge of natural history has been slow to develop. There is so much to learn that I feel at times intimidated. How to identify groups of flowers or insects or birds which closely resemble one another and can be separated only by tiny details? My response at times is to ignore the difficulty. If I live long enough, I may find the motivation to analyse the minutiae of species, but I doubt it, and in the meantime I content myself with enjoying the thing itself, whatever its scientific name.

Out walking with my daughter Amelia, I'll point out certain flowers or butterflies or birds, or whatever, which I happen to be familiar enough with to comment on, but she'll tell me quite cheerfully that she isn't interested, and I allow that an interest in natural history might develop later in her life. She was with me on Conical Hill on 4 July 2011, and we sat for lunch close to the rock. Unknown to her, I photographed her texting on her mobile phone. She obviously wasn't tuning into my profound silences (p 68); but she isn't one for solitude, and her idea of hell is being consciously alone for more than an hour. I am her opposite.

43. Amelia Martin on Conical Hill with mobile phone, 4 July 2011. Photograph by the author.

Back in 1999, I wrote a poem to the harebells on Conical Hill. It is as frail as the flowers themselves were, and describes them at the end as '... a secret trinity/as one together'. Reflecting now on the poem (which appeared in *The Silent Hollow* in 2005), I realise that it was more a farewell than a tribute, because the flowers disappeared soon afterwards from the rock. Though perennial, their hold must have been too tenuous, and no new seeds have yet found their way into a crack in that rock. I would love to return there one summer and see a few delicate blue heads nodding on their spindly stems, as though to greet me.

44. The harebell rock on Conical Hill, resembling the profile of face with gaping mouth, 13 July 2011. Photograph by the author.

When I was on the hillock on 18 August 2013, I had a good look at the rock. It is west-facing, jutting and grey-lichened, with a cleft in it which forms a ledge. (I imagine, with lazy vagueness, the numbers and species of little birds which rested and sheltered there since the first one noticed it and dropped out of the sky, before a human hand had ever touched the rock.) In my final years as a postman, when I'd sit for lunch near Kilkivan Quarry on a clear winter's afternoon, I could train binoculars on the hillock and see that very rock by the light which picked out its form, and recall past summers there, blaeberry-gathering.

Dragonfly Lochan

I walked into the south, following the march fence until I came to a peaty pool on the Glenramskill side. It lies, as such natural basins must, in a moorland hollow, and is easily missed. It has no name except the one I gave it, 'Dragonfly Lochan', from the golden-ringed dragonflies I watched there on 24 August 1997. I haven't seen any there since, but I suppose they still emerge from its placid waters to complete their life-cycle. They live for only about a month as flying insects, and daily kill and eat large numbers of other flying insects (Judy, Amelia and I, on Ben Gullion in August, saw one dart by with a green-veined white butterfly in its jaws). Fierce predators, with amazing powers of flight and manoeuvrability, dragonflies are among the fastest of winged insects, having been 'clocked' at thirty-five miles an hour. Watching them patrolling backwards and forwards at speed along forest rides on Ben Gullion, I invariably liken them to helicopter gunships; and I haven't been alone in that comparison.

Both the front and the back cover of *Kintyre Places and Place-Names* carries a photograph of that lochan, one with Cnoc Moy distant in the west, and the other with the Arran mountains blue on the north-eastern horizon. I don't believe that many photographs I've ever taken succeed in conveying intrinsic character of place, but these do, for me at least.

Benjie's Drinking Pool

By then, I knew that I had embarked on a sentimental circuit of Ben Gullion, and I descended to the back of the eponymous shoulders to revisit an even tinier pool, scarcely more capacious than a domestic sink. That one I had named 'Benjie's Drinking Pool', from times he'd quenched his thirst there. The last time I was there was in 2009, the year after Benjie's death, when for months I sought out places we'd been together, and wrote a poem, or poems, in each one, seeking the consolation of remembered times. On that day, approaching it across the level moor, I had difficulty finding it, but this time I saw it from higher ground, as a green mossy eye, and was able to go straight to it.

It is not a well, and certainly not a 'wishing well', but from the first time I went there, I conceived the notion of dropping a coin into it for 'luck'. All I had in my pockets that day was a 20-pence piece I'd picked up on Hall Street on my way to the hill, and I reluctantly offered it to the water-spirit. It seemed too much of a gift, but since I hadn't earned, but merely found the coin, I parted with it. The pool has filled with sphagnum moss – and may cease, in time, to be a pool – and I dropped the coin on the mat of moss. It didn't sink.

The Hawk's Peak

The Hawk's Peak, the second and final rock of the day, and a big one, has a name owing nothing to my inventiveness, but it has fourteen entries in *By Hill and Shore in South Kintyre*, from which may be judged its significance to me.

Everyone I ever walked Ben Gullion with has been there, and memories are as thick as bird shit on its top. On either side of the Millennium, I enjoyed many winter night-walks there, the most memorable of them under star-filled skies.

The Hawk's Peak is a prominent crag below the western shoulder of Ben Gullion, and I first heard the name in 1981 from Teddy Lafferty, who told me that Sandy Morrans took to going there in the latter years of his life when he was no longer fit to walk the Learside. Teddy remembers meeting him a few times returning from the Peak, but – as often happens – the encounters have merged into one representative memory. It's a warm Sunday, and Sandy, 'bunnet' in hand, is crossing Crosshill Dam.

Sandy was fond of frequenting a little bay north of the First Waters, known as Queen Esther's Bay, after Esther Houston, a nineteenth century cave-dweller on Polliwilline shore. Sandy, too, is commemorated in an obscure place-name, Snobs's Well, immediately north of Queen Esther's Bay. He took his water from there when 'brewing up' alone. It's more surface water than well, but Sandy scooped out a basin, and Teddy Lafferty added a pipe to concentrate the flow. The name has an occupational origin – in local dialect a 'snob' was a shoemaker, Sandy's trade. The source of the 'well' has since cut a channel through the foreshore and is effectively a small stream, but Teddy's black plastic pipe is still in place, though no longer a conduit.

After Teddy told me about Snobs's Well in 1980, I searched for months for it until I finally identified it. I was in Queen Esther's Bay on 6 July, and, while searching, found an adder 'curled on wet ground' – that wet ground was actually the 'well'! I took my kettle into the First Waters to fill it from the burn there, and, while returning with it to Queen Esther's Bay, noticed another adder on grass above the foreshore. These encounters were deemed 'slightly alarming', and I resolved to 'keep to the shore on my way home and avoid grass and bracken'. I never again saw snakes on that shore.

In Queen Esther's Bay, on 14 June 1981, John MacDonald brought me a report of the initials 'T L' carved on a stone at Snobs's Well. I assumed these must represent 'Teddy Lafferty' and decided to carve my own and John's initials alongside them, but, having examined the stone, I concluded:

> John's imagination evidently exceeds his power of observation – the 'initials' are entirely natural to the rock, but, however, do tenuously resemble 'E L'. The rock is very hard and wouldn't take a knife-blade. Perhaps, however, there is a sort of natural aptness – nature acknowledging Teddy's territorial claim here.'

I have a vague memory of seeing old initials cut into one of the rock outcrops north of Queen Esther's Bay, but I wonder now if I have been remembering young John's mistake. When wood-gathering there in March, I searched carefully for any carvings on the rocks, but found none. Elsewhere on that coast, however, visitors have left their mark. Earlier that month, in the Second Waters, with late sunlight shining on the north end of the bay, I decided to note the names and initials carved in the sandstone rocks there. As I anticipated, these were showing up plainly: 1961 E LANG/ YOGI BEAR/ G THOMSON/ J SHAW/ A McEACHRAN/ P McNAIR/ ANDY + MEG HYND 1986/ STEPHEN/ VINCENT 1980/ K HILL/ J HILL/ AH 1983/ STEVE H/ J MOHAMED/ AG/ JH/ SH/ J T GILLIES/ JEAN/ BILL 1989/ R McA/ PETER/ MARI/ ROGER/ PANTHER. Later still, I had a look at the rocks on the north side of the First Waters, but found only 6/8/95 KMcA/ C McA.

My German friend Hartwig Schutz and his daughter Wiebke, during their first visit to Kintyre in the back end of 1999, oftener frequented Ben Gullion than any other place in Kintyre, the Galdrans (which Wiebke especially loved) excepted. With my love of both memorials and words, I suppose it was inevitable that my two cherished companions should each leave behind a landscape reminder (but in their own language).

His was a small protruding rock on a forest path which took us to The Hawk's Peak. He tripped on it spectacularly one night, and it became *Hartwig Stein*. For years afterwards, I'd step across it and recall the name and its origin, but the route it obstructed, and indeed the Peak itself, finally fell out of favour and I haven't seen it for many years. On 19 November – a clear, frosty night with a bright moon – the name *Wiebke's Kreiss* ('Circle') was attached to a round patch of greater woodrush to the east of the Peak, a spot which had given us some shelter on nights when the summit itself was too windy. The patch of greater woodrush remains, but its circular form has disappeared in subsequent outgrowth.

45. The Hawk's Peak on skyline to right of eastern shoulder of Ben Gullion, with Jimmy MacDonald in foreground. On our winter route to the top, 7 December 1991. Photograph by the author.

Hartwig and Wiebke's first visit to The Hawk's Peak was on 18 October 1999. On our way up, we met John Brodie heading down Ben Gullion, and he accompanied us there.

George was following that evening and caught up with us after we had left the trees and were crossing to the Peak. The sun was going down and a bright half-moon rising as I sat on the crag filling in my journal, which recorded only two Sika deer sighted. My last night there with them was on 25 November – the eve of their departure – when we passed around a glass of twelve-year-old 'Springbank' malt whisky and toasted the future. The future, as it turned out, would cement our friendship, and visits have been exchanged over the years.

46. *The author with daughter Bella on The Hawk's Peak, 30 March 1996. Photograph by Sarah Martin.*

'Foot and mouth' restrictions

That farewell glass was secreted in a rock crevice, and nearly 18 months later I retrieved it for a celebratory drink with George and Sandy McSporran. That evening – 16 May 2001 – on The Hawk's Peak was our first time together on Ben Gullion since the 'foot and mouth' scare took hold.

On 2 March, as George and Benjie sat with me in snow and darkness on Ben Gullion, I had written in my journal: 'Up despite foot-&-mouth restrictive measures. May be our last trip up for weeks or months.' It was, but in retrospect I have to question the stringency of the measures. Farmers were understandably anxious to restrict access to their land, but was there any real necessity to close forest trails? I discovered later that certain friends continued to walk on Ben Gullion, despite the warning notices on the trail gates. In any case, the terrible disease failed to reach Kintyre.

With Benjie to walk, I had to find alternative routes, which turned out to be Kilkerran Graveyard, Kilkerran road and Kildalloig road; and these two months of exclusion from the hills brought their own limited rewards. George, Bella and I took to resting on the Look-Oot (p 147) and in the Wee Wud, which extends along the roadside from the NATO jetty almost to the Doirlinn. We became especially fond of sitting under a big ash tree in that wood.

STOP!
FOOT & MOUTH DISEASE PRECAUTION

Please do not proceed any further. Before entering any farm premises or fields, please phone the number below

TEL NO: **01586 552185**

For further information:
NFU Scotland website : www.nfus.org.uk
MAFF helpline 0845 050 4141

47. Foot and Mouth warning notice on Narrowfield gate, 2001.

The restrictions were actually lifted five days before the McSporrans joined me on The Hawk's Peak. I was in Kilkerran on the long-awaited day, 11 May, and climbed the graveyard wall on to the hill, something I'd several times longed to do during the two months Ben Gullion was out of bounds. I was to have met George and Sandy that evening, but while browsing in the old section of the graveyard I saw a white car, which resembled the McSporrans' Daihatsu Charade, come through the gates and do a circuit of the graveyard before going back out. The driver was a woman, whom I supposed to be George's wife, Margaret, and I guessed that she was looking for me to tell me that George and Sandy wouldn't be coming. I also correctly guessed the reason – they were on a Coastguard call-out. So, I sat with Benjie on a crag near the top of the trail, noting 'bees buzzing around pink blaeberry flowers', and stating the obvious: 'It's great to be back.'

Fin Rock

The first time I sat on Fin Rock, on 3 June 2002, I described it in my journal as 'the prominent Silhouette Rock on Kilkerran', which, to judge by the initial capitalisations, appears to have been an earlier, forgotten name, formed from distance. It is visible on the skyline from the south side of town and resembles a jutting dorsal fin. A description of that day – a Monday bank holiday, which was followed by a further holiday to mark the Queen's Jubilee – appears in *By Hill and Shore in South Kintyre* (p 183), therefore I'll mention only that Judy, Bella and Benjie were with me and that we walked from Narrowfield across the face of Ben Gullion and through the forest ride which, in 2007, was turned into the uppermost cycle path.

The three photographs I most value of Benjie all show him standing on a rock. The earliest was Sandy McSporran's taken at The Hidden Crag (p 174), then there was Hartwig Schutz's at Sròn Gharbh in 2007 (p 4), and finally George McSporran's in 2008 at Fin Rock. I am not certain why a rock should figure in all these favourite photographs. They are certainly all fine photographs, but I have other fine photographs of Benjie, some of them with me in them. I suppose the explanation is connected with the permanence of rocks. I can return to any of these rocks and find the photographic image of Benjie superimposed on the rock itself for as long as I wish to keep it there (which won't be long – I'm sentimental, but not, I hope, morbid!) So, it's back to the tricks of memory – willed and welcome.

48. Benjie on Fin Rock, 8 August 2008, his last time there. Photograph by George McSporran.

Fin Rock is on Kilkerran ground, across the fence from Ben Gullion forest and not far from the Piper's Cave of garbled legend. In the early 1990s, for a few years, there was an earlier Benjie on that hill, a pony Judy and I bought for our eldest daughter, Sarah. If I correctly recall the origin of her fascination with horses, she was with her younger sister Amelia and me at the Paddling Pool play-park one afternoon and heard a clip-clop-clip-clop. Then, to her excitement, a horse and its rider appeared.

49. Pony-riding at Kilkerran, 2 February 1992. L.-R. Jane Gallagher, Catherine Gallagher, Amelia Martin on Benjie, Judy Martin and Sarah Martin. Photograph by the author.

I began taking Sarah and Amelia to Kilkerran graveyard for picnics soon after that vision of the horse. We always sat with our backs against a grassy embankment overlooking Kilkerran farmhouse, at the back of which were stables. We'd often see the pony girls leading their horses into the stables or grooming them outside. These afternoons in the graveyard remain fresh in my memory. Our standard snack was a packet of 'Space Raiders', accompanied by a carton of 'Umbongo'. There may have been those who considered a graveyard rather a curious picnic spot, but to me it was ideal – quiet, clean, easy to reach, and occupied by a host of relatives and friends whose lingering influences touched me, if not my daughters.

Sarah wished for a pony, so we bought her one, and he came with the name 'Benjie'. When my sister Carol and I, as children, would pester our mother for a pet, her response was always: 'When you grow up and get a house of your own, you can have as many pets as you want.' Aside from budgies, which were something of a Martin family tradition, and, besides, required little attention, we were denied pets, for reasons I would understand only when I myself became a parent. Sarah was probably too young for the pony, and her attention shifted. The burden of care for the pony then shifted to Judy and me, and we finally parted with Benjie; he was given to a horse-lover in Carradale.

Still, his being on Kilkerran for a few years familiarised us with the hill, and I have many fond memories of gathering blaeberries with Sarah and Amelia in those summers. When I returned there on 10 June 2011, after an interval of some fifteen years, the memories assumed an emotional immediacy as I recognised the turf-dykes and hill-slopes where the girls and I gathered berries and enjoyed our little picnics.

I had a vague memory of being there with Mike Smylie, whose presence in Kintyre I'll later explain. I remember the rock we sat at – it's south of Fin Rock, on the same hillock – and that something odd took place there. I discovered what that 'something' was while reading through my journal for 1993 – the use of a gas stove! It is something of a novelty to me in the hills, though Judy has occasionally taken hers on picnics, especially when our daughters were young. And my father always took his 'Primus' paraffin stove in its green metal box, packed with paraphernalia, to Kilchousland for family days on the beach in the 1950s and early '60s. Often, a dinner would be cooked there, with water for the tea and the tatties taken from the well above the storm-beach on the south side of the sea-wall. The sandy beaches on both sides of that wall were frequently packed with picnickers, but visitors are now rare and the well is silted up and overgrown.

On that day with Mike, I fetched 'peat-coloured' water from the Rocky Burn for our picnic tea. The date was 22 August 1993, Sarah's sixth birthday, and she was with us. We picked a couple of pounds of blaeberries for eating with cream at her birthday party that evening.

I next sat at that rock on the evening of 7 May 2010 with George McSporran, but didn't, at the time, realise that I'd been there before. There is an account in *By Hill and Shore in South Kintyre* (p 277) of the hour we spent there, sheltering from a cold north-westerly wind and facing into the south. We enjoyed three memorable sightings of birds – a drifting heron, a high and rapid peregrine falcon, and a cuckoo which repeatedly and comically botched its call.

Mike Smylie appeared for the first time in Kintyre in 1992 with his boat, the *Perseverance*. Her birthday, like Sarah's, was on the 22nd, but of June, and she was eighty that year. She had been built in Campbeltown in 1912 at Bob Wylie's boat-yard, where the Jobcentre building now stands. On the day after, I noted at the Inneans: 'Here with Mike Smylie of the Perseverance, whose eightieth birthday was enjoyably celebrated yesterday.'

We set off for Machrihanish on the 10 o' clock bus and walked the coast. As we were climbing out of the Galdrans, we spotted the Greenpeace ship *Solo*, which was in the area conducting a whale watch, but she was too far out in haze to photograph. During our descent into the bay, Mike noticed an animal 'with a bushy grey tail' disappearing around a rock. Neither of us could figure out what it was, but years later I reached the conclusion that he'd seen a mink, a species which had begun to be become numerous all over Kintyre. In the bay, we found and disentangled a good length of lobster creel line, which Mike coiled and carried back to Campbeltown for his boat. He noted in my journal before we set off: 'A beautifully calm place to walk to as my first hike out into Kintyre. Thanks Angus (and for the coffee).' He too had brought coffee, which flavoured, with almonds, a Terry's Mocha plain chocolate bar. It cost him 95p in Woolworths that day, and the wrapper is still stapled into my journal.

Benjie the dog replaced Benjie the pony as Sarah's pet in 1996, and she transferred the name to him. He and I, and others with us, have spent many hours on and around the rock. George's photo was taken on 8 August 2008: '08/08/08', as I observed in my journal. That was Benjie's last time there – he was dead before the year ended. In the photograph, the rock is splashed with crow droppings, dark from the blaeberries the birds had been feeding on.

That fruit is what took – and takes – me so often to Fin Rock and the moorland around it. It's a pleasant spot for gathering, and I've never seen a stranger there. One by one, its features have entered my consciousness – the quiet heathery hollow; the little burn that ends as marsh close to the forest; the rowan where we'd cross the burn; the grassy slope which was a resting-place when the Rock itself was too windy to sit at; the rhododendron close by, another sheltering place, which, as it has grown, has become, like the Rock itself, visible from town; and a spot next to the forest fence, which also became a sitting-place.

In 2005 I wrote a poem at that spot. It came in minutes and I called it 'Evenings' and published it in *Rosemary Clooney Crossing the Minch*. I'd been gazing uphill and remembering a walk with Amelia and Bella in May 2001, which took us up the old peat road and on to the hill to the spot at which we

50. Mike Smylie, a visitor from Anglesey, with rope found washed ashore in the Inneans Bay, 23 June 1992. Photograph by the author.

stopped. I was transported in memory back to that evening and its clear light, and 'saw' us together again on the hill. The poem was the response.[26]

Soon after Benjie's death, I lashed a length of sea-sculpted driftwood to a fence-post there, with 'A Hundred Silences' painted on it. On 4 April 2009, a warm evening, I fell asleep under the stick, my head resting on a pillow of heather. When I woke I saw George McSporran heading uphill and away from me. Ordinarily, I'd have called to my old friend and either joined him or waved him on, but I knew he'd be making for the trig point on Ben Gullion to fulfil his ambition of logging sixty visits there in that year of his sixtieth birthday. He hadn't seen me and I let him go.

A fortnight later (18 April), while in a little hollow east of Fin Rock, another human presence entered the landscape – Jimmy MacDonald. The strange thing was that I'd been remembering an evening in May of the previous year when we sat there with our dogs 'in hazy evening light/... as cotton grasses swayed around us/each with its little banner of purity'. While alone there that evening in 2009, I heard a cough which I recognised as Jimmy's. I rose in puzzlement and scanned the hill, not seeing anyone until I heard my name called, and there was Jimmy and his dog Kosi returning home from a day at Balnabraid. He joined me for a chat and then continued on his way. I stayed long enough to write a poem, 'Jimmy's Cough', which was published in *Haunted Landscapes*, and from which the brief quotation comes.

Fin Rock, and its environs, is where Benjie's posthumous presence lingers most strongly, and it remains, five years on, a place for quiet reflection. Nine of the forty-two poems in my memorial volume to him, *Haunted Landscapes*, were written there. In these painful compositions, the relationship between place and memory is articulated with as much honesty and insight as was permitted me at the time. As I remarked in the booklet's introduction: 'In the months after Benjie's death, I walked the hills and shores of south Kintyre seeking – and finding – consolation in our old haunts. Consolation came also from the poems, which, whatever their merits, were written, I now understand, to heal a damaged spirit.'

In a curious way, the poems themselves have become, for me, integral to the landscapes they evoke (and this applies to my poems in general). I revisit certain places, and the harvest of memory yields not only the poems written there, but also fragments of the days of their composition. Thus, the creative act extends its influence beyond the thing created.

The Willows

The last place on Ben Gullion I'm going to in this part of the book is The Willows. George McSporran suggested the name, and it is apt – a thicket of willows grows out of the west-flowing burn in front of our sitting-place. George and I were there on 25 September and were surprised by how much the trees were now obscuring our view; but once the leaves are shed we'll see through the branches. There isn't much to see there, anyway, apart from trees. Most of them are spruce, but on the hill beyond there is a scattering of lodgepole pine (*Pinus contorta*). 'Scattering' isn't a great description of anything which has been planted, but these trees are set so much apart that they have scarcely changed the hill. That's one reason I like them. Another reason – they are individually recognisable, unlike spruce, which all look the same, especially when crowded together. Then there's the history of the tree – as 'lodgepole' might suggest, it was used in the construction of *tipis* by the North American buffalo-hunting tribes, who travelled great distances to cut supplies in high places such as the Black Hills and Bighorn Mountains.

The notion that the ancestors of these little wind-twisted pines grew on the American continent and were connected with the culture of the Cheyenne, Comanche, and Cherokee – all tribes beloved of childhood fantasy battles on that same hill, before a foreign tree was ever planted on it – never fails to excite my imagination. Twice I have sat and contemplated these pines on the facing hillside and tried to articulate in a poem my sense of wonder at their presence there, but each poem failed its inspiration, and the only bit that worked was the title, 'Immigrant Spirits'. I may yet find a framework for expression, as the Plains nomads found, in these trees, the framework of their lodges … or maybe this is it.

51. *Lodgepole pines on Ben Gullion, taken from The Willows, 6 May 2012. Photograph by the author.*

These duds (and others) aside, The Willows has been productive as a writing place, yet I didn't occupy it until 23 March 2008. Benjie then had merely nine months to live, which seems incredible because his 'presence' there is still absolute. Our first time there is clear in my memory. It was a Sunday of sleet showers slanting in from the west, and we sat in the shelter of sitka spruce and were comfortable. We would return together often, and Jimmy MacDonald and George McSporran, too, acquired the habit.

Soon after Benjie's death, I began building a cairn there, of stones lifted from all the other places we had frequented in his lifetime. At first, I was painting the place-name on to each stone in black enamel, but with the passage of time the stones have been added unmarked and are smaller. The cairn is modest and will remain so – if it were to expand too much, it might attract the attention of vandals. The Willows is remote, but nowhere on Ben Gullion can now be considered private. That peaceful spot is separated from a bike trail by merely a short hill-slope and a belt of spruce, and just as I chanced upon it, so too might others less respectful.

(On 22 December 2013, the fifth anniversary of Benjie's death, on my way through that strip of spruce to the cairn, I found a discarded plastic 'Irn Bru' bottle, and feared the worst, but there was no sign of interference when I arrived there. Actually, there are so many fallen trees in that part of the forest, as in many other parts, that there is no longer a direct route to The Willows. I sat there on a day reminiscent of that first day – westerly wind and driven sleet showers, which soon afterwards turned to snow.)

On 23 March 2009, the first anniversary of that first visit with Benjie, I made a little pilgrimage to the spot, and, on my way through the trees to reach it, I happened to notice several tufts of fur at my feet – they were Benjie's, who was by then buried in the pets' cemetery at Narrowfield. I must have snipped them there in the last months of his life. He had always hated being clipped, and was so traumatised after one experience that I resolved to do the clipping myself and spare him the ordeal. But he was no more willing to be clipped by me than by a stranger, and the method I devised was to carry a pair of scissors in my rucksack and to stealthily snip whenever I saw him distracted. It was always a work-in-progress, but kept him reasonably neat without unduly upsetting him. I lifted one of the tufts and stapled it on to a page of my notebook and have never seen the rest again. Not that I have looked – such a strange happenstance was meant for one day.

Jimmy MacDonald was at The Willows during the snows of March 2013 and photographed the whitened scene. It's all there in the photograph – the cairn; the driftwood marker at the cairn, with its legend, 'Destroy me, wind and rain/when all has been forgotten'; the naked willows; the grassy clearing beyond the burn, and the lodgepole hill beyond all. A print of Jimmy's picture hangs on my living-room wall as a reminder of our days there.

A trip to Cara

I was still in bed, though not asleep, when Duncan Macdougall 'phoned on 26 August. Judy was indoors and lifted the phone, otherwise it would have gone unanswered. Duncan, she said, when she came through to the bedroom with the 'phone, was asking if I would be interested in a trip to Cara. The same offer had come up the previous year and I'd declined it, but this time I said 'Yes'. To be honest, I had thought immediately of how this book might be enhanced by a visit to Cara. I had never been there, nor had any of my close friends except Murdo MacDonald, whom Duncan had taken the previous summer. And after I'd done the trip and spoken of it to friends, they all seemed to have been harbouring a secret desire to visit the little island!

Sandy McMillan – now retired in his native Campbeltown after a medical career – was also going and would collect me in his car at 11 o' clock. I packed food and a flask of tea in my rucksack, and checked that it also contained notebook, binoculars and camera. Looking back now, I should also have checked a few books and files for the history and lore of Cara, but there wasn't time for that. As Duncan would later explain, his final decision to cross to the island with passengers is always made on the day, once he has satisfied himself that the weather forecast is favourable. The year before, he and Murdo had a rough crossing on the way back.

52. Duncan Macdougall at the helm of Faoileag *crossing to Cara, 26 August 2013. Photograph by the author.*

Duncan was born at Glenbarr, and had settled back there after running the shop at Tayinloan until his retirement. When Sandy and I arrived at the ferry car-park at Tayinloan, Duncan was parking his car and boat-trailer. We accompanied him to the slip, where his fifteen-foot fibreglass boat, *Faoileag* – Gaelic, 'Seagull' – was already in the water, climbed aboard and were off across the Sound of Gigha. The bird life was scant that day, as far as we could see – a gannet sitting on the water and some shags and immature black guillemots.

Duncan took the boat into Port an Stòir ('Port of the Storehouse'), a creek in the north of the island, put Sandy and me ashore on the rocks, then moored the vessel. The ruined building there is perhaps too close to the shore to be a dwelling-house, and I now regret not having had a look around it. It is, presumably, the 'storehouse' of the place-name, but what was kept there? Kelp and wool immediately come to mind.

Duncan led us by a track to the island chapel, a ruin of late medieval construction. The Rev R.S.G. Anderson's *The Antiquities of Gigha* (pp. 114-17) contains a good deal of interest on the chapel, including a petition dated 9 June 1456 'in the island of Kara beside the Monkshaven', and a second identical petition, of 14 June that year, which identifies the place as 'the chapel of St. Finla in the island of Kara'. This 'Finla' (Gaelic *Fionnlagh*) remains, after due research, so historically elusive that I decline to speculate on his identity; but Anderson has scraps to offer.

Close to the chapel stands a substantial renovated two-storied dwelling-house, built around 1773 for the tacksman of Cara, who leased the island from the Macdonalds of Largie. The tacksman in the late eighteenth century was one Alexander MacMarcus, master of the ship *Beaufroy* and suspected of being prominent in the smuggling of foreign spirits into Islay and Gigha.[27] A short distance south-west of the house, an overgrown mound, which Duncan showed us, turned out to be, when we clambered on to it and looked into it, a circular corn-drying kiln of the type often found attached to ruined farming townships in Kintyre.

Cara, which is to the south of Gigha, is merely a mile long and less than half-a-mile broad, and in no time at all, it seemed, we were sitting on top of the Mull enjoying a late picnic lunch. *Maol Chàra* is the Gaelic for that distinctive lump on the south end of the island. It is, at just 185 ft, the highest point on the island. *Maol* has several topographical applications, but its primary sense is 'bald', and 'Cara' has been interpreted as Norse *Kari-ey*, 'Kari's island'. Who 'Kari' was, if the interpretation is correct, will never be known, but the assumption that he lived on or had claim to the island may be allowed.

53. Sandy McMillan and Duncan Macdougall (R) on the Mull of Cara, 26 August 2013. Photograph by the author.

'Cara', in the twentieth century, became a female personal name, and according to *The Oxford Names Companion* (p 721) it derives from Italian 'beloved' or Irish Gaelic 'friend'. I suspect, however, that some Caras whose parents have connections with Kintyre or Gigha owe their name to the little island. The first 'Cara' I ever heard of was a road-sweeper in Campbeltown, Davie Gilchrist, but his was a nickname, marking his family's former residence on the island.

By the time we reached the Mull, sunlight had broken through the cloud, transforming the island with intenser colours. From the top, there was a fine view south to the Kintyre Mull, which was catching streamers of mist blowing in on the westerly breeze from Ireland. Less than an hour later, all that remained of mist in Kintyre was a patch drifting across the north side of Creag nan Cuilean, but the coast and hills of Antrim were hidden in a white spouting wave of it.

54. The author on the Broonie's Chair, Cara, 26 August 2013. Photograph by Sandy McMillan.

After we'd eaten, Duncan led us straight down the eastern slope of the Mull to the Broonie's Chair. Approached from above and examined from close proximity, the rock doesn't much resemble a chair, but from the south-east it distinctively does. Few people, other than spontaneous visitors from yachts, set foot on Cara without having heard of the Broonie. As Sandy and I were about to clamber ashore at Port an Stòir, someone remembered that hats should be removed and a greeting delivered. Since Sandy didn't have a hat, I gave him mine for the brief ceremony, and we both muttered 'Good morning, Mr Brownie'. Anderson specifies only that 'the laird and minister were expected to lift their hats in salutation to it, as they stepped ashore from their boats', but the custom is now widespread. As Alex McKinven records in his history of football in Campbeltown, *Kit and Caboodle* (p 205), the virus of the superstition even spread to Campbeltown Pupils A.F.C, whose players and supporters, when passing Tayinloan en route to away games, would 'wave in unison' to the 'wee man', to ensure that luck was with them in the fixture ahead.

I am not, myself, immune from superstition. In fact, in addition to the superstitions I've had from childhood, I'll adopt the superstitions of others, and even create my own ritual observances, made to measure, as it were. Most folk, having been shown a rock shaped like a seat, will want to sit on it, and I wanted to sit on the Broonie's Chair, but since it's the Broonie's and since I'm superstitious, I hesitated. I seemed to recall a photograph of Dr Kenneth MacLeod sitting on the chair, but as he was God's representative on Gigha at the time, did he enjoy divine protection from the spirit's infamous malevolence? I conferred with Duncan, who assured me that most of the visitors he took to Cara were keen to sit on the chair, and did so. I suppressed my irrational anxieties, climbed on to the rock and sat. Since the Broonie is Cara's greatest asset, unless you have Campbell blood in you, I'll return to him and examine the traditions which keep his memory alive on the island (Appendix 6).

55. *The Mull of Cara, from north-west, 26 August 2013. Photograph by the author.*

While I was on the chair, Duncan and Sandy went as far south as they could safely go – which wasn't far – until the rock wall which forms the end of the Mull appeared in sight. The cliff isn't high, but it's dramatic. Shags nest there in large numbers in the breeding season, which was past; and below the areas of the cliff which offer nesting and roosting space, the smooth rock faces were whitened with excrement as though a gang of painters had been up on scaffolding with pots of whitewash. The other obvious feature of the cliff is a huge hole, which Duncan had been told was caused by a meteorite strike, but the *Old Statistical Account* of Gigha and Cara records that the rock fall was caused by a lightning-strike in the autumn of 1756, during a nocturnal hurricane.

That the noise of the rock falling was heard, and the shock felt in their houses; that the sea rose so high against the rocks on the west side of the island as to be carried over the whole breadth of it in heavy showers; that the houses were all unroofed, and the stacks of corn overset; and that all the people were obliged to extinguish their fires, and take shelter in the only slated house on the island, which fortunately suffered no damage.

I have no opinion on the cause, but the cavity is certainly remarkable ... and the tons of rock which once belonged in it are piled unmistakably on the shore below.

On our way back to the boat, I noticed around forty geese on the shore below us. I carelessly assumed that they were all Canada geese, but Duncan, who was ahead of me with Sandy, had already counted eight greylags in the flock. The latter didn't stay around to be looked at, but flew off north cackling. These geese were in a beautiful bay which maps identify as Poll an Aba, 'The Abbot's Pool'. Anderson (p 117) finds in this name 'a recollection of some ecclesiastical primate of Iona', but this may be too adventurous a suggestion, even with the nearby medieval chapel in mind. Place-names aren't always what they seem to be, and, to my knowledge, no authentic tradition survives to colour the name's background.

The Kintyre Antiquarian Society's *Place Names of Gigha and Cara* (1945) is noticeably lean compared with the two booklets on Campbeltown and Southend parish place-names which preceded it. The introduction to the booklet reveals why, in a singularly (for those restrained times) barbed remark: 'The Committee had no intimate knowledge of the natural features to which the Names applied. They asked and hoped for help on this point from Gigha, but that help was not forthcoming.'

I am puzzled, however, as to why none of the committee, not least its avid and industrious convenor, Duncan Colville, saw fit to visit the islands and see for themselves the 'natural features' with which they were familiar only from maps.

'Aird Fhada', the stony arm which juts into the sea on the south side of the Poll and secures it as a natural harbour, is interpreted in the Antiquarian Society's compilation as 'Long Height or Headland', but it is clearly (even from maps) neither a height nor a headland. It is a low-lying point, and the simple interpretation is 'Long Point'. (Gaelic *àrd* can mean either 'height' or 'point', and sometimes only familiarity with a feature so named can resolve the ambiguity.)

Two rocks to the north-west of Poll an Aba are interestingly named. A tidal rock, Eilean na h-Achrach, is 'Anchorage Rock', and Sgeir Mhic Ghaiche is 'MacGeachy's Rock' in the O.S. form. MacGeachy was once a common name on Gigha, but families of that name are now concentrated in Campbeltown, some of them by migration from Gigha in the nineteenth century.

The *Aska*

Back at Port an Stòir, Duncan proposed showing us the whole island from the boat, and we headed south again and around the Mull, which was all the more impressive from the sea. Mid-way up the west side, he steered out from shore so that Sandy and I might have a closer look at a shipwreck he'd pointed out to us from land, as two black lumps – which, left to myself, I'd have assumed were rocks – repeatedly revealed by the motion of the swells. These metal chunks of an engine are the sole visible remains of some 4000 tons of ship, and as Duncan dodged his boat around the wreck, my imagination began to sink, reluctantly, into that vast sea which rolled under the little boat's hull and over the *Aska*'s remains. How much more of her was there, underneath? Duncan, I am sure, knew exactly what he was doing, but imagination can be a fearsome tool when it starts to grind away. And it was grinding again, soon afterwards, as we rounded the north end of Cara, close inshore, and I was looking at hundreds of kelp tentacles all around the boat, waving hypnotically and invitingly – *Come join us*! It would appear, in retrospect, that I, a non-swimmer, am comfortable in small boats only when I am not aware of what's under them, unless it's sand and it's close to shore and shore's where I'm going!

The *Aska* must surely have been one of the most spectacular shipwrecks in local history. When she grounded off Cara she was ablaze, and the slow approach from south-west of that floating inferno must have been an awesome sight to all who witnessed it. Built for the British India Steam Navigation Company in 1939, to ply between Calcutta and Rangoon, she was big, a cruise-ship with 200 cabins and space for more than 2000 deck passengers, to which add a crew of 180. When war broke out, she was requisitioned as a British troop-carrier, and in that capacity left West Africa in September 1940 with 300 French troops, 50 British and a crew of 184, mostly of Indian nationality. She was bound for Liverpool and voyaging alone, her top speed of seventeen knots freeing her from convoy participation. But when she reached the north coast of Ireland on 16 September, having eluded U-boat predations in the open Atlantic, she was attacked off Rathlin Island by a Luftwaffe bomber. Six officers and six other crew were killed instantly by the first direct hits, and when the *Aska* caught fire she was abandoned without further casualties.

A week later, aground off Cara, she was still burning, and salvage crews standing by were powerless to act. By the time the fires burned out, she was being pounded by heavy seas, and the salvage operation was abandoned. Subsequently, however, she was 'heavily salvaged for scrap'.[28] That chunk of engine – said to be the flywheel – has become her memorial. It is strange to think that 4000 tons of ship could be reduced to just that little reminder of a cataclysmic war.

A visit to Cara in 1953

I conclude with an account of a trip to Cara sixty years before mine. It appeared in the *Campbeltown Courier* of 24 September 1953 under the title 'The Brownie Haunts Cara', and its author was John Herries McCulloch, described as 'of the Scottish *Daily Express*'. I had looked at the article over thirty years ago for its reference to goats on Cara, and remembered it and looked again at it. I'd never heard of McCulloch, but my initial impression on reading the article was that he had a farming background and a connection with Galloway.

Sure enough, as I found out by internet searching, he was born in Galloway and worked on farms in Canada after he emigrated there as a young man. He would later attend the University of Toronto, from which he graduated with a B.Sc. in Agriculture. He then turned to journalism and continued in that career when he returned to Scotland. I was surprised at the number of books he'd written, at a time when getting published wasn't as easy as it would become with the arrival of computer technology. His work clearly continues to be admired, not least the three books he wrote about sheepdogs, one of which, *Sheep, Dogs and Their Masters* (1938), evidently remains a classic of its genre.

His idealistic vision of Cara's renaissance as a working farm has proved to be just that, and he might struggle now to recognise the island as the one he explored sixty years ago. Its green acres have been invaded by bracken, the 'fat rabbits' appear to be extinct, and only the goats remain. During my brief visit, I saw merely two, but during the circumnavigation of the island in Duncan's boat I counted around forty, some all-white and others with the dark colourings of native feral stock (introduced, Duncan said, from Jura). In 1879, Cara was described as 'A good Grazing Farm, capable of carrying about 130 Sheep and 10 head of Cattle, or thereby.'[29]

Here is McCulloch's report, visionary effusions and all.

Just to shed some of the culture which fell so heavily on me during the Edinburgh Festival, I went down to Kintyre. There I sailed to a strange and beautiful little island where there is no culture at all, and where the only music is the thin bleat of a wild goat, or the nocturnal piping of a Brownie – if you have ears for that kind of music. The island is Cara. It lies a mile south of Gigha and a man could walk round it in an hour. It is as sweet a fragment of Scotland as you will ever see, with acres and acres of natural pasture as green and springy as a lawn, and a two-storied house which was built on a slope with its windows looking out on Kintyre. Its back is to the winds of the Atlantic.

And high up on the miniature Mull of Cara – it is only 185 ft. high – there is a chair and table of rock which are used by the Brownie who took up residence on the island soon after it rose from the sea. If you do not believe that you should not read another word of this piece.

John McMillan took me across the Sound of Gigha to the island in his motor boat. Two pretty sisters from Grangemouth, who were holidaying on Gigha – Evelyn and Margaret Bell – had heard of my repeated attempts to arrange a crossing, which had to be made in good weather because of the bad landing places, so they took the chance to join us as deck-hands. They had met McSporrans for the first time on Gigha, and when they encountered the name of McVanish they were ready to believe anything about Cara.

The last man to live in the house of Cara was Angus McGougan, and he used to have a place set at the table for the Brownie. But Angus has been dead for many years, the house is now empty and neglected, and the Brownie has the whole island to himself.

And it is no use telling me, with the scorn of a town-bred man, that I cannot produce anybody who has seen the Brownie. For a Galloway or Kintyre man knows that a Brownie is a good-natured and helpful sprite who haunts farm-houses and appears only at night – when the moon is in the right quarter.

Since nobody has spent a night on Cara since Angus McGougan left it, how can I name anybody who has seen the little man? But if you care to spend a night in the house of Cara to vindicate your scepticism, it could probably be arranged with Captain John MacDonald, the owner of the island. He lives at Gortinanaine, over in Kintyre.

We anchored the boat to the rocks at a tiny cove and explored the island. It comes easily to the feet, for not many rocks break through the turf, and there is not a tree or bush to be seen, which makes it oddly different from Gigha, less than a mile away. It used to support 100 sheep, but all it supports today is a swarm of fat rabbits and a herd of wild goats. We walked into the house and found that the goats now climb upstairs and use the bedrooms as lounges.

At one time cattle must have been raised on the island, for there are well-dyked little infields and the ruins of farm buildings. Indeed, quite a bit of the land could be cultivated as easily as the productive land of Gigha, and it would probably produce as good crops. At first glance, it looks like a good farm lying idle. It's not as simple as that, of course. It took me a week to arrange my crossing to the island. Each time I was ready, the weather became rough and made the landing too difficult.

Before a farmer could succeed on Cara, he would need a pier, and a boat big enough to carry livestock over to Gigha or Kintyre. It could be done, of course, and with a sturdy boat and a landing-place an enterprising man could hardly fail to make a good living, for he could augment his income by fishing for lobsters. They are plentiful around the island, and of very high quality.

The right sort of man may come along. He will not pine for the flesh-pots and the carnivals of culture. He will be resourceful and a hustler, but not so active and self-sufficient that he will forget to go up to the Mull sometimes, when the long twilight is falling across the Sound of Gigha, and sit down with respect in the Brownie's Chair and make a wish. When that man appears on Cara, the island will bloom again.

A larch and a rowan

There must have been a bad gale between 18 December 2011 and 8 January 2012, but I don't remember it. Whenever it happened, it blew down many trees on Ben Gullion. On the former date, I was in a place I called 'Crosshill Vista', and returned to it on the latter date, only to find that two larches had toppled across it. The place itself is quite ordinary to look at; most places are, until something or someone transforms them (even should that transformation be in the mind). Situated between a strip of larches and the gully of a stream, it is a corridor of pale grass in winter and of green bracken in summer. It leads uphill from a walkers' track and joins a cyclists' track. On the upper corridor are two low grassy mounds, probably formed by Forestry Commission workers when the trees were planted in 1979. When I was first attracted to the place, I'd sit at the lower mound, but shortly afterwards I decided I preferred the upper one, which was next to a fair-sized rowan growing from the upper edge of the gully.

I went there often for years, mostly in winter and sometimes with friends, but more often with only Benjie. The place was of Ben Gullion, though definitely lower hill, and could be reached quickly and easily. I was never bothered there by other walkers or cyclists, whom I would merely hear or see, and it became a place in which poems would come to me unfailingly. In truth, I became so habituated to writing there that I dragged out poems which I recognised as stillborn even as they emerged, and I'd curse myself for having sacrificed an hour I might have devoted to simple contemplation. But, of course, the very state of contemplation tempts one to pursue a track of thought which promises the perfect written end.

On 28 August, George McSporran 'phoned me to suggest an evening walk on Ben Gullion. I agreed and said that I'd bring along a saw and that we could make a start on clearing Crosshill Vista. It wasn't just that one of the trees was blocking the 'vista' itself – encompassing the east end of the reservoir, Cross Hill, and the hills to the north – but the same tree had crashed into its native neighbour, the rowan, and was lodged in its crown.

For anyone with superstitious tendencies, the rowan is *the* tree you simply do not interfere with at all. Its magic is so strong that it was the tree to plant close to the door of farmhouse or cottage to repel witches (what measures country folk adopted when they migrated into town I never learned: perhaps the evil forces could not follow them). I have recorded and discussed rowan superstitions elsewhere and will skip the particulars here, adding only that respect for the rowan's supernatural reputation is, even now, a potent legacy among some country folk. Yet, I have known an incomer remove an unwanted rowan from his garden and survive the act – a case, perhaps, of 'Know nothing, fear nothing'.

George's son Sandy had come along and took a spell at the sawing. We made one cut through the larch close to the rowan, then Sandy climbed the rowan to try to dislodge the severed length and topple it down into the gully. That bushy top proved difficult to budge – some of its branches were locked with the rowan's and others were stuck in the ground – but we sawed away at the branches and finally managed to dislodge the top by pulling and rocking it. Then we sawed off another length of trunk, thereby opening up our sitting-place, and the view from it. Sandy began on a third cut, close to the base of the tree, but by then the evening light was fading and midges were at us, so he gave up.

By then, too, I had begun to agonise over our violation of the larch, which had been my idea. What right had I to interfere with a natural accident? The larch had blown over, but sufficient of its roots remained in place to feed the upper trunk, whose growth continued green and vigorous. Before commencing our operations, I'd apologised to the rowan for the impending damage to it; but it had comfortably survived the larch's fall on to it, and the larch had survived its own fall.

Fate, if you like, had united the two, and I had come along and separated them, one to live and the other to die.

My companions offered sensible reassurances – the rowan is native and the larch alien, and the larch's weight might in the end have uprooted the rowan – but I remained troubled, in my obsessive way, and returned to the spot four days later to inspect the remaining length of larch for signs of life. I found two little tufts of growth close to the severed end, and when I next spoke to George I suggested we postpone completion of the final cut in case the tree should prove capable of surviving, even in these most pathetic of circumstances.

Larches, of course, aren't typical conifers. All larch species have the same peculiarity – they shed their needles in autumn, having first turned them a beautiful yellow-orange colour. And as winter nears its end, the emergence of the little green tufted buds on the Ben Gullion larches intimate, for me, the coming spring. If it were possible to accurately count both larch and rowan on Ben Gullion, I wouldn't be at all surprised if there were now greater numbers of the native species on the hill. Since its afforestation and the virtual exclusion of sheep, rowans have been sprouting all over. Many of them have seeded in such exposed spots that they'll never attain more than a few feet in height, but their powers of endurance are undoubted, and even the little ones can bear fruit. The rowan in Gaelic is *caorunn*, which is cognate with *caoir*, 'blaze'. Anyone who has looked at a well-grown tree laden with bright-red berries will understand why, and those birds which rely on the berries for food – not least the migrants from hard winters in the north, quick-winged foraging fieldfares and redwings – respond to these colour-splashes on an otherwise drab landscape as we might to the neon signs of city restaurants.

'Sheggans' and Seamus Heaney

Returning from Crosshill Vista to our bikes at Knockbay, we passed a 'camp' of wild irises, which for years has been our 'window' on the seasonal fortunes of that lovely and – in the structure of its floral organs – extraordinary flower. 'Camp' is Gerard Manley Hopkins's word, from his journal of 1873, and earns my admiration. What I see behind that choice is a military camp, for the big pointed leaves of the irises are like 'drawn swords', as a nineteenth century botanical writer observed. Geoffrey Grigson maintained that the wild iris, or yellow flag, its other 'standard' name, had 'become a poet's plant by the nineteenth century', and I'll turn soon to a poet whose achievement crossed from the twentieth into the twenty-first century, Seamus Heaney.

That 'camp' to which I refer is on Knockbay land, in a damp corner between the bottom Ben Gullion forest trail and the farm road. George and I often pass it heading on to, or returning from, Ben Gullion, and we watch for the appearance of the big yellow flowers in late May or early June.

There are two names in Kintyre for the wild iris, 'sheggan' and 'shelister'. The first is a form of Scots 'seggs', which covers a range of botanical species and is related to English 'sedge'; the second is Gaelic *seilisdeir*. That dual identity has intrigued me for years, and I return to it repeatedly in my regular *Kintyre Magazine* feature, 'By Hill and Shore'. I make no apology for recalling the subject once again, for that evening George and I stopped to look at the iris colony. The flowers were withered by then and only the leaves remained. We remarked on a poor flowering summer for the sheggan, and then passed on. Perhaps, however, we simply hadn't been among them enough; my June and July, certainly, had been devoted more to cliff and moorland habitats. When I returned home and checked my e-mails, I found one from Agnes Stewart, in which she mentioned the death of Seamus Heaney.

Sheggans and Seamus were already conjoined in my memory. In a poem of Heaney's – 'To George Seferis in the Underworld', published in the *Times Literary Supplement* of 19 March 2004 – I had noticed the word 'seggans' (he was not afraid to spice his poems with dialect words from his rural boyhood in County Derry). The word, however, wasn't glossed, so I wrote to him, care of his publisher, Faber & Faber, to ask him what he meant by it. I wasn't optimistic that he'd reply. Famous people – and he was famous even before his receipt of a Nobel Prize in 1995 – don't always welcome the attentions of strangers (who, if not psychopathic stalkers, might be autograph-hunters with investment in mind).

Letters, I suppose, are judged on their merits. In my case, a linguistic enquiry, and no sinister implications there. I received a reply, and was grateful for the generosity of a busy man. The message was written on a card – privately published by Peter Fallon at the Gallery Press in 1995 – with a reproduction of a Felim Egan watercolour on the front and three lines from Heaney's poem 'The Strand' printed on the inside. The message was dated 16 July 2004, and there was no address, which I understood entirely – a prolonged correspondence was not on offer. The message:

> Very grateful for your field-worker's knowledge of the "seggans" word – it was what we called sedge. I'd no idea of the Gaelic connection. Speaking of using the old words, I always remember John Montague's report of the praise he got from the poet Patrick Kavanagh, after he'd done a poem on the old people he'd known in his youth. "You got in the bag apron," says Kavanagh. All good wishes – Seamus Heaney.

The 'Gaelic connection' Heaney alluded to was a misunderstanding – probably I'd also mentioned *seilisdeir* in my letter – but it was clear from his reply that his 'seggan' was a kind of sedge, a group of grass-like wetland plants, and not the wild iris. Montague and Kavanagh were, of course, fellow-poets of Heaney's and both also Irish. Kavanagh's idiomatic style, with its easy evocation of places and people in his native Monaghan, exercised a powerful influence on Heaney's own artistic development.

What intrigued me most about the two Kintyre words for the one flower was the historical significance. *Seilisdeir* was the earlier native Gaelic word, while 'sheggan' was brought in with the plantation of South Kintyre by Lowland settlers in the seventeenth century, a political scheme which was paralleled in Heaney's native Ulster, but with infinitely more damaging social consequences. In Kintyre, the two conflicting communities, and cultures, were effectively integrated by the mid-nineteenth century; in Ulster, the division persists and continues to manifest itself in hatred and violence.

I put my thoughts on that dual persistence into a poem which I titled 'Wild Irises, Knockbay', and dedicated to 'Seamus Heaney's "Seggans" of Ulster'. Somewhere, I contended, an 'invisible boundary' must exist, with 'shelister' north of it and 'sheggan' south, but that dividing line could no longer be determined in the absence of 'the old ones' who had 'gone on to their underworld/and taken the language into silence'. The poem, as I recognised fully only after its publication, failed the subject, and failed it badly. I had struggled to make my ideas cohere, and when I had revised the piece to a point at which no further revision seemed possible, I pretended to myself that I had done enough. The poem should have been discarded, and the subject revived after that flawed effort had receded in memory, but I published it in *The Silent Hollow*, in 2005, and sent Heaney a copy of the booklet.

He replied, on a picture postcard of Victor Hugo photographed in 1884:

> Well, of course, I liked page 7, but there were other favourites, from the title poem through to the "Hasp" and "A Name". Glad too to see you're still sticking to the pipe ... Many thanks for sending the book – Seamus Heaney.

The dud poem was on page seven, and I very much doubt if he found much to admire in it, but 'like', like 'nice', is a fuzzy endorsement. The reference to my smoking habit relates to the photograph of me printed on the back cover of the booklet, standing, pipe in mouth, with Benjie, in the ruins of Smerby Castle in October 2002. With that message, the brief correspondence ended. I am certain he would not have wished it to continue. Still, I have these hand-written messages from Heaney, which, perhaps, come to think of it, are what I really wanted all along.

'Shelisters'

I am still on the dialectal trail of the irises. 'Sheggan' I seldom hear now from anyone, except myself and George, and we scarcely count, since we are conscious of breathing life into a dying name. 'Shelister', however, is fit and well in its homeland, North Kintyre. I was at Rhunahaorine School in July, to conduct a little 'workshop' on Gaelic place-names with the pupils. Afterwards, since the day was fine, the head teacher, Ruth Reid, led us up to the nearby site of old Largie Castle. On our way there, we passed a wet corner of a field with irises in it, and I asked if there was a local name for the flowers. 'Shelisters' was the reply, and I was told that 'boats' were still shaped from the leaves. Ruth later told me that she had learned how to make the boats from a teacher on Lismore, Frieda MacGregor.

I'd first heard about 'shelister boats' from a native of Tarbert, Iain Sinclair, who was holidaying at Polliwilline in July 1996. My daughter Bella and I went over to his caravan and were given a demonstration of the various styles of boat which could be made by bending and twisting the leaves. We later tried them in a pool on the shore, and then in the open sea, and they performed admirably.

George Campbell Hay wrote a comical poem, 'The Crew of the Shelister', which was broadcast on Children's Hour in

1948, along with commentary. The commentary would have been needed, because the poem is dense with dialect words and obscure details on boats and ring-netting, all of which would be quite incomprehensible to anyone who lacks a fishing background ... and a Tarbert one at that! The poem tells of a fishing trip in which everything is miniaturised to the scale of the boat itself. It is very accurate in all its detail, and very clever too. I have heard bits of it recited in Tarbert as though it were a product of folk tradition, but its authorship became indisputable with the publication of Michel Byrne's *Collected Poems and Songs of George Campbell Hay* in 2000.

I consulted Alexander Macbain's *Etymological Dictionary of the Gaelic Language* for the underlying meaning of *seilisdeir*, but there was no enlightenment from that quarter. Cognate forms in Irish, Middle Irish, Welsh and Old British were presented, and a Late Latin form, *alestrare*, for comparison. Douglas Clyne, however, in *Gaelic Names for Flowers and Plants* (p 101), offered this explanation:

> Seilisdeir m, from *sol*, the sun, and *leus*, from the Latin word *lux*, light. The endings *tar*, *dear*, or *astar* are common in plant names – as *oleaster*, *cotoneaster* – and mean *one of a kind*. Thus seilisdeir means the plant of light – *fleur de luce*.

That little word *leus*, in the above quotation, I recognised from Tarbert fishermen's vocabulary I collected in the 1970s. It has almost certainly faded from memory there, since it had a very specific application in the ring-net fishery, which is itself now history. In the nocturnal search for herring in the sea-phosphorescence, or *losgadh*, a single fish sighted in the water was a *leus*, Gaelic for a light or glimmer.[30] And so, it would appear, the more one advances on the trail of knowledge, the more one stumbles on beginnings.

In Grigson's *The Englishman's Flora*, among the forty 'local names' he listed were the following relatives of *seilisdeir*, 'laister' in Cornwall and 'shalder' in Devon and

Somerset. For how many millennia back would one have to go to find the ancestor of the word *seilisdeir*, and where in the world would it be? These questions excite my imagination, and reinforce my gratitude that in *seilisdeir* we have an old warrior, his sword still held in readiness, who refuses to be vanquished by the successive waves of Scots and English would-be usurpers. May he stand fast on the battlefield of language for many generations more!

56. 'Sheggans'/'Shelisters' at Knockbay, 22 May 2011. *Photograph by the author.*

My interest in etymology was stimulated forty-odd years ago by an old volume I bought in a Glasgow second-hand bookshop, Archbishop Trench's *On the Study of Words*. One name in particular caught my attention and stuck in my memory, 'daisy', which is 'day's eye', from Old English *daeges eage*. According to the *Concise Oxford Dictionary*, the explanation is that the 'disc [is] revealed in the morning', but I cannot think of many flowers whose 'discs' don't close at night and reopen in daylight, and I prefer Archbishop Trench's elucidation (p 60):

> For only consider how much is implied here. To the sun in the heavens this name, eye of day, was naturally first given, and those who transferred the title to our little field flower meant no doubt to liken its inner yellow disk or shield to the great golden orb of the sun, and the white florets which encircle this disk to the rays which the sun spreads on all sides around him. What imagination was here, to suggest a comparison such as this, binding together as this does the smallest and the greatest!

'Shelister' leaves are tough and durable and are suitable for weaving into mats and lightweight baskets, and local salmon fishermen, in pre-refrigeration times, used them for wrapping fish in. I recorded these practices in an article in the *Kintyre Magazine*.[31] Jim McAlister's grandfather, Duncan, was a fisherman at Garbhchroit and sent salmon to market in wooden boxes with the fish wrapped in leaves to help keep them fresh. Jim, who was brought up at Acra, Grogport, knew the wild iris as 'shelister'. For Archie Graham at Peninver, further south on the east side of Kintyre, the name was 'sheggan'. He recalled that the leaves were handy for wrapping individual fish. They'd be spread lengthwise on the fish, enclosing it completely, then secured with twine and trimmed to make a neat parcel. With a label attached, the fish would be despatched on the afternoon bus to Glasgow and collected at that end. As I remarked in my article: 'This use of organic material, free and naturally regenerating, may be contrasted with present-day plastic packaging, which consumes energy in its manufacture and ends up as litter or in land-fill sites.'

There is another old botanical survivor in Gaelic that I wish to introduce, but before I do I'll mention a further word for the wild iris recorded by Grigson. It is 'cheeper', and he ascribes it to Roxburghshire and explains it thus: ' ... from making a cheeping noise with the leaves.' This rather spare explanation might well have puzzled me, but I know exactly what is meant. Wet your index finger and thumb with spittle, grip an iris leaf well down its length, then draw your hand steadily up to the tip. The resultant sound should surprise you, and if it doesn't it'll certainly delight any children in the company and excite them into competition with one another in generating the loudest and funniest noises. 'Cheeper' is probably as good a name as any, but had I been inspired to create one myself, I'd probably have chosen 'squeaker' or 'screecher'. I no longer remember whether the practice was demonstrated to me or whether I discovered it for myself, but it won't fail to entertain – my daughters will attest to that!

Finally, where might that invisible boundary, separating the two words, have been? I suggest, from late twentieth century evidence – admittedly incomplete – that Grogport to Glenbarr would be a fair reckoning.

Ròideagach

I presented the word *ròideagach*, enclosed in a little anecdote, in *The Ring-Net Fishermen* (p 140). I had recorded it, on 25 May 1978, from Robert Ross, a retired Tarbert skipper, while taping him on local dialect. I had it in my mind for long enough that he'd introduced me to the word, but he hadn't. A much older fisherman, Hugh MacFarlane (born in 1884), had brought it up earlier that month. Hugh described the plant to me, but couldn't put an English name to it. Robert did, and gave me the anecdote as well. Since

1974, when I began my researches into ring-net fishing, I had become familiar with hundreds of dialect words, most of them from Gaelic, but this one was new to me and I never heard it again.

Its survival, I now realise, hung on a thread, and that thread ran from Hugh MacFarlane and Robert Ross to me, at which point its passage through oral transmission probably ended. Early in his life as a fisherman – between 25 April 1949 and 12 December 1952, to be exact – Robert Ross crewed on the Tarbert ring-netter *Mairearad*. Her skipper was Archie McDougall, and the skipper of her neighbour-boat, the *Fionnaghal*, was Archie's brother Donald. That family was known in Tarbert as the 'Toms', to separate them from the other McDougall families in the village, who had their own by-names. I was told that the first to be given the name 'Tom' was their father, Donald, from his frequent use of Gaelic *tom*, which in fishing terminology described a bunch of herring seen or heard in the water.[32] These McDougall brothers seem to have had a robust Gaelic vocabulary, though they weren't Gaelic-speaking in any strict sense, and Robert, in his years of fishing with them, himself acquired a little stock of Gaelic words additional to those in common currency. The little story the word survived in was this. A ring-net boat was close inshore searching for signs of herring in the dark, when the man on the bow called aft to his skipper: 'Keep her off – I can smell the rojagach!'

The plant is bog myrtle (*Myrica* gale) – with fir club moss, it is a badge of Clan Campbell – and it is the strongest smelling of the moorland flora. I have seen the scent described as 'eucalyptus-like', but I'd be hard-pressed myself to attempt a description. The aroma comes from a resinous substance exuded by multitudinous tiny glands all over the plant. Rub a leaf between thumb and finger, then smell the scent from your skin – it's powerful. And that is the point of the Tarbert anecdote – the *ròideagach* is so strong-smelling that its scent, wafted out to sea, was a warning that land was near. It was told as a joke, but behind the joke lay a whiff of reality.

Bog myrtle had a range of traditional uses, not least as protection from midge and flea bites. It is now processed commercially as a natural insect repellent and for use in cosmetics. Bog myrtle – or gale, 'its proper English name', as Grigson put it – also gave flavour to ale and beer before the popularisation of hops, and continues to be used in beer as well as in spirits.

Ròideagach is a variant of standard *ròid*, but more than that I haven't been able to discover. As with *seilisdeir*, preceding, my imagination has seized on this Gaelic survival-word. How many generations of Gaelic speakers in Kintyre did that word pass through on its way to the extinction which Hugh MacFarlane and Robert Ross arrested? What is its status now – living or dead? I doubt if it has survived meaningfully in Tarbert, but I keep it going myself in conversation, when the opportunity comes up, usually when hill-walking; and a few Gaelic speakers have picked it up from me. Yet, is it truly mine to nurture and transmit? Its last refuge, to my knowledge, was Tarbert, so how can I lay claim to it?

Well, that's how words are spread and take hold in communities. If one person adopts a word, because it sounds attractive or gives expression to a concept otherwise ill-served, and introduces it to friends in natural conversation, and it takes hold and spreads, then good – that's the way words and phrases travel! That most of these words and phrases now arrive via electronic media is deplorable to the likes of me, but that's the way of modern society, and no amount of condemnation will arrest the trend.

Strange as this admission may appear, the only location I could claim to find bog myrtle in lies on the north side of Craigaig Water close to the sheep-fank (p 129) ... until, that is, I had a walk to the lochs above Killean with John MacDonald on 13 June.

A walk above Killean

We took the 11.30 bus to Killean and started out on the Kintyre Way. I'd gone that way twice in 2012, first with Amelia, Judy and Murdo MacDonald, and then with Judy alone, scrutinising and photographing places for *Kintyre Places and Place-Names*. I shall state immediately that the rare species of bird, of which John and I enjoyed several sightings, will not be flying into the following account. I am keeping it out, in the interest of protecting its sanctuaries, and in so doing omitting the ornithological successes of the day. A case of conscience over-ruling conceit, and the reader being left to wonder. If it is any consolation, reader, you'll probably gain more enjoyment in guessing the species than my descriptions would have given you.

I have known John MacDonald for most of his life. I first met him at Kilchousland when he was about eight years old, and he remembers my showing him hermit-crabs in a rock pool. I broke up oatcake, sprinkled it into the water, and we watched the crabs feed on the crumbs. At John's age, seashore life – and hermit-crabs in particular – had also fascinated me. Another ploy was to collect empty winkle shells on the beach, drop them into rock pools and wait for crabs to discover them and begin checking them out as replacement homes; sometimes a shell would pass the test, and I'd see the crab lift its soft abdomen out of the old shell and into the new, usually after several tentative moves.

Days later, I posted John a little book on the seashore to encourage his interest in natural history. He was living in John Street at the time and I would probably have forgotten him, but in 1978 the MacDonald family moved into the newly renovated house next door to mine in Crosshill Avenue. Early in 1980, John began accompanying me on hikes and was a frequent companion until the middle of 1983, when his younger brother, Jimmy, took his place. Both still accompany me from time to time, but – strange to say – never together.

On that day, John was with me and would be showing me some lochs he'd fished since his teenage years. But there would be no fishing for John that day – we were walking, and committed to catching the late bus home at Muasdale. The day was dull and remained so until the final half-hour of the walk – as we were descending Clachaig Glen, the sky cleared to blue and let the sun out.

I don't enjoy the uphill slog from Killean. Going back that way is more pleasurable, and not only because it's all downhill, but also because the views to the west are open and alive. Although this was merely my third walk from Killean, a routine had already been established – with the 'uphill slog' completed, lunch at Loch an Eich. First time there, on 12 April 2012, we'd sat – Amelia, Judy, Murdo and I – in a heathery hollow overlooking the loch. I notice in my very brief journal entry for that day that 'sleet was falling' while we sat. Amelia and I climbed the hill at the loch, Cruach an Eich ('Stack-shaped hill of the Horse'), to examine the cairn on its summit, and I photographed her standing beside it, for the book. Hilltop cairns are rarer in South Kintyre than in North, for reasons I cannot even conjecture.

Like boulders (p 125), cairns could serve as boundary-markers; they could mark resting-places where funeral processions had stopped; or where a person had been found dead; and the biggest of all cairns, which are over four thousand years old, were built for communal burial over many generations. Massive cairns like these invite the theft of stones for other building purposes; small cairns encourage the addition of stones to make them bigger and to bring the donor good luck.

A cairn, certainly, is a simple and effective means of leaving one's mark on a landscape, for any reason, or for no particular reason at all. I have built only one small cairn in my lifetime, to Benjie. Stone structures of any description can be difficult, if not impossible, to interpret. Twinning-pens, for example, may be found anywhere in the hills. They are small drystone enclosures which shepherds built to confine a ewe, which had lost her lamb, with a lamb which had lost its mother. In theory, by putting the two together in such a confined space, the ewe was compelled to let the lamb suckle from her, and, from that intimacy, would ultimately adopt the orphan. Once identified, the twinning-pen, wherever subsequently encountered, is unmistakable. Similarly, but on the coast, low-walled drystone enclosures – too small to be fishermen's seasonal huts – puzzled me until I heard about duck hunters' hastily assembled hides.

57. Twinning-pen at back of Ben Gullion, with Cnoc Moy and the Slate on western skyline, 20 May 2012. Photograph by the author.

Judy and I were back at Loch an Eich on 21 April 2102, but I don't recollect that we found the original sitting-place, and I could not decide where it might have been when John and I left the track and made our way to the loch. This failure nagged at me slightly because, ridiculous as it may seem, occupying a resting-place which feels comfortable and right is, for me, almost an act of consecration; and when I return there, it is to worship, if you like, at a shrine of memories.

58. Close-up of twinning-pen in Largiebaan Glen, 8 April 1984. Photograph by the author.

John and I ended up on the very shore of the loch, next to a clump of bushes, under which I took shelter when a shower of rain came. While we were there, a green van pulled up on the road and the driver began watching us through binoculars. I then began watching him through binoculars, an exercise which I am certain yielded no useful information to either party. I guess he suspected us of being deviants from the Way, perhaps anglers or egg-thieves.

Loch an Eich is 'The Horse Loch', but the horse wasn't an ordinary animal. It was a water-horse, a dangerous supernatural creature which could kill a man or woman without remorse. That one was supposed to have eaten all the trout in the loch, but I have been assured by anglers that there are trout there. Perhaps the evil beast has gone the way of fairies and 'bockans' and all the other mythic beings which infested the ancestral landscape. Rev D. J. Macdonald had this to say about the loch in 1908:

> The legend goes that a horse, on the way to the fair, bolted, shook off the 'hems' at Braids (or the braes), the collar at Tigh an t-sùgain, and then disappeared into this loch. It has no trout. The horse is supposed to have devoured them. When a proposal was made to restock the loch, it was objected that it would serve no purpose. They would all fall a prey to the horse. A shepherd reported that he saw the track of a horse in the snow, after which piece of circumstantial evidence, sufficient to convince the most sceptical, nothing remains to be added![33]

John and I next stopped at Loch Losgainn ('Toad Loch'), and I saw there my first white water-lilies in a lifetime, not just in Kintyre, but anywhere. South Kintyre has few natural lochs of any description, partly owing to topography and partly to agriculturally-inspired drainage schemes over the past three centuries, particularly in the low-lying Laggan, or Moss, to the west of Campbeltown. The flowers were few at that early stage of summer and not fully opened, since they spread their petals only in sunlight, and that day was dull; but I was close enough to one to be able to photograph it. Lily flowers can grow to eight inches across, making them the largest of any native plant in the British Isles. John had been familiar with water-lilies ever since he began trout-fishing in the North Kintyre lochs, and reeled off the names of other lochs in which he'd seen them, including the two we'd visit next, Beag ('Little') and Mòr ('Big').

We sat and ate again at Loch Beag, on a knoll at the west side which I'd chosen as the ideal spot, but in reaching it I blundered into marshy ground and soaked the insides of my new and (for me) expensive boots. I'd fill them shortly afterwards, just past Loch Mòr. We'd noticed, as we passed that loch and headed towards Clachaig Glen, what appeared to be the foundations of a hut and associated dykes. Having looked at the structures and passed on, I then decided I ought to record them, so we turned back and I took the photographs I wanted.

Mindful of the time and the bus we had to catch at Muasdale, we were hurrying back to where I'd left my rucksack when I walked into a bog-hole. I was in over my boots and I stuck there, and then toppled slowly forward. I had my camera in one hand and, wishing to protect it from a ducking, I landed on my elbows and was thoroughly immobilised. I remember firing off a volley of curses, and when I finally extricated myself and turned towards John, who was behind me and had observed the fall in tactful silence, I noticed he was smirking guiltily. I had to laugh myself, but I was in a mess with mud and water.

As we headed downhill towards Clachaig Glen, the bog myrtle appeared in huge thickets. I was almost intoxicated with the sheer profusion, which continued even beyond Achaglass ruins.

Rubha Dùn Bhàin

I again jump forward in time, to 10 October, and also breach the terms of the book's summery title; I shall do so twice more, with greater justification. Justification for this? It ties up a few 'loose ends'.

A trip out to Rubha Dùn Bhàin was Jimmy MacDonald's idea, and he invited me along. I was last there with him and Judy on 14 June 2012, when we later took the opportunity of visiting the ruins of Innean Gaothach ('Windy Cove'), a Campbell settlement to the south.[34]

Judy was unable to accompany us on our 2013 trip to the cliffs, but drove us almost to Glenahanty, where I logged an overdue ornithological 'first'. As I was lifting my rucksack out of the boot, I heard a harsh call, which Jimmy identified as a jay's. These woodland crows have been around Kintyre for years; I had noted and published the reports, but as yet hadn't seen any. Jimmy was already scanning the hillside, which had been felled, and was able to locate three birds amid the tree stumps. With his directions, I focused my binoculars and picked out the birds in that ravaged landscape. Jays, like all members of the crow family, are very intelligent. One of the Canadian jays, Clark's nutcracker (*Nucifraga columbiana*), is said to be capable of memorising the locations of at least two thousand food caches.[35]

Past Largiebaan, as we turned off the Kintyre Way to cross the stretch of moorland to the belt of sitka spruce between us and the cliff-edge, I identified a thicket of bog myrtle – a further record of that plant which had been intriguing me all summer. I had to conclude that it is commoner than I had supposed and that I just hadn't been noticing it.

As we walked the grassy margin on the landward side of the turf-dyke along the cliff-edge, I noticed an abundance of old cow-pats and immediately thought of choughs – this was the very stuff which might help tempt them back! Futile speculation? The nearest thriving colony is on Islay, and, as Philip Watson had revealed in a lecture the previous evening (p 271), there is one breeding pair hanging on in Rathlin, which is nearer still to Kintyre. Since the chough disappeared as a breeding species from Kintyre, individual birds have occasionally been reported, but as yet there have been no signs of re-colonisation. It may, of course, never happen, but I wait and watch in hope. Re-colonisation has been effected by human agency in the south-west of England – could choughs from elsewhere also be released in south-west Kintyre?

The day was sunny, but with a brisk, cold northerly breeze, so Jimmy and I had difficulty in finding shelter on the cliff-top. When we finally settled into the most comfortable spot we could find, overlooking the Rubha, or 'point', from the south, we were rewarded with a flurry of raptors: buzzard, red kite, kestrel, and sparrow-hawk. The kite was a special sighting, not least because we were looking down on it as it swung around below the sheer rock-wall of the promontory, the bright sun highlighting its plumage colours. (I had seen my first ever red kite in October of the previous year from Ben Gullion, but it was soaring high over me in silhouette and only its forked tail revealed its identity.) Jimmy was able to take several photographs, and, when he examined them minutes later, noticed a coloured tag on each wing. He subsequently informed me that the tags indicated that the bird had begun its life in Central Scotland in 2006. We had been in 'the right place at the right time'. As I remarked to him, 'The raptors are queuing up to be noted', but, as is often the case, not another bird of prey appeared all the time we remained there.

Expected sightings included ravens, hooded crows, and rock doves, but there was an unexpected bonus: a dozen whooper swans, brilliant white and in formation, flying over the Atlantic towards the North Antrim coast. Their airborne presence is usually betrayed by their persistent calling – the 'whoop' which gave them their name – but they were miles out to sea and we heard nothing. Most of the whooper swans which pass over Kintyre in early autumn are migrants from Iceland, heading to habitual winter quarters further south, but in wet seasons, when the Laggan is a plain with many reflective eyes of tempting water, they may descend in their hundreds to break their journey by resting and feeding. Small numbers winter annually in Kintyre and may be seen, feeding, grooming and resting, on all the lochs and reservoirs with which I am familiar in the south of the peninsula. Occasionally, sick or injured birds are unable to undertake the return flight to the Icelandic breeding grounds, and linger through the summer.

Rock doves – up to twenty of them – were a continual presence on and around the cliffs. I particularly noticed them

– not for the first time – on the surface of a distinctive square-shaped rock lodged well below the cliff-top. I estimated its dimensions as 12 by 12 feet and about 5 feet deep, but Jimmy's comparison with the roof of a small garage is probably more suggestive. The rock had clearly broken away from the upper cliff and been arrested in its descent by a snub of rock, which has been holding it in place for perhaps hundreds or even thousands of years. Jimmy said that so far he hadn't been able to identify where the rock had been dislodged from. As rocks go, it's a beauty, but I wouldn't want to be anywhere below it if it finally breaks loose and resumes its downward journey. If and when that happens, will there be even one human around to notice its departure?

Barr Glen

On 8 September, Judy and I took the 3 p.m. bus to Glenbarr and set off into Barr Glen. It was our first time there on foot, and, though we failed to reach our intended destination, we were glad we'd seen the glen in its early autumnal colours. Brambles were ripening by the roadside, and as I walked I was picking the biggest and ripest of them, along with a few hazel nuts. I hadn't eaten since a mid-day bowl of cereal, and the berries were welcome, but by the time we passed Kilmaluag I was ready for something more substantial.

There was a light drizzle by then, and I suggested that we stop for a bite and a cup of tea. An old gate leading into trees soon appeared to our left, and we crossed it and sat under a venerable ash. Even when the rain turned heavy, we stayed dry under the tree's still-leafy branches. There was a line of boulders piled at our backs, and I guessed they'd been tumbled there during field-clearance generations ago. We took a look, before we left, at what lay beyond the boulder zone, and, sure enough, there was a field with sheep grazing in it. Barr Glen, to judge by the big smooth riverside fields, must have been a grain-producing valley of some note; and I know, from historical research and from oral tradition, that in the nineteenth century no small part of the barley crops went to the distillation of illicit whisky.

Amod steading is one of the prettiest rural buildings I've seen anywhere in Kintyre. Its appeal, to me at any rate, is partly architectural and partly positional – it stands at the very roadside, presenting a clean face to the passer-by. An outbuilding next to it has a date-stone incorporated high in the gable with 'AD 1879' crudely carved in it.

William Gilchrist

Amod was the birthplace in 1811 of William Gilchrist, who would become a successful printer and publisher in Glasgow, and a friend of the Islay poet William Livingstone, an edition of whose Gaelic verse Gilchrist published in 1865. He later moved with his parents, Archibald Gilchrist and Peggy McMillan, and older brother John, to Drumnaleck, near Clachan, and from there to Glasgow, where Archibald, in 1839, was recorded as a 'spirit dealer'. Kintyre was behind them, but not their Gaelic identity.

By 1871, Gilchrist had a staff of twenty-six men and boys in his Glasgow print works. He was producing posters, pamphlets, programmes, playbills, broadsheets, tracts and advertisements, as well as books in Gaelic and in English. A bound volume of posters printed on his presses is held by the National Library of Scotland in its rare books collection. He was also a shrewd investor, his portfolio including shares in property, Canadian railways, and, closer to his origins, the Campbeltown and Glasgow Steam Packet Joint Stock Company.[36]

Gilchrist's birthplace would have been a long, narrow steading with a fire in the middle of the floor and a thatched roof. Perhaps its stood on the site of the present Amod;

perhaps it was elsewhere within the boundaries of the farm, and all that remains of it is a mound of overgrown and forgotten stones. There is one certainty – he wouldn't recognise the present Amod if he could return in the twenty-first century for a look around the glen of his birth. He died in 1879, the very year on the date-stone of the 'new' Amod.

Garvalt

Just before Arnicle, we turned on to the track to Garvalt, on the north side of the glen, and found it closed off by a high fence with a notice pinned on one of the corner posts: 'Danger! Unsafe Building. Keep Out.' The roof of the main structure has collapsed and big chunks of roughcast have been dropping off the wall.

In the earliest record of the place I have seen, for 1502, the name is spelled 'Garwald', but nothing much is known about anyone there until John McCallum took John McIntylior in Dippen, Carradale, and his son Donald, to court over the theft of five stone of butter belonging to him. On 18 December 1686, the McIntyliors were ordered to pay McCallum £12 Scots for the butter and casks, and were also fined £20.[37]

At a ceremony in Glenbarr School in the summer of 1943, Dugald McMillan, shepherd in Garvalt, was presented with the Highland and Agricultural Society's Silver Medal for thirty years' service with the Macalisters of Glenbarr.[38]

Five years later, the shepherds at Garvalt, James Hunter Scott and William French Scott, a father and son from the Borders, lost their jobs for poaching salmon in Barr Water. They pleaded guilty at Campbeltown Sheriff Court, on 8 December 1948, to taking nine out-of-season fish using an acetylene lamp and gaffs. The Procurator-fiscal, A. I. B. Stewart, argued that 'no one in their senses would eat salmon at this time of year, as they are full of roe', and suggested that poached fish were being 'sent out of the district'. The suggestion was denied by James Scott, who claimed that he didn't know about a close season: 'We took them home to eat ourselves. I have three of a family and we were short of meat and needed some.' He said that he and his son were still at Garvalt, each earning £4 19s a week, until replacement shepherds could be found. James was fined £2, with the alternative of twenty days in jail, and William £1 or ten days, with fourteen days allowed for payment of the fines.[39]

The stream that runs past Garvalt is called Allt Mòr, 'Big Burn'. Not much imaginative power went into that naming effort! Gaelic *allt* also went into the name of the farm itself, *Garbh allt*. The adjective *garbh*, 'rough', has been encountered already in Sròn Gharbh, 'Rough Point', but here 'wild' would be a truer interpretation, thus 'wild burn'. It certainly expressed itself plainly that day, rushing and roaring downhill, its waters the colour of weak tea.

We hadn't gone far past Garvalt when I noticed big clumps of shrubbery growing on the bank of a ditch. It was bog myrtle. Judy immediately requested a decent-sized sprig of it to keep midges at bay, and I fetched her one, and a smaller sprig for myself. She tucked hers into the top of her jacket, and I stuck mine in my cap, but its efficacy was questionable. So late in the year, the leaves had dried out and lost their potency, as I confirmed when I rubbed them and smelt my fingers: the scent was faint compared with what it would have been in summer. We would encounter, as John MacDonald and I did on our June walk not far from the head of Barr Glen, veritable thickets of the shrub.

We had been heading for Stockadale, an interesting little Norse-named ruin at the head of the glen, but when the track past Garvalt ran out, our enthusiasm also ran out. We were both weakened by colds, and the sight of marshland and coniferous plantations every way we looked persuaded us that this was not going to be the day we reached Stockadale. Forty years earlier, in a treeless landscape, we could have gone straight to the ruin in the time left to us, but the prospect of seeking routes through spruce plantations, and over the tussocky and often marshy margins of these plantations, persuaded us to try again another day and perhaps from another direction.

59. *Carradale Girl Guides in Barr Glen, c. 1983. L-R: Gillian Ramsay, Doreen Rennie, Dawn Campbell, Shona Ogilvie, Audrey Martindale, Louise Purdie, Lorna Edwards, Sheila Henderson, Catriona McKinnon, and Ann Purdie. Photograph by Judy Martin.*

Judy had been in the glen thirty years earlier with a party of Girl Guides from Carradale. It was a 'scorching hot' day, and they were to have met up with Anne Littleson and her Glenbarr Guides, but the heat was too much for some of the Glenbarr girls, Judy later heard, and the get-together never happened. She and Gillian Ramsay and the nine Guides had a picnic at Arinanuan, on the opposite side of the glen from Stockadale, and then returned to the cars and Carradale. A photograph Judy took that day shows a landscape torn up for trees, but evidently not yet planted. The girls are posed in a line on a desert-like surface, no doubt also connected with forestry operations. I see on the distant horizon a hazy-blue *cruach* – a hill resembling an elongated peat-stack – and I also see, at the girls' feet, a Tesco carrier-bag, which is puzzling, because the Tesco supermarket in Campbeltown wasn't built until 1993, and it wasn't Tesco's then – it was Wm. Low's.

So we faced back down the glen, close to the end of which, as night fell, the houses with their lit windows seemed cosy and inviting. Passing Skernish, with its horses and outdoor array of old agricultural implements, I remembered Adam MacPhail, who had farmed there, and who, with his tales of witches, water-horses, giant serpents, and much else, was one of the most interesting of all the old country folk I tape-recorded in the late 1970s. Back at the bus shelter at Glenbarr, Judy and I watched the pale after-light of the sunset fade over Islay and the Atlantic until the bus appeared out of the darkness, twenty minutes late owing to a road accident at Arrochar.

Sròn Gharbh II

I was sitting on Knock Scalbert on 13 August, contemplating, among other matters, this book and the shape it was taking, when my thought-dogs dug up a little coincidence which I am pleased to develop, though it may impress no one else. There are two places named Sròn Gharbh in Kintyre – which isn't exactly the coincidence that interests me – one of them south of Machrihanish and the other east of Tarbert. This book began with Benjie on Sròn Gharbh (south) in 2006 and ends with him above Sròn Gharbh (north) in 2007.

In 2008 I published, for private circulation, a booklet titled *Laggan Days*, in memory of the poet George Campbell Hay. Among the little photographs on the back cover was one, taken by Judy in September 2007, of Benjie and me on a heathery knoll. East Loch Tarbert, Garval Point and Barmore Island are all in the background, and I judged that the photo was taken above Rubha Maol Daraich and captioned it accordingly. My good friend of thirty-odd years, Archie Smith – a 'Dooker' by birth, upbringing and continuing affiliation in the annals of memory – knew better and corrected my error. Therefore, Benjie and I, in that photograph, are 'above Sròn Gharbh'.

The three of us were heading that day for Laggan Loch, following the Kintyre Way from its starting point at Tarbert, and I explained the journey in my introduction to *Laggan Days*. In 2010, Archie Smith had sent me three photographs of the loch, printed on a single page. That loch is identified on maps as Loch na Machrach Bige, 'Loch of the Little Plain', but is more simply known in Tarbert as 'Laggan Loch'.

In the first of Archie's photographs, taken in July 2005 from a Forestry Commission track, the loch is hardly visible in the east. The second photograph, with Archie's dog Dileas ('Faithful') in the foreground, was taken at the loch shortly before Archie visited me, for the first time, on 1 September 1981. I was unmarried then, living at 24 Crosshill Avenue, and my first book, *The Ring-Net Fishermen*, had just been published, which was the reason for Archie's visit. The final photograph, in black and white, was taken in the spring of 1957, before Archie left Tarbert for the Forestry Commission School in Benmore, Perthshire, and his late brother, Malcolm, occupies the foreground.

For complex reasons, these photographs tore at my emotions. My responses were no doubt partly connected to my memories of George Campbell Hay, who had walked these Laggan hills from boyhood, and whose 'spirit' must, I reasoned unreasonably, linger there. I had never, to my knowledge, seen Laggan Loch, and decided that 2007 should be the year I returned to the Laggan hills – Malcolm Smith had been there with Archie fifty years before, and I was last there twenty-five years before. Numerically – or superstitiously – the trip had to happen in that year.

I had walked that coast twice in the early 1980s, but hadn't given it much thought since then; neither had I given much thought to George Campbell Hay nor to herring fishing (and I didn't want that theme stealing back into my poetry, being certain that I had written it out). At the end of August 2007, however, these influences all resurfaced and fused to produce the burst of energy which created the poems in *Laggan Days*.

On Sunday 8 September 2007, Judy and I drove to Tarbert intending to walk to Laggan Loch, but we didn't reach it. I had misjudged the time we'd take to get there and back, and we set off too late; the day was grey, with rain showers, and we wouldn't have seen the loch at its best; and the further we went, the less fair the hike seemed on the ageing Benjie. Having passed Allt Beithe, 'Birch Burn', we continued just long enough to allow us a glimpse of the mist-shrouded summit of Cruach an t-Sorchan – 'Stack-shaped hill of the foot-stool' – which had loomed large in Hay's memories of his early years.

In 2009 we tried again to reach Laggan Loch. The date was 6 September, but I had difficulty in finding the entry in my journals. When I did find the date – thanks to Judy's having pulled it out of cyberspace in an e-mail I sent to Jimmy MacDonald the evening before – and checked the journal, I discovered why I'd failed to find the entry when flipping through the pages: it consisted of less than half a page. The reason was that rain fell for most of the day, the weather forecast which Judy consulted having failed us. When I found and read out the entry to her, she remembered being impressed by my dedication as I sat in the rain scribbling urgently, so that something of the outing might be recorded at the time.

We had managed to improve a little, but only a little, on our previous distance, and I remember our sitting in a quarry at the furthest point we reached, eating lunch and looking through sheets of rain at Cruach Lagain. The little loch of our desire was beyond that hill, but by then we were so wet and miserable we decided, without regret, to turn back. Jimmy MacDonald was with us that day, but Benjie was not. On our way out, I'd laid a copy of *Laggan Days*, enclosed in a plastic sleeve, on the knoll above Sròn Gharbh where he and I were pictured in 2007. I hoped someone would pick it up and look at it carefully enough to find the image and connect it with the place, but I have no idea what became of it. Perhaps wind and rain disposed of it – yes, litter! – but it was a heartfelt offering to the memory of a companion who had once travelled that way with us.

Laggan Loch at last

I finally reached Laggan Loch on 28 September 2013. Since the previous attempts had both been in September, I felt that this one should be too, but I almost ran out of time. John MacDonald was keen to come, since he had fished every loch in Kintyre with the exceptions of Loch na Machrach Bige, its neighbour Loch na Machrach Mòire and a few other little ones in that area. He works on a Campbeltown trawler, and a Saturday was the only day that would suit him for the outing; but the weather that September was poor, with prevailing rain and mist, and there was no suitable Saturday until that last one. When it came, however, it was perfection, as sunny and as warm as a day in summer; aptly, a day like the day that opens this book.

John and I caught the 8.30 bus to Tarbert – an early start for me, but not for him – but we were without Judy, who had other commitments, and we missed her map-reading skills. My attention to such matters is perfunctory, and so it proved on that day. We made good time after a breakfast halt at the picnic table in its grassy 'siding', passed the quarry where Judy, Jimmy and I had sheltered four years earlier, and kept on going until John expressed concern. After a look at the map, we decided to cut off the Way and find Loch na Machrach

Mòire, and from there orientate ourselves to Laggan Loch. (It was a time-wasting blunder, which a closer examination of the map earlier in the walk would have prevented; the obvious departure point from the Way was behind us, as we would later realise.) After fifteen minutes on a strip of moor, we found ourselves, perplexingly, back on the Kintyre Way. We began searching for Loch na Machrach Mòire – which kept itself concealed in trees – and I was on my way to Skipness, with the Arran mountains in full view ahead, when John, who had been prospecting further back, called me to a halt. After a further look at the map, our position became clearer and we decided to climb a nearby hill, from which, we reckoned, Laggan Loch might be visible.

60. John MacDonald casting a line at Laggan Loch, 28 September 2013. Photograph by the author.

We were half-way up the hill when John noticed a fringe of blue water in the distance. We agreed that it must be Laggan Loch and hastened towards it over a stretch of moorland which led us through a marshy 'tongue', as John described it, between plantations. We followed the edge of the westerly plantation and when we turned the corner, there was the loch. Photographs were taken where Archie Smith had snapped his brother Malcolm in 1957, then we skirted the eastern shore of the loch towards one of two little promontories on which we had decided we would sit.

61. Looking back on Laggan Loch, 28 September 2013. Photograph by the author.

I arrived there alone, however – John was already assembling a fishing rod. I watched him casting time and again, but not so much as a nibble came his way, and he finally gave up and rejoined me. Minutes after sitting, he held up a red berry he'd found beside him and asked if it was edible. It was a cowberry – I'd noticed the plant, with its glossy evergreen leaves, all around the loch – and I suggested he try it. He pronounced it 'tart' and then found one for me, which I ate and found not only tart but rather dry. After refreshment, he resumed casting from the promontory, again without success. 'The jury is out on this loch, whether there's fish in it', was his verdict. In the meantime, I had been watching and photographing dragonflies and damselflies – some of them mating – and logged four species there. I could have done with longer at the loch, to meditate – preferably in solitude – on Campbell Hay's past presence there, but, thanks to our misjudgements en route, time was short.

We left at 3 p.m., to catch our bus at 4.55, choosing a westerly route which took us from the north end of the loch over tussocky ground to the foot of Cruach Doire Lèithe – 'Stack-shaped hill of the grey oak-grove' – where we found and followed an old fence which mercifully took us back on to the Kintyre Way. That, we agreed, was the route we should have taken to the loch, and would take if we ever returned. By then, we were left with an hour and fifteen minutes to get back to Tarbert, and we believed, almost to the last, that we'd manage it. Gallingly, however, we missed the bus by eight or nine minutes. We'd lingered beside the track to admire four peacocks – the only butterfly species observed all day – gathered on the still-fragrant flowers of buddleia, and that diversion was probably the difference between success and failure.

In the final stage of the walk, which had almost turned into a jog, I couldn't help but reflect that to other walkers, who began to appear the closer we approached the castle, I must have looked like one of those 'heads down' fanatics that I myself profess to despise! I was all set to hitch-hike home from Tarbert, but John had a meal to cook for a friend who would be arriving at 8, so he ordered a taxi to take us back to Campbeltown. I shan't divulge what the journey cost him, but I reckon the fare exceeded my entire expenses on food, tea and tobacco for that entire summer in the hills. It had been a wonderful summer ... and it was over.

62. *Benjie and the author above Sròn Gharbh (Tarbert), taken looking north, 8 September 2007. Photograph by Judy Martin.*

Appendix 1

Holding on to Time: Poetry and Midden Refuse in the Life of Angus Martin (1991)

Angus Martin

Craigard rightly opens this piece. It is the name of the house in which I was born in 1952. It has been empty for nearly two years now, but on most days of the week I sit there in my Post Office van, looking across Campbeltown Loch to the hunched shoulders of Ben Gullion. I eat my piece there, and, when I'm in the business of poetry, work on the typescripts which I carry around with me. Occasionally I'll even write a poem there. Craigard is a grand house, but I didn't know its grandeur for long because it was then the maternity hospital for the Campbeltown district, and I was soon on my way to a post-war housing scheme – the 'Steel Hooses' – closer to the hill, but further from the sea.

The sea, for as far back as I can remember, has been a part of my life, first in imagination, then in reality. Before I left school at fifteen to become a fisherman, the sea and the fishing were preoccupations, and much of my free time – in all weathers – was spent hanging about the Old Quay.

My father was first a fisherman and then – after wartime service in the Royal Navy and several years as a mining engineer at the coal-field at Machrihanish – a merchant seaman. I didn't, as a boy, see much of him, but I thought a lot about him, and was reminded of him by the many picture postcards that reached me from his ports of call. I thus acquired a fair knowledge of geography, but not much knowledge of my father. While he was home, however, I soaked in his yarns about the sea and fishing, and I decided early on that there could be no other life for me.

The reality of the life, however, was less romantic, and five years of fishing – on and off – were sufficient for me. When I left the job in 1978, I was already turning into a vegetarian (my family and I are now vegans) and had begun to dislike killing fish – not an ideal state of mind for a fisherman.

Four generations of Martins preceded me at the fishing, and they were real fishermen: boat-owners and skippers, many of them. I have paid tribute to them in my supernatural poem 'The Captains', of which this is the final verse.

> Let me shake your hands. Goodbye, captains.
> Be careful out there, where you are bound.
> Perhaps you have forgotten certain dangers –
> fingers of gloomy shore and the sunken teeth of reefs –
> and remember there are new lights everywhere.
> You'll manage, I daresay, but do not tell me where
> you're going, or I may wish to go with you,
> a passenger just – no skills to serve you with –
> sitting below, hearing the tongues of the sea
> and the creaking of the skiff's old bones,
> a boy in the bilgy dark, hunched at a mug of tea,
> far from home, my captains, very far from home.

Dalintober was their home, a village physically apart from Campbeltown until the late nineteenth century, and a community spiritually apart beyond that. Up until the Second World War, Dalintober had its own fishing fleet, which lay at moorings across the loch from Campbeltown.

My first book, *The Ring-Net Fishermen* – a product of my collaboration with the artist Will Maclean – was the history of a method of herring fishing evolved by the men of Kintyre.

It was a beautiful method, and the boats were beautiful. In the early 1970s, as a fisherman myself, I experienced the end of the job. I also caught, in that decade, the last of the old men who had known ring-netting before mechanisation destroyed the old ways. I tape-recorded many many hours of their knowledge, a big intake of diverse lore, some of which has seasoned and become poetry.

The same with research I did for two subsequent books about Kintyre. My informants then were old farmers and shepherds, and elements of their lives too have reappeared in my poetry.

Fishing themes have persisted since (in 1985) I began writing poems again after a silence of twelve or thirteen years. These themes have persisted because in a book of some 100,000 words I failed to realise the mystique of fishing. In my poetry I have come closer to an expression of it, but I cannot claim more than that.

I have managed better, I think, with the other main part of my heritage – the land. It's more on my mother's side, and I have concentrated on my farming ancestors in the Southend district of Kintyre: MacKays, MacKerrals, MacEachrans, MacCaigs, and the rest, old native stock, with roots deep in the land. I have managed better because I know less about farming than about fishing, and have never been a farmer – i.e., I'm not burdened by experience and tradition, and am satisfied with small insights.

The legacy of farming is much more tangible than that of fishing. At Dalintober I can look at

> ... sea-walls with mooring-rings intact;
> the stumps of net-poles
> rotting in the ebb;
> boot-sculpted slabs descending into water;
> street corners where they'd gather
> in the lee of weather,
> notching out an edge of stone
> honing knives.

There isn't much else – boats and all are gone.

... But the sea? I look out at times from land
to it, and what is it? On the surface,
effacement of all history.

I can go, however, to ancestral hill-farms and find these places much as they were when my people left them. True, the houses are ruined, and encroachment of forestry has destroyed much of the grazings. But the land remains – the same soil that generations of ancestors cultivated, and it holds tokens of their time there.

The collection of midden refuse has been for several years a hobby of mine. The interest isn't as unhealthy as might at first appear. The middens have been abandoned for as long as the farms themselves, and only the hard elements remain, purified by time: fragments of china and clay pipes, shells of shellfish, bones ... These I gather into envelopes – each marked by date and location – and place in the bottom of a display-cabinet, a means, I suppose, of holding on to time. My poems too – or many of them – are commemorative.

The need to record certain kinds of experience (and the little shoots of philosophical insight that grow from them) is one of the main forces behind my poetry; but I'm not always able to take a subject and write about it immediately. Some ideas have taken years to grow into poems, and usually appear unexpectedly.

The best of my work, I think, surfaces quietly from the dark pool of the unconscious. I catch a phrase from the disturbance of my thought, pull on it, and up come phrase after phrase until a poem entire lies fresh on the page, like a gleaming fish. But the majority of the poems I write are puny and unpalatable. They can't be returned whence they came, and I sometimes regret an idea wasted; but if the idea is strong, it will offer itself again: different fish, same species.

On the first day of this year, I walked to Balnabraid with a friend, Sid Gallagher. My MacKerral forebears were tenant-farmers there from 1770 until 1838. Sid watched me gather shards around the ruin and then suggested that I create a mosaic with all the pieces in my collection. I have no real intention of doing so, but the suggestion turned into this poem two evenings later.

> From all the china fragments
> I have gathered in my years
> of prowling round deserted habitations
> kicking down molehills and picking over
> the exposed earth of middens
> some day a mosaic will materialise
> when I take to the floor and surround
> myself with the thousand pieces.
>
> These will resolve themselves into
> the image of a ploughman steering
> a beautiful ship of horseflesh and iron
> through a breaking sea of the earth
> with the sun about to set itself
> in the six red shards from Cashan.

I had already made a poem about the gathering of shards. It appears in *The Larch Plantation*, and its title is 'Erradil'. I wrote it during an evening snow shower, on 3 April 1990, at the ruined steading of that name. My great-great-great grandmother Amelia MacKay was born there. These are the first and last verses.

> There is snow with the last of the sunlight
> coming down through the neck of the glen,
> and my pockets are heavy with shards
> of china, each glaze-veined
> with the dark earth's ageing ...

> Here is a curved, blue-patterned
> rim fragment of a drinking bowl;
> perhaps your young girl's lips were on that bowl
> when someone called you from the fire
> and startled you,
> 'Amelia! Amelia!'

Many of my poems are biographical, in a sense. *The Larch Plantation* contains poems written about my grandfather, Duncan Martin; my father, Angus Martin; an aunt, Carrie; an ancestor, Malcolm MacKerral; the Kintyre poet who was my friend, George Campbell Hay; an old Tarbert fisherman, Hugh MacFarlane, and a Campbeltown tradition-bearer and distant cousin, John Campbell, both of whom I recorded extensively, learned much from, and became very fond of.

Genealogy, too, has its role in my verse. Without my interest in remote ancestors and the places they inhabited, a field of inspiration important to me would have been inaccessible. The wider subject is an occasional passion with me, and I have amassed a great body of data on Kintyre families. I happily share – and am frequently asked to share – it with the returned descendants of emigrants. I charge none of them for my services, but some buy a book or two of mine.

The poetry itself appears almost anywhere. I often write at my own fireside after my wife and daughters have gone to bed and the house is peaceful, but if I feel inclined to write earlier in the day then I can retreat to a hut at the end of the garden. The hut is furnished with an old writing-desk, table, chair, small gas heater, paraffin lamps and a stock of candles. I take out pipe, tobacco and a flask of tea, and am happy to sit out there in all weathers. It is a very private place, and no visitor is encouraged to find me there. But I seldom stay longer than two hours. I find writing taxing, and a couple of hours is long enough to spend grappling with the forces of the unconscious.

At other times I'll write when I'm walking alone on hill or shore, or cycling. The very act of walking, or cycling, stimulates creativity. And there are certain places conducive to writing – Point, a ruined steading overlooking Davaar Island and accessible by bike in fifteen minutes, is one of them. Two of the later poems in *The Larch Plantation* were written there.

At Polliwilline, near Southend, my wife and I have a small caravan. The location is perfect for us and our daughters – for us, miles of rough, cliffy coastline to the north, rich in fauna and flora, and for them a safe and sandy beach in front of the caravan, with green countryside round about it.

I go there occasionally on my own during writing phases, and spend a night or two. I miss my daughters intensely at first, but once I have attuned myself again to solitude, and the girls' bedtimes have passed, I feel better and usually manage to write. The subjects are as diverse as the thoughts that come to me. Poems might materialise from a gull, or an owl crying in the night, from a memory, or from an outbreak of imagination.

The last night I spent there was only a week ago, and I wrote eight poems. None is particularly good. I'd walked eleven miles of lonely coast to get there, and on the day after walked the miles back, in a freezing wind and snow showers. The walk was more satisfying than the poems I carried in my notebook, but life can be like that: sometimes the journey is more rewarding than the destination.

The Scottish Book Collector, Vol. 2, No. 10, April-May 1991 (editor Jenni Renton).

Appendix 2

A Trip to the Largieban Caves

'Ariel'

On Friday last a party of us set out from this to pay a visit to the Largieban Caves. Having procured a guide at Largieban, we proceeded to the Caves. Our course led us to the top of a precipice at whose foot they were situated. Wild and rugged was the scenery around, almost perpendicularly steep, the precipices below. The guide led us a little to the one side of the precipices where there was an incline covered with grass, and rather more divergent from the perpendicular. Down this we proceeded without any great difficulty, and then advanced to inspect the caves. These are in number three. The entrances are large and spacious. Hanging from the roofs of the caves like inverted pinnacles are some beautiful stalactites formed by the filtering of water through limestone beds. Here the sparry concretions hang like a sheet of water that had been frozen in the act of falling, there they assume the form of a small yet beautiful stalactitic pillar; while yonder, stalactite and stalagmite combine in forming figures the most grotesque.

The height of the caves is very variable, at one time we were compelled to crawl on hands and feet, at another, we were in a large vaulted chamber.

The Duke of Argyll visited these caves last summer, and, with the extensive knowledge of Geology which His Grace is well known to possess, he must have taken from these many a valuable geological specimen.

After some time spent in wandering through their dim recesses the time drew near for us to leave. Outside the cave the prospect was one of wild and rugged grandeur. We were standing at the foot of a frightful precipice of tremendous height. To our left were rocky eminences and craggy steeps. High up on the front of a cliff there were written as with Nature's pen the two letters N and S. These were caused by protruding seams of quartz, and formed a very close resemblance to the letters. Now commenced the most toilsome and dangerous part of our journey. Our route led us up the front of the cliff, opposite to that which we had descended. At one time we were climbing cliffs, holding [on] only by some small ragged points or boulders, at another time we were crossing narrow ledges of rocks, on the very edge of a precipice, at every time we had to be very careful of where we placed our feet, as a stone dislodged, or one false step would have hurled us over jagged rocks far down into the sea below. In this difficult manner we reached the precipice's top, whence we easily performed our homeward course, well pleased, as every one would be, with the trip to the caves.

Argyllshire Herald, 23 May 1862.

Appendix 3

A Journey to Cnoc Moy

'Communicated'

One of us, on a previous visit, had attempted to reach Cnoc Moy, the highest mountain near the Mull and, within a yard or two, the highest in all Kintyre: but the attempt had ended in vague wanderings in a sea of mist, from which he had been extricated by a straight line course at right angles to the wind from the Atlantic. But this time the affair was to be successful. Two of us were to support one another in the attempt, provisions were taken for the day, the map was closely examined and the gradients and probable course noted, and our climbing legs put in order by an ascent of Ben Gullion. Nevertheless, to reduce the work, the actual start was to be made from Machrihanish.

Behold us then on the Machrihanish shore, photographing Gigha and distant Jura, on a morning not altogether clear but the clearest after many days of rain, and so past Lossit Park. At the upper end we pause on a little bridge, shut in by the trees which fill the glen and seem hardly to receive room for the burn below. They form an arch looking over a ripening field of corn which rises gradually towards a distant farmhouse. Then on past High Lossit, climbing somewhat reminiscent of Ben Gullion, till we come to Skerry Fell. There is a threat of rain in the air, but here we catch sight of Cnoc Moy, and nothing shall keep us from it, unless it be a deluge strong enough to wash us off our legs. Before us at what seems quite a short distance is a gap in the hills, and we decide to make for that. Briskly we descend, quickly losing three or four hundred feet of height, and leaping burns, large and small, standing patches of water, over mingled grass, moss, and heather. We take a sharp dip to Craigaig Water, and, crossing it, find a path winding up. It is beautifully sheltered, the sun shines out, and there straight in front of us is a delightful little cascade. The hollow, the stream, the cascade, all so compact, so little compared with the miles of hills, make us feel happy with ourselves. Not only do we sing, but we take a photo of the cascade.

As we come up out of the hollow, a thin cloud comes over the sun. We have sight of Cnoc Moy and the gap in the hills seems miles and miles away. We plod steadily on, rising ever rising. Water and moss, red-tinged grass with flax-like seedlings. More plodding, more water. But all things come to an end. We are on the flank of the Sleit. We sit down and eat our lunch. We have a magnificent view, which I should now describe were it not that the view from Cnoc Moy is the same but more magnificent still.

We round the flank of the Sleit and meet a wind coming up the long glen. Breeze is no name for it. It is strong as a breeze, but in its chilliness and its steadiness as well as its force it more resembles a forced draught. But now we have a full view of Cnoc Moy. The Sleit falls to a valley some 500 feet below us and then Cnoc Moy rises steeply, darkly and steadily for at least 900 feet of actual height. Nature rewards those who get thus far by marking its actual summit with a little extra round curve, superimposed on an almost perfect crescent which falls away and gives the mountain a base some two miles long in the valley. There is no ruggedness about this mountain and its wonderful symmetry is a delight to the mind, at the same time that its deep olive green is restful to the eye. But as one rests there, studying it again and again, one begins to think that its smooth face conceals the secret of its great size, and then suddenly realises that its summit is cushioned somewhere high in the sky.

Down some 500 feet to Gleneadardacrock we go, through waterlogged grass, and now we are on Cnoc Moy. It is like climbing a ladder, a ladder without end. We pant for breath. I remind my companion that the air is rarer at these great heights [sic]. Now we are on the peat and we wonder however we could have thought the mountain smooth-sided. More water, and in the distance we think we see the top. A last effort and we are there. Across the valley is the gloomy Sleit with a tumbled mass of summits behind it and those of Arran behind all; Jura and Islay we see, and seem to look down on Gigha, while the people on the Machrihanish links remind one of those on a street as seen from a skyscraper. The water of the North Channel is smooth and we can even see the streak of water behind Rathlin Island and between it and Antrim, and far behind that on the horizon is a lofty land which we have never glimpsed before, but which can be none other than Donegal. South and East all the hills are laid out at our feet like nothing so much as those descriptive models in relief of mountains, rivers and seas which one sees in schools. At the end of the Glen, are Sanda and its adjacent islets, but alas! from them even as we look an arrow of white vapour comes. The arrow moves up the Glen, and seems to hug the Sleit, and as it moves it leaves behind it a growing trail of little clouds of white vapour. It passes on and seems to stay its career a mile or so out over the Atlantic. We shall see no more and even now the white vapours seem to be gathering round to attack our own hill. Reluctantly we descend, and as we climb the flank of the Sleit we feel rain. It begins to drip from wherever upon us it is possible for water to drip, it creeps insidiously into our boots. More water comes over the cascade than we saw on our way up. We are now literally walking in water. And so for a couple of hours we continue. But what matter. Of one thing we are certain, Cnoc Moy was worth it.

And so home, where hot water, a good meal and some of the wine of the country lead us gratefully to a night's repose.

Campbeltown Courier, 27 August 1921.

Appendix 4

A Winter Adventure in Glencoe

Alexander M. Honeyman

To all those – and they are many – who are unsmitten by the disease called mountaineering, the idea of camping in the dead of winter in the mountains of Glencoe will appear little more than a stunt, particularly as the Scottish Youth Hostels Association has recently erected an exceedingly comfortable hostel on a most convenient site at the foot of the Glen. We are all, of course, members of that Association, but, although by no means scornful of the comforts of the hostel, we decided to camp. The 'bus fare to Glencoe is 16/-, so we also decided to cycle.

I had to meet my pals, Gordon and Patrick, at Glasgow Botanic Gardens, at 6 a.m., which necessitated my leaving home at 4-30 a.m., literally in the middle of the night. When I mention that I was up till 3 a.m. packing food and equipment and trying to find the most convenient way of fixing it securely on to my bicycle (in consequence of which I had about half an hour in bed), it will readily be believed that any attempt to cycle all the way to Glencoe before dark the same day was doomed to failure from the start. But, as is the case, the enthusiasm which accompanied the preparations for our holiday closed our eyes to the possible set-backs which lay ahead.

Anyway, I joined my companions at the appointed time and, by the coming of day, we had entered the Vale of Leven in high spirits, whistling more or less in harmony with the small army of message boys who are wont to throng the streets at this hour. We did not continue for long in this joyful state of abandon. It had been snowing at Loch Lomond, but now it was thawing, and the air was absolutely laden with moisture. The mist, which hung like a wet blanket over the hills and loch, was even more penetrating than rain and we were soon soaked to the skin. The 'bonnie, bonnie banks' were just twenty-four miles of sheer misery. In the eight miles between Ardlui and Crianlarich the road climbs about 600 feet through Glen Falloch, and a fully loaded bicycle has to be pushed about three miles of this. We all but fell by the wayside. At the top of the hill, two miles from Crianlarich, we lay down on the driest spot within reach, which happened to be the middle of the road, till an approaching vehicle sent us scurrying, or should I say, crawling, to the roadside. Even in this state of near-exhaustion, we still regarded Glencoe as our destination, each one afraid lest he be the first to admit defeat.

Crianlarich has a Youth Hostel. Simultaneously we realised that to pass it would be madness. We were not mad; we did not pass it; we slept for sixteen hours.

When I woke the sun was shining, but, as if to offset that, I found I had a sore throat – a fact not entirely surprising in view of the weather of the preceding day. We had breakfast and left immediately. However, the change in the weather made all the difference and the toil and weariness of yesterday were things of the past. At Tyndrum I purchased a bottle of cough-cure (so called), which became affectionately known as 'Alec's wee black bottle'. We saw now the approach of the frost we had long hoped for and, spurred on by the prospect of good weather, we crossed the Moor of Rannoch and descended into the 'Glen o' Weeping'.

As we arrived the sun departed, and the moon and a host of stars took possession of the sky.

There is a shepherd's cottage at the Study at the head of the Glen, and here we had planned to leave our cycles and transform ourselves into mountaineers. Glencoe did not fail to live up to its name – the cottage was unoccupied. Housebreaking is not in our line, so rather dejectedly we proceeded a further two miles to the farm of Achtriochatan, right at the foot of the Glen. Here we learned that the cottage at the Study was never occupied in winter, but we could leave our cycles there if we wished. This was precisely what we did wish, so there was nothing for it but to cycle the two miles back up the Glen. Here by the light of the moon and a small hurricane lamp we put on our climbing boots, transferred our food and equipment on to our backs, pushed the cycles into a shed, and set out for the hills. The mountaineering proper had begun.

Even to the traveller, if any one exists who has never heard of the massacre, Glencoe appears dark and foreboding. This is in some measure due to the fact that the mighty crags which bound the Glen on its South side rise so precipitously that they appear to overhang their bases. In early descriptions of the Glen we read of travellers being in fear of destruction by the tottering crags. These crags are popularly known as the 'Three Sisters of Glencoe'. They are three enormous rock buttresses thrust out in a Northerly direction from the slopes of Bidean nam Bian (3,776 ft.), the highest mountain in Argyllshire and possibly the finest mountain group in all Scotland. The several summits of this group are so close together and screened from the Glen by the Northern spurs that no proper view of them can be had except for some other mountain top. Bidean nam Bian is one of the finest features of the view from Ben Nevis which lies twenty miles to the North.

The most Easterly of the Three Sisters is Ben Fhada, which arises directly above the Study, and which is bounded on the East by the Lairig Eilde, a path leading from the Study to Dalness in Glen Etive. The distance is four miles, and the summit of the path, approximately half-way, is 1,650 feet above sea level. Our route lay up this path.

Beautiful as the hills are on a fine sunny day, they are infinitely more so on a clear frosty night. The snowy ridges gleaming in the moonlight contrasted sharply with the black rift of the valley we had left behind. Every detail of mountain and corrie was revealed in the light of the moon. Still, we carried torches and lanterns, for the path was uneven and ice-covered, and to slip in such a place with a sixty-pound pack on one's back would mean a nasty fall. Slowly, steadily, we made height. I began to fall behind. My sore throat made breathing a rather painful process and I was obliged to stop frequently and take a sip from my bottle. There I was, trailing along behind my companions, ice-axe in one hand and lantern in the other, and on my head a woollen helmet closely resembling a sleeping cap. It occurred to me that I must have looked the living image of Dopey of Seven Dwarfs fame.

By the time I had reached the summit of the path, Gordon and Patrick had selected a site for the tents. I should not say 'selected', for there certainly was no choice. There was a small piece of ground, flat, or nearly flat, where the tents just had to go. The snow was not deep, so we didn't trouble to clear it away. The tents were pitched facing each other, one to be used for sleeping, the other as a cook and store tent. Gordon was self-appointed cook and got to work with the stoves while we got water from a small burn about fifty yards distant.

Dinner was ready. For a while we ate in silent contemplation, like some wild beasts who had run their prey to earth at the end of a long and weary day. The dirty plates were duly thrown outside the tent – the usual method of washing up – and we proceeded to dress for bed. We knew it would be cold, so we put on every stitch of clothing we had, and one by one crawled into our sleeping bags. I say one by one, as the space was much too confined to allow us all to perform the necessary contortions at one time. Inside his bag Patrick was wearing the following: four pairs sox, one suit of pyjamas, three pairs underpants, one pair of flannels, one singlet, three pullovers, one large sweater, and a camp coat! Only his nose was visible through an aperture in his balaclava.

My small oil lamp hung on the tent pole at our heads and provided us with light and a little warmth. I blew it out and forthwith the cold crept in upon us. We lay in silence. Not a sound disturbed the night save the distant murmuring of the mountain burn and our own deep breathing. We thought of the war, stern reminder of the civilisation we sought to escape. We thought of those who had called us fools, as they sank into their luxurious mattresses somewhere in the mad world we had left behind. We did not envy them. We were at peace with the world.

When we woke it was still dark. We tried to light the lamp. Half a dozen matches were struck and applied to the wick without result. The lamp was frozen. So also was everything else. I went to the door of the tent for a drink and found the water bucket frozen solid. When I spoke, my companions howled with laughter. I had a voice like Pop-eye. I took some cough-cure and went back to bed to await the coming of day. I think we fell asleep again.

We woke later to find the sun casting her warming rays on our little tent. A layer of hoar frost sparkled on the canvas above us. This was caused by our breath condensing and freezing on coming into contact with the tent walls. We crawled out of our bags and peeled off a few layers of clothing. It was a marvellous day. The ridge of Ben Fhada, 2,000 feet above us, glowed red in the rays of the rising sun. Patrick took some photographs while breakfast was prepared. We fried eggs. The eggs, like everything else, were frozen.

When put in the pan they rose up like balloons, passed through a stage when they looked like jelly-fish, and then settled down as all good eggs should. We enjoyed those eggs. But our boots; I shall never forget the sight of our boots! They were frozen solid as stone and no amount of coaxing on our part would ever get them into the shape of our feet. It took us half an hour to thaw them out over a primus. We grabbed our axes and rope and were off.

The first part of the route to the ridge was up the side of a deep and narrow gorge which was completely frozen and hung with icicles of all shapes and sizes. Up from the depths came a gentle tinkling noise; the warming rays of the sun had loosened a tiny icicle from the bondage of night. True it is, when you penetrate the mountains they reveal a beauty and majesty hidden from the eyes of him who is content to contemplate from a distance.

At the top of this gorge we found ourselves in a snow-filled corrie leading up to a snow and rock gully which we thought would provide an easy and sporting way to the crest of the ridge. Patrick went first, Gordon second, and I last. We decided the rope would be unnecessary. I paused for a rest, and gazed back the way we had come, trying to discern the tents in the valley below. There was a shout behind me, and I turned round in time to see Gordon slide towards me in a most undignified manner. He stopped himself by clawing at the snow. He was still clawing when I got up to him, afraid almost to breathe lest the snow should give way and cause him to complete the journey to the foot of the gully. Gordon had no ice-axe, which explains why he had been unable to stop himself when the snow first gave way. With the help of my ice-axe I gained the safety of a snow-covered ledge of rock, from where I lowered the rope and axe to my companion who had by now every good reason to feel bored.

Patrick was by now well ahead, apparently unaware that we were having some difficulty. He said later he saw Gordon sliding, but thought he was doing it for fun! Roped together now, we gained the ridge in comparative safety.

A scene of unsurpassed beauty met our gaze. We were now somewhere about the 3,000 foot line, and the ridge, which bounds Glencoe on the North, lay below our eye-level. Beyond it we could see the long hollow wherein lies Loch Leven and, further still to the North, the lofty and shapely peaks of the Mamore Forest were dwarfed by the enormous bulk of Ben Nevis, the monarch of Britain's hills. To the East, over the valley we had just left, lay the Buchailles of Etive, and beyond them the loftier peaks of the Black Mount.

There are many who would be content to let the eye wander over this magnificent spectacle, but we must complete the ridge walk to the summit, 700 feet above us. As yet the view out to the western ocean was hidden from us by the Bidean Massif itself, but once on the top we should have an unobstructed view in every direction.

For 300 feet or so we climbed very steeply, then the ridge levelled out and became little more than a walk. To our left the ground sloped gently away to Glen Etive, but, on the right, great cornices overhung the gullies, and the rocks fell precipitously for 1,000 feet into the corries which drain into Glencoe.

Carefully avoiding the edge of the cornices we found ourselves on the final slope leading to the summit. A few hundred feet of easy but exhausting snow-slope were ascended and soon we stood by the summit cairn. For the time being we were warm with the exertion, but while recovering our breath we became aware of the cold. The afternoon was drawing on and an icy wind blew flurries of powdery snow in our faces. Hungrily we devoured sandwiches and chocolate while Patrick took photographs till the feeling went out of his fingers.

We gazed around us. To a height of about 3,000 feet the land was covered with a sea of mist through which the loftier summits appeared like islands in an ocean. To the West we saw the mountains of Mull and Morven. A little to the North, over Ardgour, the Cuillins of Skye were faintly visible. To the North, Ben Nevis dominated the view, towering above Loch Linnhe and the Great Glen. A large group of mountains penetrating the mist in the North-East indicated the Cairngorms. Turning towards the South we saw in succession Ben Lawers, Ben More, Ben Lui, and due South the summits of Ben Cruachan were clearly visible over the intervening ranges of hills.

We could have sat for hours and let our eyes wander over half of Scotland, but heavy banks of cloud were rolling up from the South, a timely reminder of the approach of night.

I have seldom seen such a beautiful sunset. In the West the sky was aglow with fiery reds and yellows, contrasting with the grey mists boiling in the depths of the valleys. To the North and South more sombre shades of pink and violet prevailed, while behind in the East the deep purple was falling fast.

Descending by a subsidiary ridge we caught sight of the tents –and something more. A herd of deer was advancing with unfaltering step towards our camp. A horrible dread filled our minds. Should the deer be more hungry than timid we might well be eaten literally out of house and home. We waited in suspense and to our relief saw the leader of the herd give the sign of human habitation a wide berth and make off up the hillside.

Our rate of descent decreased as it became increasingly difficult to see the ground in front of us. It was quite dark when we reached the tents; the moon made several unavailing attempts to bathe us in its silvery light, but each time was forced to retire behind the gathering clouds. In spite of the impending change of weather the frost still reigned supreme. Our little burn was frozen. Not a trickle of water could we see. We had to descend a further two hundred yards to get enough water to fill the bucket. The welcome sound of sizzling chops met us on our return.

By 8 p.m. we had dined, disposed of our plates in the usual manner, and struggled into our sleeping bags. That night was, if anything, colder, and several times we were obliged to warm ourselves by kicking as violently as the restricted space allowed. When the sun rose, we were quick to get up and thaw ourselves out in its warming rays.

Patrick had to be home on the following day, and moreover there was every sign of an approaching thaw, so, after devouring the remainder of our food, we struck camp and set off down the path. We set foot on the road almost forty-eight hours after leaving it, satisfied, however, that we had not sought in vain the companionship of the hills.

The question will still be asked – Why do people climb mountains? Personally, I climb because – though I cannot attempt to explain why – I enjoy it.

Possibly Mr J. S. Smythe, the well-known mountaineer, in his attempts to formulate his philosophy of the high places, gets very near the truth when he writes: –

'The hills have a capacity for blending into a harmonious whole the physical, mental and spiritual qualities of man. *That is why men climb.*'

Colvilles Magazine, April 1940, pp. 83-86.

Appendix 5

A Song for Jamie's Wedding

Willie Mitchell

Though lang the way an' stey the brae
Up Jamie tae your steadin'
Be't wat or fair it's I'll be there
Tae toast ye at yer weddin'.

My wife I doot'll no' get oot,
I'm tellin' ye in fairness,
She's thrang, ye see, an' canna lea'
Her twa bit bonnie bairnies.

But still, she sen's her best respects
'Twas kind o' ye tae mind her,
She hopes when Polly ye annex
A useful wife ye'll find her.

For me, ye ken my dearest wish
Is that ye'll aye be jolly,
God bless your hearth wi' loads o' mirth
But never Melancholy.

Appendix 6

The Cara Broonie and relatives

There is no certainty as to who or what the Broonie was (or is). The Rev R.S.G. Anderson heard that he was 'the ghost of a Macdonald murdered by a Campbell', but I prefer the version that he was a supernatural mercenary who sold his killing skills to Clan Donald and attached himself to the Largie branch of that family.[40] *Ùruisg* is sometimes offered as a Gaelic equivalent of 'brownie', but to that creature a different appearance and different habits are generally attributed. There are two rocks named Creag an Ùruisg in remote glens in south Kintyre, and on these the solitary *ùruisg* must have been glimpsed by long-ago evening travellers.[41]

Broonies were rarely seen, but were active among humans when they felt their services were needed; and they served only powerful families, in Kintyre at any length. The name 'broonie' is Scots for brownie – yes, the organisation for little girls is the same – and Dwelly gives the form *brùnaidh* in his dictionary of Gaelic (p 132). *The Concise Scots Dictionary* (p 67) defines 'broonie' as 'a benevolent sprite, supposed to perform household tasks in the night', but latterly, also, as 'a more malevolent goblin'. The Cara Broonie was a bit of both.

'Baigwell' of Carskey

Another old Macdonald family in Kintyre, that of Sanda, was also supposed to have its 'broonie', in the estate mansion at Macharioch, and the Campbells of Saddell had the services of one – which 'only harmed people who did bad things' – in the castle there.[42] But the best known broonie in Kintyre, the Cara individual excepted, was attached to the MacNeills of Carskey and was known as 'Baigwell' (Gaelic *Beag-bheul*, 'Little mouth'). Since there are distinct parallels between the Largie and Carskey broonies, I shall quote a letter written around a century ago by Mrs Macdonald of Sanda to John McInnes, a native of Southend, who published a poem titled 'Baigwell of Ancient Carskiey', which Mrs Macdonald was moved to comment on. The poem was published again in the *Campbeltown Courier* of 17 March 1928, when McInnes also submitted Mrs Macdonald's letter, which is reproduced in full in the *Kintyre Magazine*, No. 63, pp. 23-24.

> I am the only surviving grandchild of John Macmillan McNeill of Carskiey, and was brought up in the house with my grandparents until I was fully seven years of age, and I always spent the summers there till I was married, so the place and all its associations are very dear to me.
>
> I remember most clearly 'Baigwell's Room', of which you speak. It was on the upper landing, a small dark room, facing the head of the spiral stairs. There was, about five steps from the top, a large wide step, just by the bow window, which lighted both flights of stairs, where, when I was sent a message upstairs in the gloaming, I used to sit in fear and trembling until I could gather courage to dash past Baigwell's room, along a little passage into my aunt's bedroom, where I slept.
>
> Not that Baigwell was a wicked or unkind brownie, but the servants used to frighten us by saying, 'If you are naughty, Baigwell will come and catch you'. On one occasion I very clearly recall, my nurse, who must have wanted to get down to her big old kitchen where the other servants were dancing reels to the 'cantering' [mouth music] of an old woman, frightened me so much by the fear of being left alone and Baigwell coming to me if I did not go to sleep, that I screamed so loud I was heard down two flights of stairs. My dear old

grannie came up (a most unusual thing) and I remember her scolding my nurse, saying, 'If you ever frighten the child in this way again, it will be the last day you spend at Carskiey'. The whole scene comes vividly before me as I write. As my nurse was child and grandchild, and even great-grandchild of old retainers, this was a very serious threat in those days.

I was always told that Baigwell was a tiny person dressed in green silk, and that there was a brownie attached in the same way to the family at Macharioch – MacDonalds of Sanda, my late husband's forebears – and that these guardian fairies, or spirits, used to meet at night on Strathmore. It was genuinely believed by the old people about that Baigwell protected and befriended the Carskiey family ... We were told and believed that if the servants were careless and left their work in the kitchen not completely cleared up, Baigwell went down and roused them all up to put things in order. Probably this is the noise and hubbub to which you refer.

Similar 'inside information' appears to illumine a brief account of the Cara Broonie published in *A Short History of Largieside*, compiled by members of Largieside Women's Rural Institute in 1966. In paragraph two of 'Folklore' (p 16), he is described as 'a very industrious little chap who could be counted on to help the members of the House of Largie'. Quite often, he 'lit the fires for the domestic staff, made the porridge and swept the floors', but against that 'charming picture' there was 'the assurance of the family of Largie that far from being a helpful wee man he was a naughty rascal who loved to hide letters and documents of importance'. In paragraph three, the account suddenly switches to first person, and the author of the entire piece may be assumed to have been Mrs A. Maxwell Macdonald, one of the seven contributors.

> The stories which have been passed on orally vary in great degrees, but here is the version I learned as a small child. The Brownie lived on the Island of Cara, where his chair may be seen to this day. When danger threatened the

Macdonalds he always appeared to warn them. On their death beds the Brownie always appeared, dressed in his green suit and silver-buckled shoes and carrying a pair of grey brogans [boots] which he left at the door of the room of the dying laird.

On 9 October 2013, 'The History and Natural History of Rathlin Island' was the opening talk in the Kintyre Antiquarian and Natural History Society's winter programme. The Society's guest, Philip Watson, an Irish ecologist who has an intimate knowledge of that little island off the north Antrim coast, could have spoken on any one of several subjects, but opted to compress them all into an hour. He succeeded admirably in his presentation, which encompassed history, genealogy, natural history, marine biology and folklore. In that latter category he gave a brief account of the Rathlin 'broonie', which is known in Irish as a *gruagagh* (pronounced 'grooga'). In Dwelly's dictionary of Gaelic (p 528) *gruagach* appears with eight definitions, one of which is indeed 'Brownie'.

In Philip's recent book, *Rathlin: Nature & Folklore*, he devoted two pages to the hairy creature, whose presence in Rathlin and the north of Ireland, he suggests, was by migration 'from Scotland via Kintyre'. Like the brownie, the gruagagh's main satisfaction in life was in the performance of domestic chores, but he resented any material expression of gratitude, believing that reward signified rejection. In one Rathlin tale, a woman knitted her helper a pair of socks, 'and he left in tears, unable to accept even payment in kind'.

'Baigwell' was equally touchy. Miss Jessie Todd in Baile na Maoile – the shepherd's cottage at the Mull – in a story she told in Gaelic to Nils M. Holmer (see below), described how a pair of shoes belonging to one of the Carskey children had been left out for Baigwell, after the tracks of her bare feet had been seen in the snow; but she didn't put them on and was never seen again at Carskey, though a shepherd, soon after, saw a little woman, with a cape on her shoulder, walking in the night.

Isabella Campbell (1854-1929), who, as 'Mrs Higginson', compiled a manuscript of Skipness social history and folklore which is in the School of Scottish Studies archive, recorded the existence of a 'Gruagach' in Skipness Castle. This is her account, exactly as typed from her original manuscript:

> The Gruagach means in English the Hairy Nymph this on account of her beautiful golden tresses also called the Green Lady on account of her green gown. This green lady is supposed to have come with the Campbells and to have left with the Campbells.
>
> There is not the slightest doubt that there was such a creature in the castle at that time. There was a woman living in a room at the castle who looked after the hens, etc. She was a widow named Mrs. Barton this Mrs. Barton used to tell how the green lady used to help her feed the hens in the evening, always in the evening or at night she was never seen till after sunset she used to put her head on Mrs. Barton's knee and get her hair combed she was very small just like a child in stature who wore a green silk dress. She had neither shoes or stockings on she would help Mrs. Barton to tidy up her house. When the Campbells would be away from home, a night or two before they returned the green lady would be working in the house setting it in order for their home coming. Whether the servants had word of the Campbells coming or not when they heard the green lady working they knew the Campbells were not far off. The Campbells were in the habit of giving a ball at New Year time. At one of these balls a brother of Mrs. Barton attended to help the servants but early in the evening he felt unwell and went to bed in Mrs. Barton's room every one seems to have been so busy no one looked near him until the ball was over and then he was found nearly dead in bed. The green lady nearly killed [him] for being in Mrs. Barton's bed she was boxing him all night they took him away to his home in Lochranza. He never recovered from the thrashing the green lady gave him he died very shortly after.

Broonie Tales

The Rev Anderson, in *The Antiquities of Gigha* (1978 edition), published Broonie tales, to which Freddy Gillies added several more in his *Life on God's Island* (1999), but I'll leave these where they are and offer a set of tales, all from my own collection except for the first, which was recorded in Gaelic before the Second World War by the Swedish linguist, Nils M. Holmer. It appeared in *The Gaelic of Kintyre* (p 125) and was told to him by Malcolm MacDonald, farmer in Beachmenach, and father of Ian MacDonald, who died in 2013 at the age of ninety-three.

Malcolm said that the Cara Broonie, like himself, was a MacDonald, and that no Campbell had the courage to stay a night on the island, for the Broonie would kill him. One day Malcolm was at Cara with a drag-net for catching saithe. He had with him a Campbell, who was on the shore holding an end of the net-rope while Malcolm rowed the boat out to encircle and trap the fish. Campbell heard a splash in the water, at once threw the rope away, plunged into the sea and leapt back aboard the boat. He confessed that he had taken fright, thinking that he heard the Broonie splashing in the water.

That element of superstitious dread erupting into terror appears also in a story from Calum Bannatyne, who was born in Rosehill Cottage, near Glenbarr, in 1900. He was on Cara once as a boy to gather gull eggs. One of the men in the party – a 'joker', Calum called him – was apprising the others of the Broonie's history of violence. Calum, who had a Campbell grandmother, learned that day that anyone with Campbell blood would be attacked and 'never make any headway on Cara'. Another of the older men in the company, who was 'very fond of whisky', had a notion that there might be a bottle of the stuff stashed somewhere in the laird's house by the shepherd who had been over for lambing. They opened a window to gain entry, and some of them began trooping up the stairs to search the upper storey. The house was dark inside and someone began striking matches, but every match would instantly blow out with a 'pooh!' The stair was draughty from broken window-panes, but someone declared that it was the Broonie blowing out the matches, and they all took sudden fright and began charging back down the stairs and out through the open window. One boy impulsively slammed the window down after him, and an elderly man at his back got such a shock that he made one dive at the window and took the whole frame out with him. Everybody fled to the boat, which two or three of the boys lifted bodily off the beach and practically threw into the water. (27 March 1977)

Mrs Finlay Clark (Margaret Sheddan), in Glenbarr, had a cousin who was a table maid at Largie Castle. The cousin told her that the Broonie would always anticipate an event of importance to the Largie family, a marriage or, especially, a death. The cousin shared a bedroom in the attic of the Castle, and reported hearing a horse and carriage clattering up the driveway at dead of night – this was the Broonie arriving from Cara. 'But nobody ever saw him.' (3 March 1977)

Just as there was a room reserved for 'Baigwell' in Carskey House, there was the 'Broonie's Room' in Largie Castle. Willie McGougan admitted that he'd never seen the Broonie, though he'd been a long time at Largie. Willie was quite often on Cara and sat on the Broonie's Chair and drank from the Broonie's Well to the north of the Chair. A shepherd named Gilchrist, who was on Cara 'a terrible time ago', told some good stories about the Broonie, with whom he 'got on fine', and Willie passed on one of them to me. The shepherd and his wife sailed to Gigha one day, but the weather turned wild and they couldn't get back to Cara until the next day. Their cow had been calving when they left her, and when they returned she had given birth and the calf was tied beside her. Of course, there had been no one on the island. As Willie added, 'Ye just believe as much o' that as ye like'. (7 March 1977)

I can claim to have met someone who suspected she had encountered the Broonie. I was cycling home from the

Learside one evening in the spring of 1995, and, seeing the woman in her garden at Glenramskill, stopped for a chat. Her story emerged unexpectedly during the conversation and I memorised it and wrote it down when I arrived home. It has sat in my files since that day, but now that my friend is dead I feel that I can tell her story. I shall keep her name to myself, however, since I did not anticipate ever publishing the story and never asked her permission.

The woman used to visit Killean churchyard to tend her mother's grave there. One warm day when she was busy at the grave, she became conscious of a 'presence', and when she turned to look she saw a tiny 'overdressed' man with a swarthy face standing watching her, his hands on his hips. She remembered him wearing a buttoned-up waistcoat, jacket and a hat that was either a trilby or a Homburg. 'Did I startle you?' he asked. 'Yes,' she replied. He asked her what she was doing, and then enquired if she had seen 'the stones'. He insisted that she must, led her to the walled enclosure containing the Largie family memorials, and pulled aside the wire fencing which closed off the entrance. She had to stoop to enter, and the vault was cold inside. Remarking that he'd 'leave her to it', he withdrew. She was very disturbed – concerned that she might be attacked or her belongings stolen from the grave – so she waited a few minutes and then crept out. There was no sign of the little man, not even on the road. It had been an 'uncanny experience', she said, and when she next returned to the churchyard she found the entrance to the vault gated and padlocked.

Sources

1. *Kintyre Magazine* No. 35, p 16, & obituary *Campbeltown Courier*, 23/3/1935.
2. *Campbeltown Courier*, 8/5/1969.
3. *Ib.*, 10/10/1968 & 7/10/1976.
4. Ben Gadd, *The Rockies: Canada's Magnificent Wilderness*, Ontario 1992, p 123.
5. A. Martin, *Kintyre: The Hidden Past*, p 215.
6. A. Martin, *Kintyre Country Life*, p 108, & *Kintyre: The Hidden Past*, p 210.
7. *Campbeltown Courier*, 17/2/1934.
8. *Ib.*, 8/5/1981.
9. *Ib.*, 25/6/1932, 'A Grave in Gartnagrenach'.
10. *Ib.*, 18/6/1932, 'Kintyre Public Assistance Committee'.
11. A. Martin, *Kintyre: The Hidden Past*, p 192.
12. E.R. Cregeen and A. Martin, *Kintyre Instructions: The 5th Duke of Argyll's Instructions to his Kintyre Chamberlain, 1785-1805*, 2011, p 176.
13. *Ib.*, pp. 175-76.
14. Register of Poor, Campbeltown Parish, 26/2/1889, Argyll & Bute Council Archive, CO 6.
15. A. Martin, *Kilkerran Graveyard Revisited*, p 76.
16. *Ib.*, p 19.
17. *Campbeltown Courier*, 14/7/1966.
18. *Argyllshire Herald*, 21/6/1913.
19. *Campbeltown Courier*, 23/7/1970.
20. A. Martin, *Kintyre: The Hidden Past*, pp. 210-11.
21. *Campbeltown Courier*, obituary, 24/8/1950.
22. *Ib.*, 22/4 & 24/6/1944.
23. Register of Poor, Campbeltown Parish, 20/1/1902, *op. cit.*
24. *Argyllshire Herald*, 23/7/1910.
25. A. Martin, *Kintyre: The Hidden Past*, pp. 153-54; *Argyllshire Herald*, 23/3 & 30/3/1907 (quotation); Register of Poor, Campbeltown Parish, entry 1575, 21/3/1898, *op. cit.*
26. *By Hill and Shore in South Kintyre*, p 164, for the day and the poem.

27. *Kintyre Magazine* No. 17, p 15.
28. P. Moir and I. Crawford, *Argyll Shipwrecks*, 1997, pp. 17-18.
29. *Campbeltown Courier*, 16/8/1879.
30. A. Martin, *The Ring-Net Fishermen*, p 165.
31. No. 71, pp. 32-33.
32. A. Martin, *The North Herring Fishing*, 2001, p 17.
33. 'West Kintyre Field Names', *Transactions of the Gaelic Society of Inverness*, Volume XXVII, 1908-11 (1915).
34. Angus Martin, *Kintyre Places and Place-Names*, p 148.
35. Ben Gadd, *op. cit.*, p 90.
36. Jean C. MacLeod, 'William Gilchrist, 1811-1879, Letter Press Printer and Lithographer, Glasgow', *Kintyre Magazine* No. 70, pp. 2-5.
37. *Justices of the Peace in Argyll*, F. Bigwood, N. Berwick 2001, p 13.
38. *Campbeltown Courier*, 3/7/1943.
39. *Ib.*, 11/12/1948.
40. For that story, and sidelines, see *Kintyre Places and Place-Names*, p 279.
41. *Kintyre Places and Place-Names*, p 312.
42. Mary Brown, Edinburgh, letter to *Campbeltown Courier*, 31/3/1989.

Index

Neither 'Campbeltown' nor 'Kintyre' has been indexed, owing to the frequency of references. Appendix 4, 'A Winter Adventure in Glencoe', has only been lightly indexed.

Achadh na Sìthe, 83-84, 85
adders, 183
afforestation, 8, 165, 236
Aignish, 9, 52, 62, 73, 77-80, 120, 166
Ailsa Craig, 124, 139
Aird Fhada, 207
Allt Beithe, 240
Allt Mòr (Barr Glen), 236
Amod (Barr Glen), 234-35
An Comunn Gàidhealach, 92, 94
Anderson, Georgina, 114, 115
Anderson, Rev R.S.G., 201, 204, 206, 268, 273
angling, 22, 55, 146, 243-44
Angus, Naomi, 109
ants, 152, 154
Ardshiel Hotel, Campbeltown, 44, 86, 90
Argyll Arms Hotel, Campbeltown, 114
Argyll Colliery, 152
Argyll Folk Festival, 114
Argyllshire Herald, 78, 147, 154

Arinascavach, 173
Arkle, Peter, Penicuik, 111, 164
Arnicle, 235
Arran, 38, 68, 100, 181, 242, 272
Aska, the, 207-8
Auchencorvie, 17, 166
Auchenhoan, 122, 137
Ayrshire, 44, 94, 139, 144

Baden, 135
badger's skull, 5
'Baigwell', 268-70
Ballantyne, Robert 'Bob', Campbeltown, 47, 48
Ballygroggan, 8, 13, 18, 54, 62, 71, 72, 76, 80, 101, 125, 126, 157
Balnabraid, 122, 128, 132, 137, 195, 250
Balnatunie, 132, 137-44
Bannatyne, Calum, 128, 273
Barr Glen, 233-38
Battlefield Band, 114
Beattie family, Largiebaan, 41-42
beer, 31, 35, 106, 170
beetles and other 'bugs', 63-64
Beinn na Faire, 7, 20, 72, 133, 171
Bell, Evelyn and Margaret, Grangemouth, 210
Ben Gullion, 11, 68, 71, 128, 131, 155-57, 159-62, 165, 173-93, 195-99, 173, 212-14, 232, 240, 255

279

Benjie, dog, 4, 5, 6, 11, 14, 40, 101, 131, 139, 161, 174, 175, 182, 187, 188, 189, 193, 195, 197-99, 212, 218, 231, 241, 245
Benjie, pony, 190-91
Benjie's Drinking Pool, 182
Bignall, Eric, 52-54
binnein place-name element, 59-60
Binnein Buidhe, 59, 60
Binnein dà Néill, 59, 60
Binnein Fithich, 59-60, 61, 62, 66, 67, 70, 78
Bissett, David, Campbeltown, 114
Black Forest, 4, 135
Black Loch, 173
Blackwood, Rev B. B., 40
blaeberries, 102, 154, 155, 166, 170, 171, 173, 181, 188, 192, 193
Blake, William, 170
Bley, Carla, 89
Bloody Bay, 139
bog cotton, 76, 102, 103, 195, 256
bog myrtle, 129, 222-24, 230, 231, 236
botany, 10, 13, 39, 54, 143-44, 163, 167
boulders, 13, 14, 120, 124, 126, 128, 130, 133, 134, 135, 137
Breackanridge, Isabella, Southend, 142
Brodie, John, Campbeltown, 185
Broonie – see Cara Broonie
Broonie's Chair, 203-4, 211, 274
Broonie's Well, 274
Brown, Duncan and family, Drumlemble, 54
Brown, Eddie, 55
Brown, Pete, 89
Brown, Rab, Campbeltown, 52, 53

Bruach Dearg, 42-44, 56
Bruce, Jack, 89, 90
burnet rose, 10
Burton, Richard, 110
buses, 3, 8, 17, 35, 54, 61, 66, 70, 76, 81, 91, 92, 170, 192, 221, 225, 233, 238, 244
Butler, Mary, 106
butterflies, 37, 61-64, 167, 181, 244
buzzards, 30, 107, 122, 232
By Hill and Shore in South Kintyre, xix, 72, 122, 130, 139, 140, 182, 188, 192

cairns, 11, 198, 226
cameras, 27, 66, 67, 159
Cameron, David, 90
Campbells of Kintarbert, 97
Campbells of Saddell, 269
Campbells of Skipness, 272
Campbell, Angus, High Glenadale, 79
Campbell, Colin, Carradale, 96
Campbell, George Douglas, 8th Duke of Argyll, 72, 253
Campbell, Iain, Campbeltown, 27-29, 45, 114
Campbell, Iain, Remuil, 79
Campbell, Isabella, Skipness, 272
Campbell, James, 'killed in China by pirates', 97
Campbell, Janet, 84, 94
Campbell, John, Campbeltown, 251
Campbell, Miss Lucy, 98-99
Campbeltown Courier, 7, 48, 83, 85, 89, 91, 113, 114, 151, 165, 209, 269
Campbeltown Creamery, 165

Campbeltown Grammar School, 85, 86, 95, 130, 146
Campbeltown Journal, 99, 141
camping & tents, 20, 23, 25-26, 27, 29-30, 31
Canada, 74, 93, 209, 231
canoeists, 36
Cara Broonie, 204, 209, 210, 268, 270-71, 273-75
Cara Island, 199-211, 273-74
'Cara' as personal name, 202
Carradale, 96, 108, 109, 191, 235, 237
Ceòl, 113
choughs, 48, 50, 52-54, 231
Clachaig Glen, 226, 230
Clachan, 82, 83, 91, 94, 234
Cladh Mhìcheil, 82, 96-99
Claffey, Michael, Campbeltown, 55, 56, 57, 169, 170
Clark, Mrs Finlay (Margaret Sheddan), Glenbarr, 274
Clark, Mary, Feochaig, 145
Claymore, M. V., Irish ferry, 140
Clyne, Douglas, 219
Cnoc Moy, 22, 27, 33, 65, 159, 166, 169, 170, 181, 255-57
Cocker, Mark, 63
Coffield, Johnny, Machrihanish, 25
Colville, Alex, Campbeltown, 40, 41
Colville, David & Sons, 109
Colville, Duncan, 206
Colville, Mary – see McShannon, Polly
Colville, Willie, Machrihanish, 47, 48, 50

Comunn Gàidhealach, An, 92, 94
Conical Hill, 68, 155, 160, 177-81
Constable, John, 61
Cooper, Derek, 30
corn-kilns, 132, 201
Corrie, the, Largiebaan, 80
Coulson, Tom, forester, 165
cowberries, 244
Craigaig, 5, 15, 54, 72, 128-30, 170
Craigaig Water, 129, 170, 224, 256
Craigard House, 246
Cream, 87, 89
Crerar, Robert, Campbeltown, 146
Crossan, William, Campbeltown, 85
Crosshill Dam, 156, 162, 183
Crosshill Loch/Reservoir, 156, 165, 173
Crosshill Vista, 212-14
crows, 77
Cruach an Eich, 226
Cruach an t-Sorchan, 240
Cruach Doire Lèithe, 244
Cuillins, The, 9, 264
curlew, 173
cycling, 54, 55, 58, 146, 170, 251

daisy, the word, 221
Dalabhraddan, 141
Dalintober, 247, 248
Davies, Rob, 50
deer, 186
Dileas, dog, 239
Dippen, Carradale, 235
Docherty, Alex, Stewarton, 35-36
Docherty, Barbara elder, Drumlemble, 35, 70, 120
Docherty, Barbara younger, 12-14, 35, 120

281

Docherty, Christine, 120
Docherty, Donald, 22, 31, 46, 51, 77, 120, 121, 169
Docherty, Malcolm elder, Drumlemble, 36, 69-70, 120, 121
Docherty, Malcolm, younger, 40, 52, 132-33, 137
Dores, Inverness-shire, 108
doves, rock, 73, 232
dragonflies, 65, 181, 244
Dragonfly Lochan, 181
driftwood, 14, 23, 124
Drumchapel, 46
Drumlemble, 27, 70, 101, 102, 106, 117
Drumnaleck, 234
Duncan, Alexander, 93
Dundee, 86, 108
dung-beetle in Inneans Glen, 64

eagles, golden, 30, 31, 122, 133
Earadale, 80-81
Easter egg-rolling, 147, 162
Edgar, James, father of Jim below, 149
Edgar, Jim, 85-87, 90
Edinburgh, 33, 44, 86, 120, 130, 131, 210
Egan, Felim, 216
Eilean na h-Achrach, 207
Electric Ladyland, 86, 87
Engelsbrand, 4, 135
Erradil – see Earadale
Escalator Over the Hill, 89

Feochaig, 145, 146, 173
Ferguson, Duncan, Dalbuie, 60, 79

Fin Rock, 160, 188-93, 195
First Waters, 183, 184
Fisher, Archie, 114
fishing, commercial, 38, 45-46, 73, 219, 223, 240, 241, 247-49, 273
fishing, leisure – see angling
Fleetwood, 45
foot-&-mouth outbreak, 186-7
Forestry Commission, 165, 212, 239
foxes, 40, 72, 107, 171
frisbees, 55
fulmars, 53

Gaberlunzie, 114
Gadd, Ben, 74
Gaelic of Kintyre, The, 273
Gaelic language, 42, 82, 91-94, 142, 178, 214, 217, 219-20, 223, 234
Galdrans, 5, 102, 184
Gallagher, Jane & Catherine, Campbeltown, 190
Gallagher, Sid, Campbeltown, 250
Galloway, 139, 209, 210
Gartnacopaig, 41, 42, 44, 169
Gartnagrenach, 82, 96
Gartnagrenach burial-ground – see Cladh Mhìcheil
Garvalt (Barr Glen), 235-6
Gatt, Hector, Campbeltown, 70
Gaughan, Dick, 113, 114
geese, wild, 206
Gilchrist, Davie 'Cara', 202
Gilchrist, Mary, Tallavtoll, 93
Gilchrist, William, printer & publisher, 234-5

Girl Guides, 71, 237
Glasgow, 70, 122, 221
Glenahanty, 17, 18, 20, 41, 55, 57, 58, 75, 159, 169, 170, 230
Glenahervie, 81
Glenbarr, 200, 233, 235, 237, 238
Glenbreackerie, 18, 71
Glen Coe, 49, 109, 258-66
Gleneadardacrock, 13, 18, 42, 65, 111, 169, 170, 257
Glenmurril, 126, 132
Glenramskill, 128, 146-49, 181, 275
Glenrea, 158
Glens of Antrim, 31-33, 48
goats, wild, 11, 15-16, 44, 45, 77, 172, 209, 211
Gordon-Dean, Peter, casualty at Largiebaan, 41
graffiti, 104, 106, 184
Graham, Archie, Peninver, 221
Graham, Gordon, climber, 109, 258-66
grass-of-parnassus, 13
Greenland, 130
Greenpeace, 192
Grigson, Geoffrey, 178, 215, 219, 222, 224
Grogport, 92, 221, 222
gruagagh/gruagach, 271-72
guano, 73
gulls & their eggs, 11, 23, 54, 70, 273
Gulls' Den, 22, 31

Halbert, Bob, 43, 44
Halbert, George, Campbeltown, 44
Hamilton, Lanarkshire, 108
Hamilton, Malcolm, Campbeltown, 23, 24, 25, 106
Hamilton, Patrick, climber, 109, 258-66
Hamilton, Stewart, Campbeltown, 25
harebells, 177-78, 180
Harvey, John, Campbeltown, 106
Harvey, John, Gartnacopaig, 44
Hathway, John, 73
Haunted Landscapes, 195
Hawk's Peak, 161, 182-83, 185-86, 188
Hawthorn families, Kintyre, 150
Hay, George Campbell, 218-19, 238, 239, 240, 251
Heaney, Seamus, 215-18
Helm, Sandy, Campbeltown, 128
Henderson, Hamish, 115-20
Hendrix, Jimi, 86, 87, 89
hen harrier, 122
hermit-crabs, 225
Hidden Crag, The, 173-76, 188
Higgins, F. R., 123
Higginson, Mrs – see Campbell, Isabella
High Glenadale, 71, 107
High Tirfergus, 109, 112
Holmer, Nils M., 271, 273
Homeston, 53, 75
Honeyman, Alec M., Campbeltown, 71, 107-9, 258-66
Honeyman, Allan J. K., Hamilton, 108
Hooper, Jon, vet, 175
Hopkins, Gerard Manley, 215
Houston, 'Queen' Esther, Polliwilline, 183
Hynd, Jan, Iona and Bob, 107

Innean Beag, 13, 133
Innean Gaothach, 230
Innean Mòr, 76, 166
Inneans/Bay, 7, 13, 14, 15, 17, 20, 22, 23-31, 35, 54, 55, 64, 71, 101, 106, 111, 159, 164, 169, 171, 172, 194
Inneans Glen, 13, 18, 35, 133, 170
Inneans, variant spellings, 104-5
irises, wild, 215-22
Islay, 52, 94, 151, 152, 201, 231, 234

Jackson, Hamish, 101
jays, 230
jazz fusion, 90
Jock Tamson's Bairns, 114

Kavanagh, Patrick, 216-17
Keil Cave, 168
Keith, Winifred, Dundee, 108
Kelly, Dorothy, Machrihanish, 102
Kelly, John, Machrihanish, 102
Kelly, Peter, Machrihanish, 47, 48, 49, 50
Kelly, Robert, Machrihanish, 106
Kennedy, Tommy, Campbeltown, 146
Kerouac, Jack, 24
Kerr, Betty, Machrihanish, 101
Kerr, Eddie, Drumlemble, 23
kestrel, 232
Kilchousland, 192, 225
Kildalloig, 187
Kilkerran graveyard, 128, 152, 187, 188, 190-1
Kilkerran road, 86, 131, 187
Killean churchyard, 82, 275
Killeonan, 70

Killypole, 62, 99-101, 104, 106, 107, 109, 110, 111, 112, 115-17, 120
Killypole Loch, 28, 101, 107, 168
Kinloch, RMS, 72
Kintyre Antiquarian [& Natural History] Society, 43, 79, 206, 271
Kintyre Botany Group, 82
Kintyre Country Life, 143
Kintyre Magazine, xx, 59, 115, 140, 215, 221, 269
Kintyre Places and Place-Names, 59, 60, 72, 80, 104, 126, 128, 130, 133, 143, 155, 181, 225
Kintyre: The Hidden Past, 23, 27, 32, 77, 92, 167
Kintyre Way, 8, 17, 50, 62, 64, 74-75, 76, 157, 166, 225, 231, 239, 242, 244
kites, red, 232
Knockbay, 163, 215
Knocklayd, Co. Antrim, 46
Knock Scalbert, 71, 238
Kosi, dog, 5, 60, 195

Lafferty, James Jnr., Campbeltown, 35
Lafferty, Teddy, Campbeltown, 6, 7, 18-21, 25, 26, 34, 48, 49, 50, 53, 55, 102, 139, 183, 184
Laggan, The, 174, 229, 232
Laggan Days, 238-41
Laggan Loch, 239-44
Lagnagortan, 94
Lang family, Balnatunie, 141-42
Lang, Robert 'Roby', Campbeltown, 114
Langlands family, 141-42
Laracor, 123

larches, 165, 212-14
Larch Plantation, The, 250, 252
Largie Castles, 218, 274
Largiebaan, 9, 17, 18, 35, 36, 38-42, 43, 44-54, 56, 58, 59, 65-70, 72-76, 79, 80, 121, 166-8, 169, 231
Largiebaan Caves, 39, 40, 44, 46, 56, 72-73, 167-8, 253-54
Largieside, 91, 92, 93, 270
Larne, 89
Layde Church, 46-48
Leamnamuic, 98
Learside, 52, 63, 69, 145, 176, 183
Leitch, Mary Ann, Islay, 94
leus, 219
lichen, 11, 181
Limecraigs, 86, 95
Linguistic Survey of Scotland, 117
litter, 30, 157, 159-62, 198
Littleson, Anne, 237
Livingstone, William, poet, 234
Locarno Café, Campbeltown, 145
Loch an Eich, 226-29
Loch Beag, 229
Loch Ciaran, 94
Loch Losgainn, 229
Loch Mòr, 229
Loch na Machrach Bige – see Laggan Loch
Loch na Machrach Mòire, 241, 242
Lochend U.F. Church, 40, 85
Lochorodale, 17, 56, 58, 158
lodgepole pines, 165, 196-97
Look-oot, The, 147, 187
Lossit, 10, 11, 35, 76, 125, 126, 168, 255
Loynachan family – see Lang

Macalisters of Glenbarr, 235
Macalister, Fiona, 130
McAlister, Duncan, Grogport, 221
McAlister, Jim, Grogport, 221
Macarthur family, Campbeltown, 150-52
Macarthur, Campbell, Campbeltown, 145-50, 152
MacArthur, Hugh, Campbeltown, 20, 22
Macarthur, Mhairi, Campbeltown, 147-50
MacArthur, Willie, Campbeltown, 6, 20-25, 42
Macaulay family, Penicuik, 111-12, 164 (Niall only)
Macaulay, Colin, 89
MacAulay, Gordon, Campbeltown, 111
Macbain, Dr Alexander, 79, 219
MacBride families, 93
MacCaig, Norman, 95
McCallum, John, Garvalt, 235
McCartney, Paul, 165
MacConnachie, the name, 94
McCulloch, John Herries, 209
MacDiarmid, Hugh, 9, 10
Macdonalds of Largie, 201, 211, 275
Macdonalds of Sanda, 268-70
MacDonald, Rev Donald (1799-1851), 81
MacDonald, Rev Donald (1926-1928), 81
MacDonald, Rev Donald John (1880-1926), 81, 229
MacDonald, Jimmy, Campbeltown, xx, 3, 5, 11, 31, 33, 37, 39, 52, 53, 58, 59, 60, 66, 69, 71-2, 78, 106, 122,

285

133, 135, 137, 138, 139, 158, 185, 195, 198, 199, 230-3, 240, 241
MacDonald, John, Campbeltown, 22, 42, 44, 46, 55, 56, 57, 58, 73, 101, 102, 103, 127, 128, 169, 170, 173, 184, 224, 225-30, 236, 241-45
MacDonald, Malcolm, Beachmenach, 273
Macdonald, Mrs of Sanda, 269
MacDonald, Murdo, Lochgilphead, 75, 81, 82, 96, 97, 135, 199, 200, 225, 226
MacDonald, Rev Murdo, 81
Macdonald, Rev William, 82
MacDougall family, Glenramskill farm, 147
McDougall fishing family ('Toms'), Tarbert, 223
Macdougall, Duncan, Glenbarr, 199-208
McDougall, Gordon, Campbeltown, 69
McDougall, John, joiner, Campbeltown, 112
McEachran, Alistair, Campbeltown, 89
McEachran, David, Campbeltown, 89
MacFarlane, Hugh, Tarbert, 222, 223, 224, 251
McGeachy, Michael, Campbeltown, 29-30, 45
MacGillivray, Iain, Campbeltown, 18
McGougan, Angus, Cara, 210
McGougan, Willie, Largie, 274
MacGrory, A. P., Campbeltown, 40, 41

MacIlchattan families, 93
McInnes, John, Southend and Glasgow, 269
McInnes, Latimer, Campbeltown, 178
McInnes, Robert, Stewarton, 56, 58, 107
McIntosh, Donald, Carradale, 96
Macintosh, Margaret, Hamilton, 108
McIntylior, John and Donald, Dippen, 235
McIntyre family, 95
McIntyre, Allan, 95
McIntyre, Iain, Glenahervie, 153
MacKay, Amelia, Erradil, 250
McKellar, Neil, 43-44
McKellar, Neil Sr., 44
Mackenzie, Hector L., 130
McKenzie, John, uncle, 35
Mackenzie, Margaret (Anderson), 130
MacKerral family, Balnabraid, 250, 251
McKinlay, Graham, Saddell, 59
Mackinnon, Duncan of Loup and Balinakill, 83
Mackinnon, Duncan, of Ronachan, son of above, 83
McKinven, Alex, Campbeltown, 204
McLachlan, Duncan, Campbeltown, 23
MacLean, Ruari, 31, 53, 54
Maclean, Will, artist, 247
MacLeod, Dr Kenneth, Gigha, 204
McManus, Niall, 114
MacMarcus, Alexander, tacksman of Cara, 201

286

Macmaster, Archie,
    Campbeltown, 90
Macmaster, Jim,
    Campbeltown, 90, 120
McMillan, Alexander,
    Machrihanish, 167-68
McMillan, 'Sweetie' Bella,
    Campbeltown, 153-54
McMillan, Campbell, 114
MacMillan, Dugald, shepherd,
    Garvalt, 235
McMillan, Dr Sandy,
    Campbeltown, 75, 199, 202,
    204, 205
McMillan, Rev William,
    Erskine, 118
McMillan, Willie,
    Campbeltown, 101
McMullen, Robert,
    Drumchapel, 120, 121
Macnamara, Brinsley, 123
McNaughtan, Adam, 115
MacNeills of Carskey, 269
MacNeill, Rev John, 41
McPhail, Adam, Glenbarr, 230
Macphail, Calum, 47, 48, 50
Macphail, Iain, 50
McPhee, James, 101
McPherson, Elsie,
    Campbeltown, 18
McQuilkan families, North
    Kintyre, 84, 92-94
McQuilkan, Duncan,
    Campbeltown, 84, 85, 91-94
McQuilkan, John,
    Campbeltown, 84-87, 95
McQuin, John, sentenced to
    transportation, 141
McRobert, Jack and Jess,
    Campbeltown, 45

McShannon, Alec, 116, 117, 119
McShannon, Hugh, 73
McShannon, Jamie, Killypole,
    116, 117, 267
McShannon, John, 116, 117, 119
McShannon, Polly (Colville),
    Killypole, 117
McSporran, George,
    Campbeltown, 18, 40, 101,
    102, 122, 139, 140, 145-49,
    156, 160, 174, 186, 187, 188,
    189, 192, 193, 195, 196, 198,
    212-14, 215
McSporran, Margaret
    (Thomson), 102, 188
McSporran, Morris,
    Campbeltown, 102
McSporran, Sandy,
    Campbeltown, 18, 40, 174,
    186, 188, 213-14
McTaggart, Billy,
    Campbeltown, 105, 106
Mactaggart, Col. Charles, 98
MacVicar, Angus, author, 116
McWhirter, Francis and
    Madge, Campbeltown, 61

Machrihanish, 3, 5, 15, 17, 35,
    36, 42, 61, 66, 70, 76, 102,
    116, 168, 170, 255
Machrihanish Golf Club, 50
Martin, Amelia (McKenzie),
    author's mother, 191
Martin, Amelia, author's
    daughter, 59, 60, 66, 71, 75,
    106, 107, 109, 110, 115, 128,
    129, 135, 163, 176, 178-79,
    181, 190, 193, 225, 226
Martin, Angus, author's father,
    44, 192, 246-7, 251

Martin, Bella, author's
    daughter, 157, 163, 186, 187,
    188, 193, 218
Martin, David, Lewiston, 93
Martin, Henry, author's uncle,
    142
Martin, John, Campbeltown, 69
Martin, Judy, author's wife, xx,
    4, 5, 33, 63, 66, 71, 106, 107,
    108, 122, 135, 162, 163, 175,
    181, 188, 199, 225, 226, 227,
    230, 233-38, 239, 240, 241
Martin, Martin, 79
Martin, Sarah, author's
    daughter, 106, 107, 108, 120,
    122, 124, 163, 190, 192
Matheson, Barbara – see
    Barbara Docherty, younger
Mathieson, Donald,
    Glenahanty, 60, 79
Maxwell Macdonald, Mrs A., 270
Mayfair Restaurant,
    Campbeltown, 147
Mayo, Rear Admiral Robin,
    Campbeltown, 165
Melville, Herman, 38
*Memories of the Inans,
    Largybaan and Craigaig:
    1980-85*, 111
mice, 27
midges, 3, 63, 78, 213, 224, 236
Milloy families, 82
mink, 30, 193
Miss Lloyd's Well, 157
mist, 71, 169-73, 203, 255, 257
Mitchell, Willie, Campbeltown,
    117-19, 267
Mohamed, Jan, Machrihanish,
    55, 184

Moher, Cliffs of, 73-74
Money, Zoot, 29
Montague, John, 216
More, theme music, 87
Morrans, Sandy 'Snobs',
    Campbeltown, 183
Morrison, Norman, 82
mountaineering, 49, 108-9,
    258-66
Mull of Cara, 201-6, 210, 211
Mull of Kintyre, 37, 73, 74, 80,
    203
Munro, Neil, 178
mushrooms, 122, 123, 137, 139,
    155-56
music, 29, 87, 89, 90, 116, 117

Narrowfield, 187, 188, 198
Native Americans, 196-97
NATO jetty, Glenramskill, 146,
    147, 187
Nature Conservancy Council, 52
Neate, Timothy, 117
Nelson, Terence, Ballymena, 48
Nimmo, Jan, Glasgow, 152
Norse influences, 78-81, 236
Nottingham, 108

oars, 14, 15, 20, 21
'ocean glitter', 68-69
Old Road (Glenramskill), 108,
    146, 176
Oman, Les, Campbeltown, 113
O'Neill, John, Campbeltown,
    165
Ordnance Survey, 60, 78-79,
    153, 155
owls, 56, 107
oyster-catchers, 61

288

Paddy the pigeon, 175-76
Paterson, Tommy, Drumlemble, 54
peat-cutting, 56, 58
Perseverance, Loch Fyne Skiff, 192
photography, 4, 6, 7, 8, 10, 11, 13, 20, 21, 27, 33, 66-67, 123, 132, 159, 171, 174, 181-82, 188-89, 193, 199, 238-39, 243, 255
Picture House, Campbeltown, 149, 152
pigeons, feral, 175-76
Pink Floyd, 87
pipit, meadow, 173
place-names, 9, 42, 59-60, 78-81, 96, 104-5, 128, 143, 153, 155-56, 174, 182, 183, 185, 188, 196, 201-2, 204, 206-7, 236, 239
Place Names of Gigha and Cara, 206
poetry, 9, 10, 15-16, 56, 69, 132, 171-2, 176, 180, 182, 193, 195-6, 216-18, 240, 246-52, 267
Point, 252
Poll an Aba, 206
Polliwilline, 29, 63, 183, 184, 252
Pollock, Robert, 106
ponies, 190-91
Port an Stòir, 201, 204, 207
poteen, 33
psychedelia, 87
quartz, 152, 254

Queen Esther's Bay, 128, 152, 183, 184

rabbits, 25, 30, 209, 211
radios, 27, 28, 41, 45, 133
RAF Machrihanish, 23, 49, 102
rain, 13, 22, 24, 27, 71, 116, 137, 171, 172, 233, 240, 257
Ramsay, Gillian, Carradale, 237
Rathlin Island, 111, 231, 257, 271
ravens, 31, 59, 72, 77, 133, 167
Reid, Mhairi – see Macarthur
Reid, Ruth, Rhunahaorine School, 218
Rennie, Allan, Carradale, 106
rhododendron, 193
Ring of Bright Water, film, 149-50
Ring-Net Fishermen, The, 84, 222, 239, 247
roads (old), 13, 74, 108, 133, 193
Road to Drumleman, The, video, 152
Robb, Annie, Pitsligo, 168
Robertson, Davie, Campbeltown, 114, 115
Robertson, John 'Floorie', Campbeltown, 69
rocks, 4, 5, 6, 11, 13, 69, 162, 166, 174-75, 177-81, 182, 185, 188, 191, 233
Rocky Burn, 147, 192
Rodgers, W. R., 123
ròideagach – see bog myrtle
Rosemary Clooney Crossing the Minch, 193
Ross, Robert, Tarbert, 222, 223, 224
Rothesay, 90
rowans, 143, 212-14
Royal Hotel, Campbeltown, 113, 114, 115

289

Royalist, sail training brig, 11
Rubha Dùn Bhàin, 39, 53, 54, 69, 73, 77, 230-33

Saddell Street, Campbeltown, 27, 94
Sailor's Grave, Inneans, 8, 30, 106
Saint Ciaran's Cave, 168
salmon, 221, 235
Sanda Island, 89, 257
School of Scottish Studies, 115, 117, 272
Schutz, Elisabeth, 4, 128
Schutz, Hartwig, 4, 5, 6, 40, 128-29, 135, 184-86, 188
Schutz, Wiebke, 136, 184-86
Scott family, shepherds, Garvalt, 235-36
Scottish Arts Council, 159
Scottish Wildlife Trust, 170
seaweeds, 167, 208
Second Waters, 29, 120, 124, 184
Second World War, 116, 151-52
seilisdeir – see irises, wild
Sgeir Mhich Ghaiche, 207
shags, 153, 201, 205
sheep, 46, 74, 77-78, 80, 94, 167, 172, 209, 211, 214, 227
'sheggans' – see irises, wild
shelister boats, 218
silences, 12, 18, 68, 179
Silent Hollow, The, 180, 217
Sinai Sort, The, 95
Sinclair, Donald, Ballygroggan, 23
Sinclair, Dugald, 98, 99
Sinclair, Iain, Tarbert, 218

Singing Rock, 172
Skernish, 238
Skerry Fell, 255
Skipness, 92, 93, 242, 272
Skye, Isle of, 9, 13, 14, 30
skylark, 72
Slate/Sleit, 46, 101, 102, 103, 256, 257
Smerby Castle, 133, 218
Smith, Archie K., Tarbert, 82, 239, 243
Smith, Malcolm, brother of above, 239, 243
Smylie, Mike, 191-94
Snobs's Well, 183, 184
snow, 112, 199, 250, 271
Soft Machine, 90
Solo, Greenpeace ship, 192
Song of the Quern, The, 56, 171
Southend, 116, 142, 170, 248
sparrow-hawk, 232
spruce, 46, 165, 175, 176, 196, 231, 237
Sròn Gharbh (Machrihanish), 3-6, 8-12, 14, 15, 20, 21, 66, 81, 135, 189
Sròn Gharbh (Tarbert), 238, 239, 241, 245
stalactites and stalagmites, 72-73
Stewart, Agnes, Campbeltown, xx, 10, 17, 20, 25, 42, 61, 101, 117, 215
Stewart, Allister, Campbeltown, 17, 20, 42, 101
Stewart, A.I.B., Campbeltown, 235
Stewart, Archie, Campbeltown, 114

290

Stockadale, 236
stone-knapping, 153
Strang, Peter, Gobagrennan, 101
supernatural experiences, 130-31, 275
superstitions, 182, 204, 213
Sutherland, Alison, 130
Swanney Farm Cheese Ltd., 165
swans, whooper, 107, 232
Sweetie Bella's Quarry, 153
Swift, Jonathan, 123

Talamhtoll, 93
Tarbert, 222-23, 239, 240, 244
Tayinloan, 81, 82, 200, 204
tea, 9, 13, 14, 53, 55, 139, 192, 233
Third (Soft Machine), 90
Thomas, Captain F. W. L., 79
Thomson, Arthur and Jenny, Machrihanish, 102
Thomson, Don, Drumlemble, 23
thrushes, winter, 214
Tiree, 150
toad, 171
tobacco, 9, 92, 157-58, 218
Tocher, 115, 117
Todd family, 42, 271
tom, 223
Tòn Bhàn, 4
Trench, Archbishop Richard Chenevix, 221
trout, 229
Trudy, dog, 122
twinning-pens, 226-28
Uamha Ròpa, 40
Uigle Burn, 173
ùruisg, 268

vandalism, 162, 164

Walker, Steve, Campbeltown, 104
Wallace, David, Campbeltown, 47, 48, 50
water & wells, 22, 102, 144-45, 152, 157, 158, 165, 183, 192
water-horses, 228-29, 238
water lilies, 229
Watson, Philip, Bangor, 231, 271
Watson, Prof. W. J., 59
'Wee Green Hill', Glenramskill, 147
Wee Wud, 187
Weigh-house, 112, 113
Weigh-hoose Folk Club, 113-14
Weir, William, Talavtoll, 94
wells – see water
West Coast Motors, 92
whins, 162
whisky, 24, 31, 93, 106, 107, 118, 132, 165, 174, 186, 234, 257, 273
Whistlebinkies, 114
Wilcoxson, F. J., sculptor, 83
Willows, The, 196-99
wind, 9, 13, 14, 212, 256
witches, 178, 213, 238
wood fires, 14, 24, 111, 128, 173
woodrush, greater, 185
Woolley, J. S., 117
Wordsworth, William, 68
World Fishing, 45
Wurttemberg, 135-36

291

Lightning Source UK Ltd.
Milton Keynes UK
UKHW022036150221
378828UK00010B/2556